Dr. and Mrs. Edward Hempel

Robinson

Fenner Brockway

Cearbhall Ó Dálaigh

Ronald Reagan

Douglas Corrigan

Neil T Blaney

Mary McAleese

Hillary Rodham Clinton

Tomás Ó Fiaich

Leslie Howard

Doncha Ó Dúlaing

Donogh O'Malley

Elizabeth R

Erskine Childers

Maud Gonne MacBride

Jimmy Carter

John, Count Mc Cormack.

awaharlal Nehru

Joannes Paulus PP. II

THE
PRESIDENTS'
LETTERS

For letter writers everywhere and in memory of my parents, Florence and Daniel G, and my brothers Gerry and Barry, who wrote some of the best.

THE
PRESIDENTS'
LETTERS

AN UNEXPECTED
HISTORY OF
IRELAND

————◆————

Flor MacCarthy

NEW ISLAND

THE PRESIDENTS' LETTERS

First published in 2021 by
New Island Books
Glenshesk House
10 Richview Office Park
Clonskeagh
Dublin 14 D14 V8C4
Republic of Ireland
www.newisland.ie

ISBN (print): 978-1-84840-769-5

Cover image credits: see image credits, pp 286 and 287, except for drawing of President Michael
D. Higgins on front cover which is reproduced by kind permission from Sacred Heart NS,
Huntstown, Dublin.

The editor and publisher have made all reasonable effort to trace copyright holders and obtain
permission to reproduce visual and quoted material. Please contact the publisher if any copyright
appears to have been infringed.

Book and cover design by River Design Books, riverdesignbooks.com
Edited by Susan McKeever
Proofread by Jane Rogers
Printed by L&C Printing Group, Poland

New Island Books is a member of Publishing Ireland

In partnership with:

CONTENTS

HYDE (One term: 25 June 1938–24 June 1945)

Douglas Ross Hyde (Dubhghlas de hÍde), the first President of Ireland, was chosen by an all-party agreement. Hyde was an academic, writer, politician and diplomat from a Church of Ireland family in Co. Roscommon. He attended Trinity College, Dublin, where he became fluent in French, German, Latin, Greek and Hebrew. In 1893 he co-founded Conradh na Gaeilge (the Gaelic League), to promote the Irish language and culture he was so passionate about. He was Professor of Irish at UCD, and wrote widely using the pseudonym *An Craoibhín Aoibhinn* ('the pleasant little branch'). Hyde was seventy-eight and already retired when he was asked to become president; he suffered a stroke two years later, which confined him to a wheelchair. He was married to German-born Lucy Cometina Kurtz (named after the Great Comet of 1860), and they had two daughters.

O'KELLY (Two terms: 25 June 1945–24 June 1959)

Seán T. O'Kelly (Seán Tomás Ó Ceallaigh) was the first President of Ireland to win a contested election. He was born in inner-city Dublin and in 1916 was jailed for his part in the Easter Rising, along with his wife, Kit Ryan (later a Professor of French at University College Dublin). A lifelong politician, O'Kelly was a founder of Sinn Féin and later of Fianna Fáil; he was Ceann Comhairle of the first Dáil, and became Ireland's first Tánaiste. When Kit died in 1934, O'Kelly received a papal dispensation from the Vatican to marry her sister, Phyllis. He made the first State Visit by an Irish president, to the Vatican, in 1949, and was re-elected unopposed for a second term in 1952. Weeks before leaving office, 'Seán T', as he was known, made the first State Visit by an Irish president to the USA.

DE VALERA (Two terms: 25 June 1959–24 June 1973)

Éamon de Valera was the first president born outside the State and the most prominent Irish political leader of the twentieth century. At the age of two he was sent from New York to be raised by relatives in Co. Limerick. He grew up to become a teacher, and was a leader of the 1916 Easter Rising, for which he was sentenced to death and later released. De Valera founded Fianna Fáil and became Ireland's first Taoiseach; he was elected president in 1959. On his re-election aged eighty-four, he became the world's oldest elected Head of State, retiring at the age of ninety. 'Dev', as he was known, was married to children's writer Sinéad Ní Fhlannagáin for nearly sixty-five years until her death in 1975, seven months before his own. They had seven children.

CHILDERS (Died in office during first term: 25 June 1973–11 November 1974)

Erskine Hamilton Childers, Ireland's only president to die in office, became Head of State of the country which had executed his father in 1922 during the Civil War. Childers Sr, an English-born republican and writer of spy thrillers, asked his then sixteen-year-old son to forgive the signatories of his death warrant. Childers studied at Cambridge before joining *The Irish Press*. He was a Fianna Fáil TD from 1938 to 1973, when he was elected president, promising a more inclusive and forward-thinking presidency. He died suddenly after only eighteen months in office and his funeral saw the largest-ever gathering of monarchs and rulers on the island of Ireland. He was survived by his seven children and his second wife, Rita Childers (née Dudley) who was briefly considered as his successor for the role of president.

Ó DÁLAIGH (One term; resigned: 19 December 1974–22 October 1976)

Cearbhall Ó Dálaigh (Carroll O'Daly) became an agreed president following the death of Erskine H. Childers. He was brought up in Bray, Co. Wicklow and was a graduate of University College Dublin, where he showed a keen interest in the Irish language and the arts, and where met his wife, Irish scholar Mairín Nic Dhiarmada. After a brief stint at the *The Irish Press*, Ó Dálaigh's legal career took off: he became Ireland's youngest-ever Attorney General, Chief Justice, and Ireland's first judge at the European Court of Justice in Luxembourg. He was appointed president in 1974, but resigned less than two years later following a clash with the government, which he felt had not been supportive. The Ó Dálaighs retired to Sneem in Co. Kerry, where Cearbhall died of a heart attack two years later.

HILLERY (Two terms: 3 December 1976–2 December 1990)

Patrick John Hillery (Pádraig J. Ó hIrghile), a GP from Spanish Point in Co. Clare, is the only president to have been twice elected unopposed. As a Fianna Fáil TD, he held a succession of ministerial portfolios including Foreign Affairs, when he helped to negotiate Ireland's entry to the EEC in 1973. He was Ireland's first European Commissioner and became a vice president of the then-Commission of the European Communities. Hillery married an anaesthetist, Maeve Finnegan, whom he'd met when they were students at University College Dublin; they had two children. Following Ó Dálaigh's resignation, Hillery was elected unopposed in 1976 and again in 1983, after being persuaded to stand by the leaders of the three main political parties. After leaving office in 1990, Hillery retired from politics.

ROBINSON (One term; resigned: 3 December 1990–12 September 1997)

Mary Therese Winifred Robinson (née Bourke; Máire Mhic Róibín) was the first woman and youngest President of Ireland so far. She was born in Ballina in Co. Mayo, studied law at Trinity College Dublin, then went on to attend Harvard Law School. She married fellow TCD law student and cartoonist Nick Robinson; they have three children. Robinson became Professor of Criminal Law at the young age of twenty-five; she was elected to the Seanad and made a name as a human rights campaigner, academic and politician. In 1990 the Labour Party proposed her for Ireland's first presidential election in seventeen years, which she won, aged just forty-six. By halfway through her term her popularity rating reached an unprecedented 93 per cent. A few months before the end of her term, Robinson resigned to take up the post of United Nations High Commissioner for Human Rights.

McALEESE (Two terms: 11 November 1997–10 November 2011)

Mary Patricia McAleese (née Leneghan; Máire Pádraigín Mhic Ghiolla Íosa) was the first president to come from Northern Ireland and the world's first woman to succeed another woman as president. She graduated in Law from Queen's University Belfast, and was Professor of Criminal Law at Trinity College Dublin. In 1979 she joined RTÉ as a journalist and presenter before returning to Queen's, where she became Pro-Vice Chancellor. She is married to dentist and politician Martin McAleese and they have three children. McAleese was chosen to run for president by Fianna Fáil and at the age of forty-six, after a bitterly contested election campaign, became Ireland's youngest-ever president (by a few months). She went on to be re-elected unopposed for a second term in 2004. In 2011 she hosted Queen Elizabeth ll on the first State Visit to Ireland by a British monarch.

HIGGINS (Two terms: 11 November 2011–present)

Michael Daniel Higgins (Mícheál Dónal Ó hUigínn), is the ninth and current President of Ireland. A politician, poet, sociologist, author and broadcaster, Higgins received in excess of one million votes in his second presidential election, more than any candidate, in any election, in the history of the State. A long-time Labour politician for Galway West, he is the first president to have served in both Houses of the Oireachtas; from senator, to TD, to Minister for Arts, Culture and the Gaeltacht. Higgins is fluent in Irish, speaks Spanish, and has written on a wide variety of subjects from human rights, to social justice, to football. 'Michael D.', as he is affectionately known, is married to actress and political activist Sabina Higgins (née Coyne) and they have four children. In April 2014, he made the first State Visit by an Irish president to the United Kingdom.

INTRODUCTION

T his book was written out of curiosity. Who writes to the President of Ireland, I wondered. What are the letters about, where are these letters now and what might they reveal – about us and about how Ireland has changed since our first president sat down to open his morning post in June 1938?

The answers – often surprising, sometimes shocking – I'm sharing with you here: a selection of 315 letters, telegrams, cards, memos and notes, including one crumpled, but incredibly historic envelope. Most have never been published before; a handful have never been revealed in public until now.

Over two years of joyful discovery in archives and private collections I've found the correspondence I expected to find: letters of congratulations, of resignation, of sympathy; letters between Heads of State, and letters commuting a death sentence. But among them I also found letters of love and of loss; begging letters and threatening letters. There is correspondence written in such anger that the pen has ripped through the page and some so hilarious that I almost got kicked out of the reading room of the National Library for laughing out loud.

There are letters sent from palaces, parliaments and prisons; from war zones, refugee camps and homeless shelters. Communications arrived at Áras an Uachtaráin from places as diverse as the headquarters of the United Nations in New York to the shadow of the Acropolis in Athens, sent by 'a humble well-wisher'.

The list of letter-writers reads like a who's who of the twentieth century and beyond, and includes John F. Kennedy, Princess Grace of Monaco, Nelson Mandela, Fidel Castro, Indira Gandhi, Richard Nixon, Charles de Gaulle, Queen Elizabeth II, the Dalai Lama, Muammar Gaddafi, Louis le Brocquy and Seamus Heaney.

But, of equal importance to me, are the letters sent by citizens of Ireland to their president, whether posted from West Cork or Western Australia. It's clear that, right from the start, Irish people have turned to their president in times of celebration and of tragedy, to mark a big occasion or ask a small favour.

If a letter made me exclaim, 'I *never* knew that', it made the cut. There are lots of these: President de Valera's message in Irish, flown by Apollo 11 astronauts to be placed on the surface of the moon; the note banning Maud Gonne from any future garden parties at

Áras an Uachtaráin; the letter written (but never sent) by President Ó Dálaigh offering himself in place of IRA kidnap victim Dr Tiede Herrema; the heartbreaking poem about peace by Buncrana schoolboy Shaun McLaughlin, six weeks before he was killed in the Omagh bombing. I found a fascinating and very funny description of his election campaign by President Childers; letters from children in post-World War II Germany and a scurrilous description of poet Patrick Kavanagh, who wore 'a green woollen jumper' and 'sandals without socks' to a presidential reception. I read about Seamus Heaney's delight at hearing, while on a Greek island, that he had won the Nobel Prize in Literature; the letter of thanks from four-year-old Princess Caroline of Monaco for the gift of an Irish pony; the letter of sympathy from President Higgins to Shane MacGowan on the death of his mother Therese, herself an award-winning singer … the list goes on.

So that the letters can speak for themselves we've set them in context with writers and historians introducing thematic chapters: from political correspondence to letters on the arts; from correspondence with the Irish diaspora to the famous visitors' books at the Áras, which themselves are full of surprises.

The earliest entry here dates from just before President Hyde took office in 1938; the most recent is a message to Bob Dylan from President Higgins marking their eightieth birthdays in April/May 2021. To complete the collection, former presidents Mary Robinson and Mary McAleese have each chosen some noteworthy letters from their own presidential files. And there are letters from the files of President Michael D. Higgins, though with the current presidential term only halfway through, you have until 2025 to get your letter into a later volume.

Finally, I couldn't resist including some of the many wonderful photographs, newspaper clippings and drawings which accompany the correspondence in the archives and which help to bring these letters and their stories to life.

I hope you enjoy them!

Flor MacCarthy
September 2021

Chapter 1

Power Play
Politics and the Presidency

David McCullagh

The president's role in politics is easy to define: he or she doesn't have one – at least not in active party politics. Although there is no constitutional or legal bar on the president expressing political opinions, a very strong convention has grown up over the decades since the first President of Ireland was chosen that the office is above politics.

The office was deliberately designed to be politically neutral, despite opposition fears at the time that Éamon de Valera saw the presidency as a job for himself, to guarantee his grip on power. In fact, the truth was that de Valera viewed the president as a ceremonial figurehead to represent the State at home and abroad, and as a sort of referee with very limited powers to be used only in clearly defined circumstances.

Nearly all of the president's functions are performed 'on the advice of the government'. In other words, the president has no choice but to perform the act requested. Only four powers can be exercised at the president's discretion:

The first President of Ireland, Douglas Ross Hyde, reading his correspondence in the garden at Áras an Uachtaráin in the early days of his presidency, June 1938.

- Referring legislation to the Supreme Court to test its constitutionality;
- Appointing members of the Council of State (a purely advisory body with no actual power);
- Having a piece of legislation put to a referendum before signing it (but only if a majority of the Seanad and at least a third of the Dáil request that this happens);
- Refusing a dissolution of the Dáil (but only if the Taoiseach making the request has lost the confidence of a majority of the Dáil).

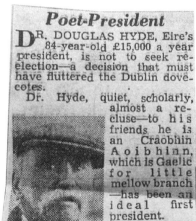

Poet-President

DR. DOUGLAS HYDE, Eire's 84-year-old £15,000 a year president, is not to seek re-election—a decision that must have fluttered the Dublin dove-cotes.

Dr. Hyde, quiet, scholarly, almost a re-cluse—to his friends he is an Craobhín Aoibhinn, which is Gaelic for little mellow branch—has been an ideal first president.

Even though all the tales told in Dublin are eventually repeated within the walls of the vice-regal lodge in Phoenix Park, he never showed any signs of being concerned by the various changes in the direction of the political winds.

Dr. Hyde

'An ideal first president' is how the *Yorkshire Evening News* described President Douglas Hyde, saying he showed no signs of 'being concerned by the various changes in the direction of the political winds', 6 January 1945.

As the first holder of the office of president, Douglas Hyde set the tone: he had not been involved in active politics so he found it easy to avoid partisanship. The main political choice he made as president was the decision *not* to use his power to refuse an election to a Taoiseach who had lost the support of the majority of the Dáil – in this case, Éamon de Valera, who had lost a vote on transport legislation and was anxious to improve his political position with a snap election. Hyde's decision, in 1944, set an important precedent, and the circumstances were carefully noted by the president's secretary, Michael McDunphy.

The next two presidents, Seán T. O'Kelly and Éamon de Valera, largely kept to the template set by Hyde – at least in public. Both had been senior politicians, but once elected they left active politics behind. However, some close personal connections with Fianna Fáil politicians led to a few interesting pieces of correspondence, including a TD's request to O'Kelly for a loan, and

UIMHIR................................

Signed copy

UACHTARÁN NA hÉIREANN

SGEUL .... General Election ....

FO-SGEUL .... May, 1944 ....

1.   Shortly after 9 p.m. on the 9th May the telephone rang in my private residence. The speaker was Mr Murray, Assistant Private Secretary to the Taoiseach, to inform me that a short time previously, at 9.5 p.m. to be exact, the Government had been defeated on the second stage of the Transport Bill, 1944 (Dáil Debates, 9.5.44, Vol.93, No.6, Col.2467), and in consequence of that defeat the Taoiseach wished to call upon the President to discuss with him the question of a General Election. The Taoiseach thought that I as Secretary to the President should also come to the Áras.

2.   =I arranged with the President for an appointment with the Taoiseach in the Áras, giving myself about forty minutes to get there by car from my home in Clontarf. Unfortunately the President's chauffeur was out and my own car not being available at the time, I set out on my bicycle. Never did the six mile journey, a continuous rise against a strong headwind, seem so Arduous.

3.   Having reached the Áras I found that the Taoiseach was already there with the President in his bedroom, the latter, a man of 84 years, having been practically bedridden for some years. I went to my office and waited there for a few minutes until the President sent for me. I found him lying in bed looking somewhat expectant.

(2006).E.10290.Wt.4380—16.2,000.2/47.A.T.&Co.,Ltd. Spcl.

4.   The Taoiseach then explained the matter to the President as follows. The Government had been defeated on a matter which had been regarded by him the Taoiseach as a major one, and in the circumstances he considered that he as Taoiseach had ceased to retain the confidence of Dáil Éireann within the meaning of Article 13.2.2 of the Constitution. He proposed, therefore, to advise the President to proclaim a General Election. He realised that the President was entitled

5.   The President looked at me, and then at the Taoiseach, and again back to me. Realizing that the

6.   When the Taoiseach had left the room the President turned to me and said immediately "I must refuse; the country does not want a General Election." I suggested that the matter was not quite so simple. If he refused, the Taoiseach would be forced by article

There was however, no single Party or combination of Parties, which could secure such a nomination, and there was consequently no practicable alternative to the existing Government. We discussed the matter at length, and finally the President agreed that the wisest thing to do from the point of view of the

Extracts from a four-page memo on a precedent-setting late-night meeting at Áras an Uachtaráin when President Douglas Hyde decided against using his power under the Constitution to prevent the calling of a general election.

DÁIL ÉIREANN

BAILE ÁTHA CLIATH
(Dublin)

2nd Dec 57

To - Right Hon Sean T O'Kelly
President of Ireland.

A Cara Sean,
You will doubtless be surprised to hear from me & it is indeed with shame & reluctance that I write but needs must,

I got my son & my daughter married last year & the expense of providing for both in the one year strained my Finances & on top of that the expense of the General Election last July & March left me worse still. I would require a loan of £700 from now until next October. when I will be able to repay it in full from the Harvest, & I wonder if you would be kind enough to let me have that amount, I find myself caught out as I have to meet immediately both My Annuities & Rates as well as Seeds Manures & other Expenses, & will have practically nothing coming in before April

DÁIL ÉIREANN

BAILE ÁTHA CLIATH
(Dublin)

2

You may be surprised that after over 30 years in the Dail I am not in a better position Financially but with an average of a General Election every 2½ years together with the cost of keeping a Rural Constituency going I must admit that I am no better off today than when I first entered Dáil Eireann with the Chief & Yourself in June 27,

I had hoped that after 30 years faithfull Service there would be some promotion which would have improved my position but The Chief in his wisdom decided otherwise.

I know I am asking a great favour from you & would not do so If I did not think you would help me I can definitely guarantee its repayment on or before October 1st without fail.

I will be in the Dail On Wednesday & Thursday this week if you wish to contact me, I would also request that you keep the contents of this letter Strictly Private

Your old Friend
Martin Corry

Martin Corry TD seeks a loan from President Seán T. O'Kelly, 2 December 1957: '… it is indeed with shame and reluctance that I write'. The former War of Independence veteran was a Fianna Fáil backbench TD for forty years.

de Valera's brief but affectionate message to a recuperating Dan Breen, the War of Independence hero and Fianna Fáil TD. O'Kelly, an inveterate gossip, did bad-mouth Fine Gael Taoiseach John A. Costello to foreign diplomats, which was disloyal but not politically significant. De Valera dabbled in internal Fianna Fáil politics when Jack Lynch faced pressure over the outbreak of the Troubles in the North. De Valera persuaded uncompromising republican Kevin Boland not to resign from Cabinet in protest at Lynch's moderate approach to Northern Ireland, and later steadfastly supported the Taoiseach when he sacked two ministers suspected of involvement in a plot to import weapons for northern nationalists, in the so-called Arms Crisis.

The fourth president, Erskine Childers, promised a more active presidency, and proposed a presidential 'think-tank' to chart the future of the country. But his desire to expand the role of the office led him into conflict with the Fine Gael/ Labour coalition government, detailed in a memorandum he wrote of a conversation with Taoiseach Liam Cosgrave. Childers died after less than a year and a half in the job, before these tensions came to a head.

His successor, Cearbhall Ó Dálaigh, also had a strained relationship with the government. He eventually resigned when he was called a 'thundering disgrace' by Minister of Defence Paddy Donegan, after Ó Dálaigh – quite properly – referred an Emergency Powers Bill to the Supreme Court to test its constitutionality. He felt that the government, and particularly Liam Cosgrave, hadn't taken the matter seriously enough, and that Cosgrave had slighted him from the start of his term of office. Resignation took courage, a quality Ó Dálaigh did not lack – previously, he had offered to take the place of IRA kidnap victim Tiede Herrema, saying he believed he could bring the kidnappers to reason, but if he couldn't, he didn't mind dying.

Patrick Hillery, his successor, deliberately avoided any public political involvement, as he strove to restore the stability and dignity of the presidency.

Cóip de Sreangscéal a cuireadh amach 11.45 a.m. 11/8/64.

Deputy Dan Breen.
67, Ballytore Rd.,
Rathfarnham Park,
Dublin 14.

Best Wishes. Old soldiers never die.

Eamon de Valera.

One-line letter from
President de Valera
to Dan Breen, old IRA
leader-turned-politician,
who was recovering
from illness, in 1964.

23rd February, 1961

A Thaoisigh, a chara,

The time has come when I must tell
the Cardinal definitely whether I intend to be, or not
to be, in Armagh on March 17th for the celebrations
opening the Patrician Year.

I am now firmly of opinion that I
should be there. The Cardinal, I know, desires my
attendance, and should I fail to respond he may regard
it as a slight.

The occasion is, of course, a great
national one, and it would seem to be the President's
duty to participate, if at all possible. Indeed, should
the President not attend, the feeling would, I think, be
widespread that he has been guilty of a dereliction.
All sorts of questions would be raised publicly, and I
do not think that adequate answers could be forthcoming.

The ceremonies will be religious, and
my being present at them should not create any special
difficulties, particularly as Protestants, no less than
Catholics, honour St. Patrick as the National Apostle.

Should the unlikely however, happen,
and the Northern authorities make objection to my entering
the Six Counties, it would be much better to be prevented
in that way than that we ourselves should default through
anticipating difficulties and consequences which might
never arise.

I have given consideration to the possible
effects of my attendance on the political relations
between the two parts of the country, and I cannot see
that my going to Armagh on this occasion could, in any
way, be detrimental. Accordingly, I would propose that
I tell the Cardinal, immediately, that it is my intention
to be present: I would be glad to know, as soon as
possible, that you agree, and that the necessary preliminary
steps to inform the Northern authorities will be taken by
the appropriate Government Department.

Le mór-mheas,

Do chara,

Sgd. E...mon de Valera

An Taoiseach Seán Lemass,
Áras an Rialtais,
Baile Átha Cliath.

Delivered by m okilly
by hand L carseials
Private sec (R foley) at
Leinster House at 1255
on 23/2/61.

Though he was (unfairly) criticised for inactivity, Hillery showed steel when required. After Garret FitzGerald's Fine Gael–Labour coalition lost a budget vote in January 1982, leading members of Fianna Fáil, including Charles Haughey, tried to contact Hillery to persuade him to refuse a dissolution, on the assumption that the party would be able to form a minority government without having to go through an election. Their calls were recorded in the logs of the Áras duty officer, but Hillery resolutely refused to talk to his former party colleagues, demonstrating his independence and that of his office.

The 1990 election of Ireland's first female president, Mary Robinson, broke all sorts of political moulds and was a significant advance for women. During her campaign, Robinson had suggested in an interview with *Hot Press*

In a letter hand-delivered to the Taoiseach, Seán Lemass, President Éamon de Valera says he would like to enter 'the Six Counties' to attend Saint Patrick's Day religious celebrations and that he has considered the possible effects it may have on the 'political relations between the two parts of the country'.

Election flyer from the 1973 presidential campaign of Erskine H. Childers, who defeated the Fine Gael candidate, Tom O'Higgins. Less than eighteen months later Childers suffered a fatal heart attack, becoming the only President of Ireland to die in office.

magazine that if then-Taoiseach Charles Haughey pursued a course of which she disapproved, she'd be able to look him in the eye 'and tell him to back off because I have been directly elected by the people and he hasn't'. This, of course, went well beyond actual presidential powers, as she well knew. But she did find ways to assert her independence in office, highlighting the issue of emigration, and controversially shaking hands with Sinn Féin leader Gerry Adams in West Belfast before the IRA ceasefire, annoying both the Irish and the British governments. She resigned as president shortly before her term concluded, after a campaign backed by the government to become United Nations High Commissioner for Human Rights.

Her successor, Mary McAleese, used the soft power of the presidency to build bridges, particularly with her native Northern Ireland. Áras an Uachtaráin became a key meeting ground for communities from the North, and she and her husband, Martin, performed valuable work in reaching out to loyalists in particular.

The current president, Michael D. Higgins, has also followed precedent in legal and constitutional terms, while at the same time using the office to highlight issues in which he is interested, particularly on questions of economic justice and reconciliation on the island of Ireland. Some of his speeches have raised eyebrows in Government Buildings; but he, like his predecessors, has been careful to keep within the letter of the Constitution and maintain the conventions surrounding the office, while at the same time using the presidency to generate debate.

Theodore Roosevelt once described the American presidency as a 'bully pulpit', meaning he believed it was a superb platform from which to advocate an agenda (Roosevelt was using 'bully' to mean excellent or first-rate). The presidents of Ireland may lack the political power of their US counterpart, but they certainly occupy a bully pulpit, should they choose to use it.

ROINN AN TAOISIGH
DEPARTMENT OF THE TAOISEACH

BAILE ÁTHA CLIATH 2
DUBLIN 2

7th September 1973

<u>Private and Confidential</u>

Dear President

I have your letter of 6th September about
<u>Peace Point</u> and I appreciate your feelings.

My basic difficulty is that <u>any</u> statement on
a subject as sensitive as the North can be
construed - whether we like it or not - as
having a strong political content. What is
good news for one interest may be bad news for
another.   I do not think that, at this point
certainly, the possibility of the Office of
President being involved in this type of situation
outweighs whatever advantages might be gained by
the association of the Office with the efforts of
<u>Peace Point</u>.

A further difficulty is the association of the
group with a public relations firm (Press reports,
which I do not think are accurate, say that it is
"run by" the firm.)   This, in itself, is not of
course objectionable but the association of the
Office of President with the fund raising
activities organised by a firm of this sort on the
group's behalf would not, I think, be desirable.
I may add that experience in the Department of
one of the members of the Dublin Committee of
the organisation has been a great deal less than
happy.

While any one of these arguments in itself may
not be conclusive, I think that, on balance, you
will agree that their cumulative effect is to
point definitely to the decision taken.

Yours sincerely

Erskine Childers
Uachtarán na hÉireann
Baile Átha Cliath 8

Taoiseach Liam Cosgrave writes to President
Erskine Childers to advise him against making
any remarks on Northern Ireland.

Draft handwritten letter by President Ó
Dálaigh in which he considers offering himself
in place of kidnapped Dutch industrialist
Dr Tiede Herrema, who was held by the
Provisional IRA for thirty-two days in 1975.
'If I fail, I do not mind dying, it will vindicate
Ireland's honour,' the president wrote.

A thorough search, I believe I could bring the kidnappers [May '76 - 15]

I have been considering the Harrema affair and Yodet Day I had done

a draft of a letter which I proposed in due process under the Constitution to issue as a message to the People

On learning of the Garda success in tracing & surrounding the kidnappers I was satisfied that my message would serve no purpose.

It now seems to me that the only way to save

ARCHIVES

PSI/211   (23)

OIFIG AN AIRE COSANTA
(OFFICE OF THE MINISTER FOR DEFENCE)
BAILE ÁTHA CLIATH, 8.
(DUBLIN 8)

22 October 1976

A Uachtarain Uasail,

Thank you for your letter of the 19th instant.

I fully accept that the gravamen of my utterance was contained in the words you quote in the last two lines of the first page of your letter. For these and for the references which additionally I made I have expressed my regret and have tendered to you my sincere and humble apology.

I feel that I should add that it is now apparent that my words are open to misinterpretation and that they have in fact been subject to interpretations which certainly I did not intend. I would be grateful if you would regard my apology as comprehending my regret for a situation in which such interpretations could arise.

Mise le meas,

Patrick Donegan

AIRE COSANTA.

Uachtaran na hEireann
Aras an Uachtaráin
Pairc an Fhionn Uisce
BAILE ÁTHA CLIATH, 8.

PSI/215   (33)

UACHTARÁN NA hÉIREANN
PRESIDENT OF IRELAND

BAILE ÁTHA CLIATH 8
DUBLIN

2

The accompanying statement and this letter (taken together) explain briefly why I feel I must now after less than two years relinquish that office.

I should record how pleasant, courteous and cordial our personal relations have been since I took office.

I would however be failing in my duty if I did not also record here - for history - that since I entered on the Presidency on 19 December 1974 - having resigned as a judge of the Court of Justice of the E.E. Communities - that on none of the occasions of your infrequent visits to Aras an Uachtarain did you, in your conversations with me, say anything to me that could

Minister of Defence Paddy Donegan apologises to President Ó Dálaigh for calling him a 'thundering disgrace' after the president referred a controversial Emergency Powers Bill to the Supreme Court.

Draft resignation letter from President Ó Dálaigh to the Taoiseach, Liam Cosgrave, saying the latter had not kept him 'even remotely' informed on matters of state, as obliged by the Constitution.

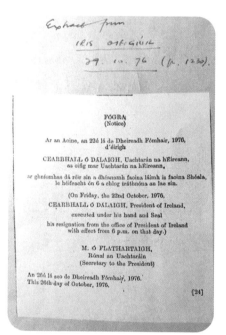

On 22 October 1976 President Cearbhall Ó Dálaigh became the first President of Ireland to resign. Hundreds of supportive messages from the public were delivered to Áras an Uachtaráin, and an unsuccessful petition urged Mr Ó Dálaigh to seek election again.

A supportive telegram sent to President Cearbhall Ó Dálaigh at the time of his resignation.

Cearbhall Ó Dálaigh standing with his dogs outside a pharmacy in the village of Sneem, Co. Kerry, in 1977. He had retired there with his wife, Máirín, following his resignation the previous October. Ó Dálaigh died of a heart attack less than two years later and was buried in Sneem following a State Funeral held in the village.

UACHTARAN NA HÉIREANN
PRESIDENT OF IRELAND

BAILE ÁTHA CLIATH 8
DUBLIN

Statement by President Hillery

In recent days it has come to my attention that there were rumours circulating as to the possibility of my resigning as President.

There is absolutely no foundation whatever for such rumours. I am not resigning.

Áras an Uachtaráin
3 X 1979

President Patrick Hillery responds to rumours that had been circulating about his personal life which had led to widespread speculation that he was on the point of resigning from office.

FROM (Date Time) ....

TO (Date Time) ....

UNIT JOURNAL

Time Received or Sent	Serial No.	Date Time of Origin	In	Out	Incidents, Orders, Messages, etc.	Action Taken
		2045	✓		From Brian Lenihan TD and Mrs Barrett. Mr Lenihan and Mrs Barrett wish to see the President on a private matter.	President not available at the moment. President informed.
		2110	✓		From Brian Lenihan. Has my message been passed to the President.	President not available but your message has been logged.
		2130	✓		From Brian Lenihan. Was Mr Haughey's message passed to the President.	Mr Haughey's message was logged. Mr Lenihan informed.
		2135	✓		Mrs Grace Brett (Kilkenny). She does NOT want another election. She wants a National Government.	

(a) Insert Name of Unit or Staff Section thus, "I Brigade Journal" or "Operations Section, etc."

(b) Refers to incoming messages only.

132181.500pads.5/80.EPC.Ltd.   G52

Date Time of Origin	In	Out	Incidents, Orders, Messages, etc.	Action Taken
			From Mr Haughey. Please log the following message and give it to the President: 'As the leader of the largest party with the support of the majority in the Dáil, I wish to speak to the President at the earliest possible moment with a view to forming a Government. Please ring me and confirm the President got my message.	President informed
2200	✓	✓	From Capt Barbour to Mr Haughey. President will be informed A.S.P.	
2200	✓		Taoiseach arrived at Áras.	

Telephone logs at Áras an Uachtaráin: Fianna Fáil leader Charles Haughey tries but fails to speak to President Patrick Hillery about government formation. His fellow opposition Fianna Fáil TD, Brian Lenihan, later denied that he too had telephoned the Áras; his subsequent admission is credited with scuppering his campaign to become Ireland's seventh president.

President Patrick Hillery hosting a meeting of European
leaders at Áras an Uachtaráin in 1979; among them Taoiseach
Jack Lynch, French President Valéry Giscard d'Estaing, British
Prime Minister Margaret Thatcher and Italian Prime Minister
Francesco Cossiga.

FAMILY TREE SCHEME

An Oak Tree
was planted
in the grounds
of
the Phoenix Park

In Honour of
President Mary Robinson

To Celebrate the Visit to
Áras an Uachtaráin
12th December 1992
of
the Lesbian and Gay Community of Dublin

HELPING
TO IMPROVE
IRELAND'S
LANDSCAPE

John McCullen
President

PRINTED ON RECYCLED PAPER

Kieran Rose, Senator David Norris and other members of the Gay and Lesbian Equality Network (GLEN) at Áras an Uachtaráin in July 1993, to celebrate the passing of the Criminal Law (Sexual Offences) Act. President Robinson said she was 'proud to sign into law' the Act which decriminalised homosexual acts. Both Mary McAleese and Mary Robinson worked as legal advisors to the Campaign for Homosexual Law Reform.

A certificate sent to President Mary Robinson by the Lesbian and Gay Community of Dublin to celebrate her hosting of an official reception for the group at Áras an Uachtaráin, in 1992.

Drawing of President Mary Robinson as news breaks of her appointment to the UN, by twelve-year-old David Horan, a pupil at Ballyguiltenane National School, Co. Limerick.

By David Horan

Dublin University Independent
Unionist Association (DUIUA)
c/o Central Societies Committee,
Trinity College, Dublin 2.

Uachtarán na hÉireann,
Áras an Uachtaráin,
Phœnix Park,
Dublin 8.

13th. July, 1998.

Dear President McAleese,

Thank you for inviting me to Áras an Uachtaráin for your
reception to mark the 12th of July. I was particularly moved by
the warmth of the welcome that I received from yourself and Dr.
McAleese on that occasion. You made me feel very much at home,
and — particularly with the musical event of the evening — helped
me experience some of the joy that I have usually associated with
St. Patrick's Day. A number of us would also like to thank you
for your speech in which you emphasised — among other things —
the part played by both traditions in the national culture and
identity; and where you set forth your vision of that shared
identity in the modern Ireland.

One cannot let the opportunity go by without acknowledging the
events of last week, which led to the terrible loss of the lives
of the three Quinn boys, Richard, Mark, and Jason at Ballymoney.
The sense of palpable shame coming out of this is felt by all of
us who are in any way associated with unionism or Protestantism
on this island.

Once again, we would like to express our deep appreciation at
what you have done, and are doing, to recognise and celebrate the
diverse traditions that we share. We wish you continued success
in this endeavour; and in wishing it, it is our hope that we on
this island may soon be lead towards a state of peaceful
coexistence.

Yours sincerely,

Secretary, DUIUA.

Letter of thanks to President Mary McAleese following her
inaugural 12 July garden party in 1998, delivering on her election
promise to 'build bridges' between communities North and
South. The letter-writer refers to the murder the previous week of
three children in a sectarian arson attack by loyalist paramilitaries
on their home in Co. Antrim.

Building bridges: a North–South
reception to mark the annual 12 July
garden party at Áras an Uachtaráin.
President Mary McAleese poses with
members of the Northern Irish Regiment
and the No. 1 Army Band.

President Michael D. Higgins addressing the
European Parliament in Strasbourg. In his
address he called for a 'radical rethink' of
how EU leaders were handling the Eurozone
debt crisis, in April 2013. 'There is nothing …
more crushing to an individual than endemic
unemployment, particularly to young people,'
he said.

Chapter 2

Foreign Correspondence

Ireland on the World Stage

Rory Montgomery

Some of the president's international duties are formal – writing to foreign counterparts to mark national days or to express condolences on deaths and disasters, for instance. However, presidents' own personalities and interests have contributed to Ireland's international reputation and growing place in the world.

The 1937 Constitution, which established the office of president, marked an important step in Ireland's journey to achieve sovereignty. That journey was completed with the entry into force of the Republic of Ireland Act in 1949, which attracted hundreds of congratulatory letters to President Seán T. O'Kelly from Heads of State and Irish people around the world. The mayors of several US cities congratulated him on 'the ending, after eight hundred years, of the occupation of Ireland'. An immediate consequence of Ireland's departure from the Commonwealth was that it was now the president who signed the credentials of Irish ambassadors taking up duty abroad – an important symbolic change.

Foreign policy can pose challenges. President O'Kelly received letters of complaint after the Taoiseach, Éamon de Valera, paid his condolences

KING GEORGE SENDS GOOD WISHES

THE President, Mr. O'Kelly, has received the following messages of goodwill on the occasion of the inauguration of the Republic:—

FROM KING GEORGE VI—" I send you my sincere good wishes on this day, being well aware of the neighbourly links which hold the people of the Republic of Ireland in close association with my subjects of the United Kingdom. I hold in most grateful memory the services and sacrifices of the men and women of your country, who rendered gallant assistance to our cause in the recent war, and who made a notable contribution to our victory. I pray that every blessing may be with you to-day and in the future."

FROM PRESIDENT TRUMAN —" On the occasion of the entering into force of the Republic of Ireland Act, I send to you and to the Irish people, on behalf of the people of the United States of America, sincere good wishes for the continued welfare and prosperity of your country."

FROM SIGNOR EINAUDI, President of the Republic of Italy— " On the occasion of the proclamation of the Republic of Ireland, bound to Italy by ties of traditional and well-tried friendship, as well as by common ideals, please accept the good wishes which, on behalf of the Italian nation and personally, I tender herewith for the happiness of Your Excellency and for the well-being and prosperity of the Irish people."

FROM AUSTRALIA—" On this occasion of national celebration, the Government of the Commonwealth of Australia tenders to Your Excellency sincere and affectionate greetings and good wishes for the happiness and prosperity of yourself and of your people. It is the earnest desire of the Australian Government that the warmest personal ties will continue to bind our countries."

FROM SAO SHWE THAIK, President of the Union of Burma.— " On this memorable day I send you, Mr. President, and through you to the Government and people of your newly-born Republic, heartiest greetings and best wishes on my own behalf and on behalf of the Government and people of the Union of Burma. We look forward with confidence to·a long and happy association between our two countries."

MR. PAASIKIVI, President of Finland, asked Mr. O'Kelly " to accept hearty congratulations and warmest wishes."

FROM THE CROWN PRINCE-REGENT OF SWEDEN—" On the occasion of the celebration of the coming into operation of the Republic of Ireland Act, I wish to express my sincere congratulations and best wishes for yourself and for the prosperity of your country."

TO THE TAOISEACH

The following messages have been received by the Taoiseach :—

FROM MR. ATTLEE, Prime Minister of Great Britain.—" On this significant occasion I send a message of greeting from the Government and people of the United Kingdom to the Republic and all good wishes for its progress and prosperity in the future. We have many ties of kinship and common interests, and I look forward with confidence to the maintenance of a close and cordial friendship between our two countries."

FROM MR. ST. LAURENT, Prime Minister of Canada.—" On the occasion of the establishment of the Republic of Ireland, I have pleasure in extending to you, on behalf of the Government and people of Canada, the most cordial good wishes for a happy and prosperous future. At this time, we cannot fail to recall the memorable contribution made by pioneers of Irish stock to the building of the Canadian nation. Remembering this, we look forward with confidence to the continuation of the friendship which has for so many years linked the Irish and Canadian peoples together."

FROM DR. MALAN, Prime Minister of South Africa :—

" With to-day's entry into force of the Republic of Ireland Act, a constitutional change has taken place which marks the fulfilment of an ideal which has long been cherished by the Irish people. In welcoming the new Republic, tribute is due both to Irish statesmanship and to the statesmanship of the United Kingdom that the fulfilment of this ideal has resulted in the strengthening of the ties of friendship and association between the two countries. South Africa, too, is gratified that the relations of the Republic of Ireland with the Union, as with other member-States of the Commonwealth, will continue to be characterised by special ties of understanding, friendship and goodwill which cannot but prove mutually beneficial amidst the difficulties and complexities of to-day's international problems.

" On this important and happy occasion I am, therefore, glad to send you the greetings of the Government with our best wishes that the new Republic, whose birth has been attended by such happy auspices, will prosper and grow from strength to strength in cordial and willing collaboration with all who share with her the common traditions of western democracy and Christian civilisation."

FROM MR. FRASER, Prime Minister of New Zealand—" On the occasion of the entry into force of the Republic of Ireland Act, in conveying to you and your Government most cordial greetings from the Government of New Zealand. I should like to reaffirm our hope that the friendly relations existing between our two countries will be fully maintained, and that the free association of Ireland with all the countries of the British Commonwealth will continue to be marked by close co-operation, mutual confidence and a spirit of good-will."

FROM PANDIT NEHRU, Prime Minister of India—" On the occasion of coming into force of the Republic of Ireland Act, 1948, I wish to convey to the Government and people of Ireland the sincere wishes of the Government and people of India. I sincerely hope that the friendship which has marked the relationship between our two countries will be maintained, and even strengthened, by close co-operation in the extension of democratic freedom to the peoples of the world which do not now enjoy it, and in the firm establishment of world peace."

FROM MR. LANGE, Acting Prime Minister of Norway—" On the coming into force of the Republic of Ireland Act, I have the honour to express to Your Excellency the good wishes of the Norwegian Government and the Norwegian people for the future of the new Republic."

Ignored by North

Apart from the ban on demonstrations by the Northern Ireland Minister of Home Affairs, Mr. Warnock, and the consequent police precautions, Northern Ireland officially ignored the birth of the Republic.

'Ireland takes her place among the nations of the world,' announced the headlines, as hundreds of messages arrived at Áras an Uachtaráin congratulating President Seán T. O'Kelly on the enactment of the Republic of Ireland Act on 18 April 1949.

Dun Laoghaire

Enthusiastic scenes marked the coming into force of the Republic of Ireland along the coastal area and other parts of South Co. Dublin. Bonfires, meetings and parades formed a background to the official salute to the Republic which took place at Dun Laoghaire.

A torchlight procession headed by a band marched from Blackrock to Dean's Grange, Cabinteely, Foxrock, Carrickmines and Cornelscourt, where the final rally was held. Bonfires dotted the countryside from Rathfarnham to Dean's Grange.

The ceremonies began one minute after midnight at Dun Laoghaire with a fanfare of trumpets and roll of drums as the Tricolour was broken at the masthead near the saluting station on the East Pier. A naval guard of honour presented arms and searchlights from corvettes in the bay spotted the Flag as it ascended the mast. Then boomed out the salute of 21 guns fired by a detachment of the 14th Field Battery at ten-second intervals. The Reveille was sounded by buglers of the Army No. 3 Band.

The playing of the National Anthem concluded the ceremony, which was witnessed by a huge concourse of people, including a goodly number of English visitors who were spending the Easter holiday in hotels in the area.

World Interest In Ceremonies

FOREIGN journalists and photographers who are attending the ceremonies include representatives of newspapers and newsagencies in Britain, the United States, France, Denmark, Sweden, Canada, India, and Australia. There are also radio news commentators from the B.B.C., American, Canadian and Swiss Broadcasting Corporations. A special film record of the ceremonies is being made by the Paramount Film Company.

The Irish Independent reports on the moment Ireland became a republic: midnight on Easter Sunday, 17/18 April 1949. The occasion was marked with a 21-gun salute fired at midnight from O'Connell Bridge. Dun Laoghaire celebrated with cannon blasts and a flag-raising ceremony on the East Pier, illuminated by searchlights from craft in the bay, followed by a torchlit procession.

to the head of the German legation in Dublin on the death of Hitler – an act over which he had no say. Presidents need to speak and write in accordance with government advice – as evidenced by the directions in the 1980s not to reply to letters from Colonel Gaddafi of Libya and Fidel Castro of Cuba. Over time, though, they have pushed the boundaries, and governments have given them freer rein – within limits.

Ireland's entry to the United Nations in 1955 greatly expanded our international horizons. In the years afterwards, diplomatic relations were established with many more countries, including those emerging from colonisation, with the Soviet Union and its satellites, and with the People's Republic of China. However, these new political and economic ties can impose their own constraints. For instance, full-throated support from Presidents O'Kelly and de Valera for the Dalai Lama and the cause of Tibet has given way over time to a much more hesitant approach, stemming from an awareness of the risks and consequences of Chinese retaliation. Ireland is by no means unique in this.

Éamon de Valera was the most internationally famous Irish statesman of the twentieth century and enjoyed

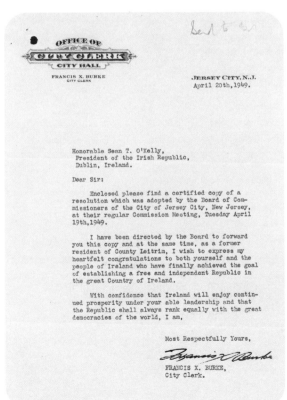

Jersey City welcomes Ireland's enactment of the Republic of Ireland Act, on 18 April 1949, having 'resisted tyranny and oppression' for eight hundred years.

BY MAYOR EGGERS

WHEREAS, the Republic of Ireland was officially proclaimed to the World on Easter Monday, April 18, 1949; and

WHEREAS, Ireland having been invaded in 1172 and for 800 years successive generations of Irish men have resisted tyranny and oppression and have continuously fought to regain their independence and establish a free Ireland; and

WHEREAS, these efforts reached their climax on Easter Monday in 1916 when the Provisional Government of the Irish Republic was proclaimed by President Patrick H. Pearse; and

WHEREAS, sovereign military forces of the mighty British Empire succeeded in suppressing this gallant effort executing President Patrick H. Pearse and 14 members of his staff for their part in the struggle; and

WHEREAS, the Constitution of Ireland as proclaimed in 1916 and reiterated this Easter Monday, 1949, closely paralleled the Constitution of the United States of America and emphasizes the adherence and beliefs of the Irish people in the principles of Democratic Government; and

WHEREAS, there has existed from the founding of the United States of America a deep and abiding friendship and affection between our people and the people of Ireland

NOW, THEREFORE, BE IT RESOLVED, that the City of Jersey City extends its felicitations to the Irish people on the culmination of their efforts to elect a sovereign independent state with the further wish that Divine Providence may see fit to ordain the abolition of the artificial border separating one part of Ireland from the other,

BE IT FURTHER RESOLVED, that copies of this Resolution as adopted by the Mayor and Board of City Commissioners of Jersey City be forwarded to President Sean T. O'Kelly of the Irish Republic and to the President of the United States of America.

This is to certify that the foregoing is a true copy of a resolution passed by the Board of Commissioners of Jersey City, N.J., at its meeting held. **APR 19 1949**

Francis Burke
City Clerk.

Jersey City was among dozens of US cities, including Chicago, New York and San Francisco, which adopted a resolution, a formal expression of the opinion of the city council, to celebrate the enactment of the Republic of Ireland Act.

A GRACIOUS O'KELLY GESTURE TO MAMIE

President Sean O'Kelly of Ireland gained an admirer with his gallant greeting of Mrs. Eisenhower at a White House dinner given for him.

O'Kelly had been in the U.S. before, as Irish ambassador in 1924–26. But this was the first time an Irish president had paid a state visit.

President O'Kelly's headline-making State Visit to the US in 1959 was the first by a President of Ireland and helped repair strained relations after Ireland's neutral stance during World War II.

particular respect in newly independent countries, as the letters he received throughout his fourteen years in office show. When he became president in 1959, he received the congratulations of many counterparts, including three former generals who were now Heads of State: Charles de Gaulle, Dwight D. Eisenhower and Francisco Franco. Ten years later he received de Gaulle at Áras an Uachtaráin on his post-resignation visit to Ireland, and in 1970 he sent a telegram of condolence to de Gaulle's widow, Yvonne.

Presidential visits abroad have become a major part of the role. The first-ever State Visit was President O'Kelly's to the Vatican, followed by his visit to the United States in 1959, after which he was warmly congratulated by people he had met, at all levels: his letters of thanks to those on the American side who had helped with the visit were described as the

'nicest ever received' from a Head of State. The number and range of visits grew enormously from the 1980s onwards, when Patrick Hillery was president. He travelled as far as Australia and New Zealand, and exchanged visits with the King and Queen of Spain; on their visit he brought them to his hometown of Spanish Point, Co. Clare.

Hillery's successor, Mary Robinson, broke new ground by using her visits to highlight issues of international concern. She reported to other Heads of State after visiting Somalia during a ceasefire in its civil war – the first visit in that period by any foreign leader. She also visited Rwanda after the Tutsi genocide. As a former anti-apartheid activist, she was warmly received in South Africa. These visits helped to further establish her international reputation, and pointed the way to her subsequent appointment as United

1842 North Capitol St.
Washington, D. C.
May 24, 1945

Ignore

President Hyde
Chief Executive of the Irish Republic
Dublin, Ireland

Dear President Hyde:

Because of Irish censorship, it is somewhat difficult for Americans to know exactly what the nature of the present Irish government is but I am enclosing an article (one of the few articles concerning Ireland to appear in America recently as most of our newsprint is devoted to countries fighting for decency and freedom) which appeared in the conservative New York Herald-Tribune about two weeks ago. You will note that it mentions the Irish swastika at half mast in mourning of the unconfirmed death of the world's leading murderer.

Things must have undergone drastic change since my grandmother left Ireland. I have constantly attempted to keep up with these changes, but since the assumption of the premiership by a non-Irish Brooklyn boy with the Spanish (Franco) name, who placed Irish foreign policy solidly in partnership with the German forces of paganism and destruction I can only hazard a guess as to the present composition of the Irish government.

I should greatly appreciate therefore your reply (in either verse or prose) to the following questions:

1. Has the sacred color of the shamrock been put to the perverted use of coloring a swastika or is the Irish swastika like the present Irish foreign policy, an exact miniature of the late Third German Reich?

2. Do the Irish people who permitted this dastardly government to remain in power expect the same consideration from the victorious democratic nations that is justly due gallant little Greece?

3. Which direction is Ireland looking for assistance and friendship these days?

4. Will there be a little three dictatorship alliance by Portugal, Spain, and Ireland?

5. Will the southern Ireland volunteers who fought with such valor and distinction in the courageous British 8th Army under Ireland's own Field Marshall Montgomery be deprived of Irish citizenship because they fought and died for the principle of justice and democracy?

6. If the answer to 5 (above) is no, is it possible that those who fought for justice will insist upon it by conducting tresson trials for those public officials responsible for the flagrant betrayal of the Irish people?

Should I receive no reply to the above questions, I and countless other Americans of Irish extraction can but conclude that the Irish swastika is still flying over the historic land of the Shamrock.

Very truly yours

Esther Hagan Taylor

Esther Hagan Taylor

P.S. I regret that the Ireland of St. Patrick, Schelly and Victor Herbert is not at San Fransisco assisting in the construction of a just and peaceful world.

'The Irish swastika is still flying over the historic land of the Shamrock,' says one of the many letters to President Douglas Hyde expressing outrage at the formal condolences paid by Taoiseach Éamon de Valera to Germany on the death of Adolf Hitler.

D D E

THE WHITE HOUSE

June 24, 1959.

Dear Mr. President:

Thank you so much for your two recent letters.

I write this note on the eve of your departure from the office of the Presidency of Ireland. I quite understand the contentment with which you face your new life, knowing that you will take with you great satisfaction in the splendid service you have given to your country. I am certain that the freedom from official responsibilities and the added leisure to enjoy yourself will give you increased happiness in the years that lie ahead. And I might add, also, that I look forward to just such a refreshing experience some eighteen months from now!

Once again permit me to tell you what a pleasure it was to have you visit our country. You made -- if such a thing could be possible -- new friends for Ireland, and your presence here reaffirmed the warm ties that the people in the United States have always felt for the people of your country.

With the hope that you and Mrs. O'Kelly will find your retirement a peaceful and pleasant adventure, and affectionate regard to you both, in which Mrs. Eisenhower joins,

Sincerely,

Dwight Eisenhower

His Excellency
Sean T. O'Kelly,
Roundwood,
County Wicklow,
Ireland.

As he leaves office, US President Dwight D. Eisenhower writes to President O'Kelly: 'You have made – if such a thing could be possible, new friends for Ireland.'

11th February, 1960.

Excellency,

I duly received your letter of 6th December and would like to convey my thanks for the appreciation expressed by Your Excellency of the action taken by the Irish Delegation at the General Assembly of the United Nations in relation to the treatment of Tibet. In taking this action, the Minister for External Affairs, Mr. Aiken, reflected the sentiments of affliction and of sympathy sincerely felt by the Irish people at the brutal invasion of your country and the treatment of its population.

We most fervently pray that God will so order events as to lead to the restoration of the rights of the Tibetan people and enable them to pursue their way of life in peace and tranquility, free from outside intervention.

I beg Your Excellency to accept my warmest personal good wishes.

Yours sincerely,

Eamon de Valera

His Excellency the Dalai Lama,
Birla House,
Mussoorie, U.P.,
INDIA.

In November 1959, the Dalai Lama thanked President de Valera for Ireland's 'courageous efforts' in raising global awareness of 'the tragic situation the Tibetan people are facing'. This was President de Valera's reply.

Nations High Commissioner for Human Rights. The fact that President Robinson was a liberal woman unexpectedly elected in what was then a conservative country in itself generated interest; when another highly articulate and assertive woman, Mary McAleese, was elected straight after President Robinson, interest was piqued further.

Presidents McAleese and Higgins continued the pattern of extensive travel. The former received Queen Elizabeth II on her historic State Visit to Ireland, although President Robinson had visited London in 1996, and exchanged friendly letters with the queen. In 2013 President Higgery paid the first State Visit by an Irish president to Britain. The three most recent presidents have placed a particular emphasis on reaching out to the Irish diaspora. President Higgins has used many of his visits to make substantial speeches expounding his social and economic philosophy and his views on development, climate change and human rights. Promoting trade and tourism has also become a more significant element in presidential programmes.

It seems certain that future presidents will follow in the footsteps of their predecessors by using the status and symbolic power of the office to highlight and promote Irish foreign policy and international relations.

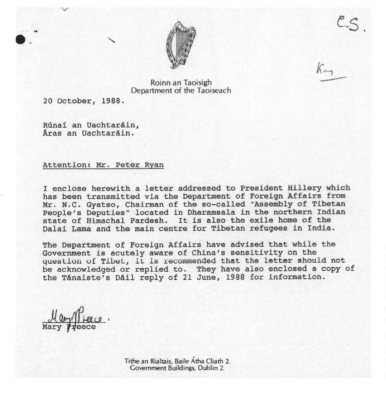

An official from the Department of the Taoiseach directs President Hillery not to acknowledge or reply to a letter from a senior Tibetan leader, and says the Irish government is 'acutely aware of China's sensitivity on the question of Tibet'.

In 1988 President Hillery became the first Irish president to visit the People's Republic of China. Ireland and China established diplomatic relations in June 1970.

Menu for a Welcome Dinner for President Patrick Hillery and his wife, Dr Maeve Hillery, during the first State Visit by a President of Ireland to Japan, September 1983.

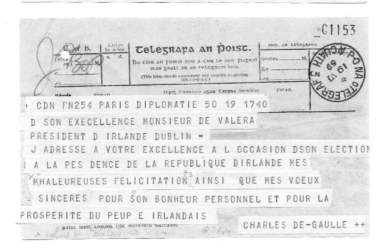

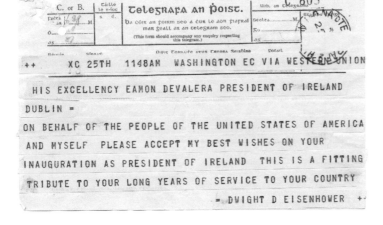

A trio of telegrams from Generals Franco (Spain), Eisenhower (United States), and de Gaulle (France) to the newly inaugurated President of Ireland, Éamon de Valera.

C. or B.	Táille le n-íoc							
	s. d.	**Telegrafa an Poist.**				uiṁ. an Telegrama		

Ní mór an foirm seo do cur le h-aon fiafruí a déanfar mar ġeall ar an telegram so.

(This form must accompany any enquiry respecting this telegram.)

Seólta............M.

Do............

Ag............

Oifig Tosnaíte agus Treoraċa Seirḃíse   Focail

Réamráḋ   Síneaḋ   [P.O. NA dTELEGRAF Á'CUATH 4 II 48]

SCDN TSA346/4   2030 ⁴ M.   BG New Delhi   98/97

Mr S T OCeallaigh President of Ireland   DUBLIN

No 121F C I

On behalf of Government and people of India I thank you Mr
President most sincerely for your affectionate message of sympathy
in the great tragedy that has befallen India stop
India is proud of the historic achievement of this great son of
hers for herself as well as of the nobility of his message to
mankind stop Like you I hope that his martyrdom may serve to
accelerate the reign over this earth of brotherhood among its
peoples.

             Mountbatten of Burma
             Governor General of India.

Louis Mountbatten, 1st Earl Mountbatten
of Burma, the Governor General of
India, thanks President O'Kelly for his
'affectionate message of sympathy' on
the assassination of Mahatma Gandhi.
In 1979 Mountbatten would himself
be assassinated when a Provisional IRA
bomb exploded on his fishing boat at
Mullaghmore, Co. Sligo.

PRIME MINISTER'S HOUSE
NEW DELHI

December 20, 1962.

Dear M. de Valera,

Thank you for your greetings.

Our hearts are heavy this year for our country is facing a most difficult situation. It is good to know that we have friends.

With good wishes for the season and the New Year,

Yours sincerely,

Indira Gandhi

'Our hearts are heavy,' wrote the Prime Minister of India, Indira Gandhi, to President Éamon de Valera. 'It is good to know that we have friends.' It was December 1962, weeks after the outbreak of the Sino-Indian war on the border with China.

GOVERNMENT OF THE REPUBLIC OF BIAFRA

Telephone: 01-373 7463

YOUR REF...........

OUR REF.... Pol. 021/79

Office of the Special Representative
30 Collingham Gardens
London, S.W.5

24th September, 1969.

     The Special Representative of the Republic of Biafra
in the United Kingdom presents his compliments to His
Excellency Mr. Eamon Devalera, President of the Republic
of Ireland, Dublin, and has the honour to transmit the
following message from His Excellency, General C.
Odumegwu Ojukwu to him:

     "Your Excellency,

     The Government and entire people of Biafra
have followed with deep concern and anxiety the
sad events which resulted in loss of lives and
property of the Irish people. May I, on behalf
of my Government and people, convey to Your
Excellency and your countrymen my profound
sympathy for this upheaval which again places
in sharp focus the yearnings of all Irish
people for national unity and self-determination.

     "We in Biafra have all the time drawn
inspiration from your peoples history and ideals
in our present struggle against British
imperialism. I am sure that the identity of
our experiences and ideals will continue to foster
greater mutual understanding and cooperation
between our two peoples.

               General C. Odumegwu Ojukwu
           Head of State and Commander-in-Chief
                 of the Armed Forces,
                 Republic of Biafra."

H.E. Mr. Eamon Devalera,
President of the Republic of Ireland,
Uachtaran Na heireann,
Aras An Uchtarain,
Thoenis Park,
Dublin.

                         /...

In the middle of the Nigerian Civil War
in 1969, the secessionist Biafran leader
General Ojukwu expressed his 'deep
concern' to President de Valera at the
escalation of violence in Northern
Ireland.

FROM: FIELD-MARSHAL THE VISCOUNT MONTGOMERY OF ALAMEIN,
K.G., G.C.B., D.S.O.

ISINGTON MILL,
ALTON,
HANTS.
TEL. BENTLEY 3126.

1 August 1967

My dear President
    I write to ask if Your Excellency will allow me to visit Dublin. A young friend of mine, Alan Howarth, is marrying a Dublin girl, Miss Chance — the daughter of Arthur Chance of 90 Merrion Square. The wedding is to be on September 23, and I would like to arrive in Dublin by air on Thursday September 21. On Friday September 22 I would very much like to pay my respects to Your Excellency, and hear your views on what is going on in the world today — which is not good.
I would stay in the Russell Hotel.

Yrs. very sincerely
Montgomery of Alamein

Lord Montgomery of Alamein, the senior British Army office known as 'Monty' who had family links to Donegal, writes to see if President de Valera is available to meet and discuss 'his views on what is going on in the world today'. The president agreed to meet him.

Teachtaireacht ón Uachtarán Childers chuig an
nGinearál Franco ar dhunmharú Admiral Carrero
Blanco.

Thug an Roinn Gnóthaí Eachtracha fios dom gur chóir
teachtaireacht a chur; aontú Roinn an Taoisigh leis i bprionsabal.

D'aontaigh an tUachtarán leis an téacs seo leanas a shocraigh
Micheál ó Floinn agus mé féin eadrainn, an teachtaireacht a chur
i Spáinnis tríd an Ambasáid seagainne i Madrid:

"His Excellency Francisco Franco Bahamunde,
Head of the Spanish State,
Madrid.

I have learned with a deep sense of regret of the tragic
death of Admiral Carrero Blanco, President of the Spanish
Government.   On behalf of the people of Ireland and on my
own behalf I wish to express to your Excellency and to the
Government and people of Spain our profound sympathy on this
grievous loss suffered by your country.

Erskine Childers   "

móf

29. xii. 73

President Erskine Childers sends a letter
of 'profound sympathy' to President
Franco on the assassination of Admiral
Carrero Blanco, killed by Basque
separatist group ETA.

THE WHITE HOUSE

WASHINGTON

January 14, 1981

Dear Mr. President:

Before leaving the White House and the office of
President, I would like to convey to you and the
people of Ireland my very best wishes for the
future. We take great pride in the close friendship
between our two countries. Just as the family
ties of millions of Americans to Ireland are
reinforced by our common attachment to democratic
principles and freedoms, so are the ties between
our two governments.

Sincerely,

Jimmy Carter

His Excellency
Dr. Patrick J. Hillery
President of Ireland
Dublin

US President Jimmy Carter, as he retires,
writes to President Patrick Hillery: 'We
take great pride in the close friendship
between our two countries.'

Mogadisho
3/10/1992

Your Excellency the President of
Republic of Ireland,

We welcome your visit with indiscribable joy of
heart and will believe that your visit will arouse international
syspathy for the suffering Somali people whose people are
suffering to an unimaginable dgree following the war to liberate
the country and people from dictator Siyad Barre and his clique
followed by conflicts and disunity of the nation caused by
underground placemen of Siad Barre.

Our gratitude for your Excellency who travelled
thousands of kilometrees to see for yourself the extent of our
people is more than some thing that can be expressed in words,
particularly the political problem that the Irish Island is
fading.

We are not unaware that your people back home
regard you as their heroine and your visit to Somalia which is
experiencing its worst calamity in its history makes your
excellency an international humanitarian hero.

It would be grossly ungrateful of us if we fail
to mention the young Irish ladies who also, like Your Excellency,
crossed thousands of kilomtres to share with us our sufferings
and living their comfortablef homes and beloved families and
country to save our people.

We pray to the Almighty to reward Your Excellency
and your people for your sacrifices to save the lives of people
in a distant country.

Finally this humble present is of no value to
Your Excellency exce_pt bring a token of our gratitude and joy
at your visit and to remind you in your life of your visit to
our country for the sake of humaniterianism.

surp risingly your visit reminds one (Somali)
that the Britidh people who knew the Somali characters and
behaviour call the Somalis ""the Irish of Africa".

May the Almighty return you Home savely,

Amen.

DAUD SABDOW MOHAMED
&
MURUG JEYLANI MOHD

A letter from Mogadishu thanking
President Robinson for visiting
Somalia and noting that the Somalis
are referred to as 'the Irish of Africa'.

President Mary Robinson writes to
the Heads of State of the UN Security
Council, the EEC and the Council
of Europe about her visit to famine-
stricken Somalia.

October, 1992

At the request of the Irish aid agencies who are particularly
active in the region, and with the approval of the Irish
Government, I recently visited Somalia and Northern Kenya to see
at first hand the effects of the famine in the region. I was
accompanied by the Irish Minister for Foreign Affairs, Mr. David
Andrews, T.D.. The conditions that I found there, on which I
subsequently reported to the Secretary General of the United
Nations, are so appalling that I feel compelled to bring them
also to your personal attention.

The scale of death and misery in the area is almost beyond belief
and the degradation and humiliation that has been visited on the
Somali people diminishes all of us as human beings. Many
thousands are dying each week and millions are at grave risk.
The international community has to assume responsibility for the
immediate adoption of the measures required to cope with this
catastrophe.

During my visit I witnessed the heroic work of the aid agencies
and the remarkable impact of their feeding programmes. Yet that
is not enough and the deaths continue daily. The amount of food
and relief supplies reaching Somalia is seriously inadequate and
security for humanitarian assistance is desperately needed.

The horrific scenes of starvation are not confined to Somalia.
In Mozambique and other parts of Southern Africa, drought and
civil war have resulted in serious food shortages and there is
now a very real risk of famine in the coming months. The
international community must take urgent measures to ensure that
adequate resources are provided to save these people. It is
vitally important, I believe, now that we have emerged from two
generations of Cold War, that the World should develop the
capacity to respond to such dreadful situations with effective
international action.

Because my own visit was to Somalia and because of the appalling
nature of what I found there, you will understand that that
country in particular is the focus of my attention. I believe
strongly that the international community has the resources to
save the people of Somalia and that those resources must be
applied in sufficient quantity and without delay so that many
more deaths will be prevented and the tragedy which is striking
a whole people will be averted.

It is my earnest request that you will bring this message to the
attention of your Government and that you and they will find it
possible to give your support to a more urgent, co-ordinated
international humanitarian response to the plight of the Somali
people utilising the full resources of the United Nations.

President   *Republiek van Suid-Afrika*

Dear Madam President

I was very pleased to hear that you have accepted my
invitation to visit South Africa and that the last week in
March 1996 will be an acceptable time for you.

Ireland has always been dear to me with its strong Anti
Apartheid Movement in the past and its unstinting support in
our struggle towards a democratic South Africa. I am glad
that our relations are ever strengthening with Embassies
established in both South Africa and Ireland and a South
African Ambassador to be appointed in Dublin very soon.

I look forward to hosting you in this country and can assure
of the heartiest of welcomes from all concerned.

With kind regards

NR MANDELA

Her Excellency Mrs Mary Robinson
President of Ireland
Aras an Uachtaráin
Phoenix Park
Dublin
Ireland

The President of South Africa, Nelson
Mandela, thanks Ireland for its 'unstinting
support in our struggle' and says he looks
forward to the visit by President Robinson.

UACHTARÁN NA hÉIREANN
PRESIDENT OF IRELAND

12 September, 2001

His Excellency George W. Bush
President of the US

Dear President,

I wish to extend to you, on my own behalf and on behalf of the people of Ireland, our deepest sympathies on the loss of so many lives in the attacks on the World Trade Centre, the Pentagon and also Pittsburgh earlier today. I was greatly shocked to learn of these dreadful assaults.

Our thoughts and prayers are with the victims and their families and I would like to sympathise with you and all the people of the United States of America at home and abroad. These are crimes against the very foundations of all our humanity.

It is our fervent hope that the rescue and emergency services will succeed in minimising the loss of life.

Yours sincerely,

Mary McAleese
President of Ireland

President Mary McAleese writes to
the US President George W. Bush
in the immediate aftermath of the
terrorist attacks in the United States
on 11 September 2001.

Chapter 3

Nearest Neighbours
Northern Ireland and Great Britain

Martina Devlin

'Everything passes', according to Oscar Wilde in an essay on art and criticism, observing how – over time – the owl built its nest in the remains of King Priam's palace, while shepherds and goatherds wandered over Troy's plains, where epic battles had once been fought.

True, of course, but only up to a point. A presidential archive – recording letters, telegrams and, more recently, emails sent to Heads of State in times of celebration, challenge and controversy – allows future generations to immerse themselves in the State's standout moments. What's past remains accessible, even if changing attitudes mean it sometimes appears incomprehensible.

Long before she used her memorable *cúpla focal* during the 2011 State Visit to Ireland, Queen Elizabeth was sending conciliatory gestures from Buckingham Palace, such as a telegram to President Éamon de Valera on his eightieth birthday in 1962. Although only one sentence

UACHTARÁN NA HEIREANN

SGEUL..............British.National.Anthem..............................

FO-SGEUL...........Playing.when.President.is.present..............................

....

GENERAL NOTE.

1.   When the President is present at a function in
Ireland no Anthem may be played in his honour except
the Irish National Anthem.

2.   If the Irish Anthem is not played, no other
Anthem should, under any circumstances, be played.

3.   If the Anthems of other countries are played in
honour of visiting teams or competitors representing
their respective countries, these foreign Anthems
should be played in circumstances which clearly
indicate their subordination to the Irish National
Anthem.

4.   The Irish National Anthem was played for the
President at the Horse Show on the occasion of his
attendance in 1938 (P.463). Subsequently, the
Anthems of all the countries of the Military Teams
competing in the National Military Jumping Competition,
including the Irish one, were played as each team
moved into the jumping enclosure. In each case the
playing of the Anthem was clearly an act of courtesy
to the competitors.

5.   A separate note is attached regarding a pro-
British demonstration which took place on that
occasion.

Fodhla—Wt. 3277—Gp. 50—500—11/'37—P 6918.
Wt. 1742—Gp. 50—5,000—7/'38—Q 3448.

Over/

long, it is of historical interest, considering the fact that in his youth he had waged war on her grandfather's armed forces.

In the early years of statehood, Ireland stood on its dignity and was vigilant about potential slights. A 1938 Áras an Uachtaráin memo stipulates that only the Irish national anthem – not the British national anthem – should be played at events where the president is in attendance.

As time went on, formal courtesies had a gradual impact. The declaration of the Republic in 1949 led to an extraordinary letter of congratulations to

President Seán T. O'Kelly from George VI, son of the king-emperor who had lost possession of three-quarters of Ireland some twenty-seven years earlier. It was gracious, to say the least.

The Welsh Republican Movement also sent its good wishes, along with a surfeit of optimism: 'Today Ireland. Tomorrow Wales. Forward the Celtic Republics.' The 'Donegal Society of Philadelphia' pledged

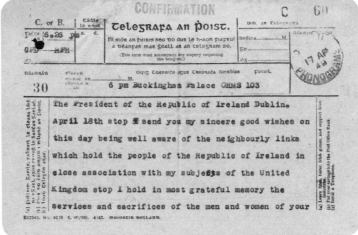

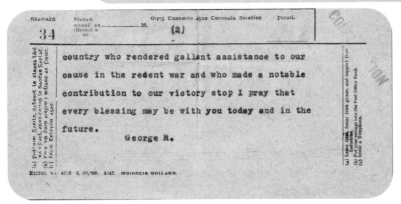

The only national anthem to be played in honour of the President of Ireland when he is present is the Irish national anthem, according to a memo dated 15 November 1938.

Telegram from Britain's King George VI to President Seán T. O'Kelly on the declaration of Ireland's independence on 18 April 1949: 'I pray that every blessing may be with you today and in the future.'

ROYAL COURT TELEGRAM

SERIAL No.	TIME HANDED IN	OFFICE OF ORIGIN AND SERVICE INSTRUCTIONS	WORDS	RECEIVED AT h. m.	DATE OR OFFICE STAMP
	10.22 PM 18/4	DUBLIN			

To   HIS MAJESTY KING GEORGE THE SIXTH
        BUCKINGHAM PALACE

I AM VERY GRATEFUL FOR YOUR MAJESTYS KIND
GRACIOUS MESSAGE OF GOOD WISHES WHICH I CAN ASSURE YOUR MAJESTY
                                    OF
WILL BE WARMLY APPRECIATED BY THE PEOPLE/IRELAND ON THIS OCCASION
OF SUCH DEEP SIGNIFICANCE TO THE IRISH NATION PERMIT ME TO EXPRESS
TO YOUR MAJESTY MY SINCERE GOOD WISHES FOR THE PEACE AND PROSPERITY
OF GREAT BRITAIN WITH WHICH IRELAND HAS SO MANY TIES AND SUCH
SPECIAL RELATIONS I EARNESTLY HOPE THAT THESE RELATIONS WILL
CONTINUE AND THAT OUR TWO COUNTRIES MAY ADVANCE TO A BETTER AND
MORE CORDIAL FRIENDSHIP ON MY OWN BEHALF AND ON BEHALF OF THE
PEOPLE OF IRELAND I PRAY THAT GOD MAY GRANT YOUR MAJESTY HEALTH
AND HAPPINESS .

        SEAN T. OCEALLAIGH
           PRESIDENT OF IRELAND .

President Seán T. O'Kelly thanks King
George VI, by return: 'I am very grateful
for Your Majesty's kind gracious message
of good wishes.'

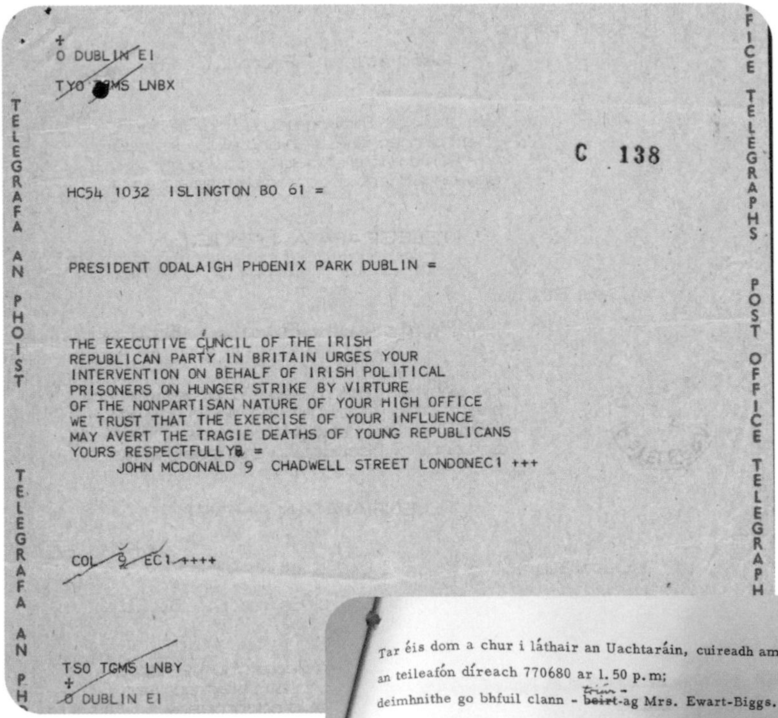
+
O DUBLIN EI

TYO TGMS LNBX

C 138

HC54 1032 ISLINGTON BO 61 =

PRESIDENT ODALAIGH PHOENIX PARK DUBLIN =

THE EXECUTIVE CUNCIL OF THE IRISH
REPUBLICAN PARTY IN BRITAIN URGES YOUR
INTERVENTION ON BEHALF OF IRISH POLITICAL
PRISONERS ON HUNGER STRIKE BY VIRTURE
OF THE NONPARTISAN NATURE OF YOUR HIGH OFFICE
WE TRUST THAT THE EXERCISE OF YOUR INFLUENCE
MAY AVERT THE TRAGIE DEATHS OF YOUNG REPUBLICANS
YOURS RESPECTFULLYB =
JOHN MCDONALD 9 CHADWELL STREET LONDONEC1 +++

COL 9 EC1 ++++

TSO TGMS LNBY
+
O DUBLIN EI

Citing the 'non-partisan' nature of the presidency, republicans in the UK seek President Cearbhall Ó Dálaigh to intervene in the 1974 hunger strikes of the Provisional IRA political prisoners.

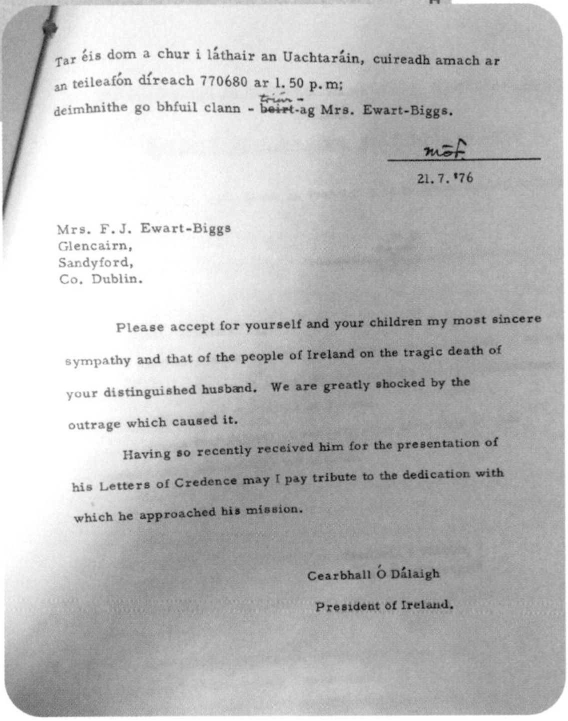
Tar éis dom a chur i láthair an Uachtaráin, cuireadh amach ar an teileafón díreach 770680 ar 1.50 p.m;
deimhnithe go bhfuil clann - ~~beirt~~ triúr -ag Mrs. Ewart-Biggs.

mó f.
21.7.'76

Mrs. F.J. Ewart-Biggs
Glencairn,
Sandyford,
Co. Dublin.

Please accept for yourself and your children my most sincere sympathy and that of the people of Ireland on the tragic death of your distinguished husband. We are greatly shocked by the outrage which caused it.

Having so recently received him for the presentation of his Letters of Credence may I pay tribute to the dedication with which he approached his mission.

Cearbhall Ó Dálaigh
President of Ireland.

President Cearbhall Ó Dálaigh offers his 'most sincere sympathy' to the wife of British Ambassador Christopher Ewart-Biggs, who was assassinated by a Provisional IRA landmine attack in Dublin in 1976.

support for efforts 'to regain the occupied territory in northeastern Ireland'. Rather more touching was a telegram from one Wendy Wood to 'Sean Kelly Dublin' in which she wrote: 'God be with you in your nationhood may partition end and Scotland also earn freedom.'

By 1952, further evidence of an entente cordiale between Ireland and Britain was emerging. Discussions were held about President O'Kelly attending George VI's funeral, but Taoiseach de Valera was opposed because a portion of Ireland 'is still foreseeably with-held from Irish control'. A compromise was struck with Áras flags flown at half-mast and flowers from the president dispatched to Windsor.

The Irish-British diplomatic relationship bedded down, in tandem with changing attitudes to the border – in the Republic, there was increased acceptance of the reality of partition. However, the blanket and dirty protests in Long Kesh, after special category status was withdrawn from paramilitary prisoners, reopened wounds in the 1970s, drawing a bustle of written protests to the Áras. One, from the Executive Council of the Irish Republican Party in Britain, urged President Cearbhall Ó Dálaigh's intervention, using 'the non-partisan nature of your high office'.

> The 2nd of September 1981. I have been in Clare for a large part of the Summer and will just dictate some of the things that occurred.

> The H-Block people organised a march on my house in Spanish Point prior to Pat Duffy, one of SDU men on me came to say would I receive a letter handed in by two of them, that the superintendent thought that would suffice and they may go away. There was nothing clear whether they were going to leave a picket on the house for the Summer or not. I agreed to this and they were to come at 10 o'clock on Saturday morning. I told the children and the O'Connors and asked Norman not to go to 10 o'clock mass as he usually was doing. There was some gardai at the back of the house. I could hear them speaking and I saw guns visible in the car.

President Patrick Hillery writes an account of an anti H-Block march on his home at Spanish Point, Co. Clare, in the summer of 1981. He said he could see armed Gardaí (Special Defence Unit) at the back of his house. He told his children a letter of protest in support of republican prisoners was handed in.

> The letter appeared to me as a doctor, on humanitarian reasons, to say my oath as a doctor was an older oath than my oath as President to remain neutral politically. The oath was to preserve human life. They really can argue on what people should do who are not involved or who are not in a position to do anything.

CONFIDENTIAL

VISIT TO NORTHERN IRELAND BY PRESIDENT ROBINSON, 18-19 JUNE 1993

I have been instructed on behalf of the United Kingdom Government to report our serious concern at the proposed inclusion in the projected visit by President Robinson to Northern Ireland of a two hour meeting in West Belfast on the afternoon of Friday 18 June.

As developed by the groups who are organising it, this event has become a very one sided affair. The list of people expected to be present includes a number of prominent members of Sinn Fein. There are some persons who have been convicted of terrorist offences or who are suspected of involvement in support for terrorist activities.

A meeting by President Robinson with such people would do very grave disservice to community relations in Northern Ireland. It would have the inevitable effect of exacerbating threats in security there. It would have a very serious and prejudicial impact on Unionist opinion. They would see it as a calculated expression of support by the President personally and by the Irish Government for unconstitutional politics.

Such a meeting would also inevitably have an impact on the political standing of the British Government in Northern Ireland and of the Secretary of State for Northern Ireland personally. In the circumstances he could not but make clear in public that such a visit, if it goes ahead, was doing so against his specific advice.

We would also be concerned about the security implications of such a meeting. The Secretary of State for Northern Ireland would also have to refer to this aspect in his public statement making clear that by proceeding with the visit the President was ignoring his advice that it might endanger life.

In addition the Secretary of State for Northern Ireland would need to make clear that full details of the proposed visit had only been made available to us three days in advance, precluding any possibility of adjusting the arrangements so as to avoid these difficulties.

The Secretary of State for Northern Ireland is well aware of the profound damage which would be caused to bilateral relations between Britain and Ireland by his having to make such a statement. He therefore earnestly trusts that President Robinson will not go ahead with this element of her proposed visit.

CONFIDENTIAL

The British Secretary of State for Northern Ireland, James Prior, advises President Mary Robinson that her planned meeting with community groups in West Belfast would be going against 'his specific advice' and might 'endanger life'.

Tensions ratcheted up in 1981 as, one by one, ten hunger strikers starved to death, including MP Bobby Sands. Protestors targeted President Patrick Hillery's family home in Co. Clare, as he recorded on 2 September 1981: 'The H-Block people organised a march on my house in Spanish Point.' One of his Garda protection unit asked if he would accept a letter from the demonstrators, in the hope of persuading them to leave, amid concerns that his property might be picketed for some time. President Hillery, who remarked on the sight of armed Gardaí at the back of his house, agreed to receive the letter in person. Its contents suggested his oath as a doctor to preserve life pre-dated his oath as president to remain politically neutral. However, the president, who had practised medicine before being elected to political office as a Fianna Fáil TD, was unconvinced.

Mary Robinson's presidency was notable for her commitment to the peace process. She did not shy away from the Troubles, and following the 1993 Warrington bombings, which claimed the lives of two children and injured many

Oifig an Taoisigh
Office of the Taoiseach

16 June, 1993.

Mrs. Mary Robinson,
President of Ireland.

Dear President,

I refer to your proposed visit to Northern Ireland later this week.

I have to inform you that late last night, the British Ambassador to Ireland delivered a note to the Secretary to the Government, expressing the serious concern of his Government at the proposed inclusion in your visit, of a meeting in West Belfast with community groups.

The reasons for the British Government's concern are set out in the note, a copy of which I enclose. In the light of the views expressed in the note which have to be taken seriously, together with the security considerations, the Government feel that you may wish to reconsider the advisability of your planned visit to West Belfast, as currently envisaged.

Yours sincerely,

Taoiseach

Oifig an Taoisigh, Tithe an Rialtais, Baile Átha Cliath 2.
Office of the Taoiseach, Government Buildings, Dublin 2.

Taoiseach Albert Reynolds warns President Mary Robinson to 'reconsider the advisability' of her planned trip to West Belfast. The president went ahead with the event, which included a controversial handshake with Sinn Féin leader Gerry Adams.

GERRY ADAMS MP
Sinn Féin
18 July 1997

President Mary Robinson
Aras an Uachtaran

A Chara

Martin McGuinness and I have provided a detailed political report and assessment to the IRA and urged them to restore the cessation of August '94. I have been told that they will respond without undue delay.

If this is secured it is critical that the objectives of the peace process are advanced as speedily as possible and that this new opportunity is not squandered the British government as happened before.

I thank you for your efforts to date in pursuit of a just and lasting peace in Ireland.

Is mise

Gerry Adams MP
President

Sinn Féin President Gerry Adams briefs
President Mary Robinson in advance of
an IRA ceasefire in 1997.

... recently reported that you in the company of the most senior member
...) of the Windsor family did attend the funeral services of the two boy
... s of the I R A in Warrington

When these three I R A terrorists were shot dead in Gibralter their cadavers were
sent by air to Dublin. . From that city they were conveyed by road to Belfast.
On the part of the journey through the free state the route was festooned with black
flags. This was obviously done to betoken respect and fellow feelings towards
these I R A murderers

It is contended that that massive demonstration did indicate the true sentiments
of the majority of the population of s ireland and I believe that your attendance
at that funeral service was a mere window dressing act

I further believe that all southern irish should only be treated as pariahs, that
they should be ostracised and totally denied all U K benefits

                                         Yours uncordially

To correct any false impression I do mention I am a Mass attending R C

Copy to The Rev: Ian Paisley M P

A hostile response to President Mary Robinson's attendance at the memorial service in Warrington on the first anniversary of the bombing by the Provisional IRA, 1993, saying it was 'a mere window dressing act'.

THE LILLIE ROAD C   LIMITED

                             MORE HOUSE

                             28 The Grove,
                             Isleworth,
                             Middlesex
                             TW7 4JU

                    Phone 081 568 9487
                          081 568 2079
                    Fax   081 758 9263

                    10/4/94

Dear President Robinson,

Thank you very much for attending the Warrington
Memorial Service. It was a tremendous support for
the Irish community in Britain to have you there. I
do hope that the anger and the love that has come
out of this tragedy will spark the beginning of an
ongoing and productive shared peace movement.

Renewed thanks for this and for the many positive
initiatives you have so far taken in your term as
President. Every blessing and every success for
the future.

Yours sincerely,

Father Ken McCabe,
Director,
More House.

By contrast to the above, a letter to Mary Robinson from Father Ken McCabe, an Irish priest and children's rights activist in the UK, who told the president that her visit to Warrington was a 'tremendous support' to the Irish community in Britain. Two children, Tim Parry (12) and Johnathan Ball (3), died in the attack.

other people, she attended a memorial service in the Cheshire town to pay Ireland's respects to the community. 'You brought the ordinary people of our two islands together,' she was assured, in a letter of acknowledgment signed by the town mayor. A postal flurry shows that while some considered her presence at the event an insult – several correspondents proposed that Irish people in Britain should be denied social welfare – most felt that she had done the right thing.

Another of President Robinson's achievements was to normalise visits by Ireland's Head of State north of the border. In 1993, a planned trip set alarm bells ringing because her itinerary included a cultural centre in West Belfast, where Sinn Féin members, including Gerry Adams, would be in attendance. Unionism bristled, the Secretary of State for Northern Ireland objected, and Britain leaned on the Irish government.

The Albert Reynolds–Dick Spring coalition proved susceptible to pressure. As Taoiseach, Mr Reynolds wrote to the president enclosing a letter from the British Ambassador outlining 'serious concerns' and complaining that attendees would include people convicted of terrorism. The list of negative repercussions predicted by Britain included everything but the sky falling in. The Irish government advised President Robinson not to go but she went anyway, and an historic handshake took place between her and Mr Adams. Such acts of leadership paved the way for the Good Friday Agreement.

Parity of congratulations is the subtext of a pair of letters from Mary McAleese sent in October 1998 to John Hume and David Trimble, following the news that they were to share the Nobel Peace Prize. Both letters are broadly similar, heartfelt endorsements of the peace process. Curiously, Mr Trimble is addressed as 'Dear David', whereas his fellow recipient is 'Dear Mr Hume' – but bureaucracy rather than any lack of warmth from the Áras appears to be the likeliest reason. One of the most significant letters received by President McAleese during her tenure is dated 5 March 2011, from 'your good friend Elizabeth R' – salutation and signature both handwritten – accepting an invitation to Ireland. Queen Elizabeth followed through promptly with an era-defining State Visit that May.

By 2014, when Michael D. Higgins was president, all was sunshine and rainbows between the two countries – two years before the Brexit vote was to cause a certain souring. There was much fanfare about his reciprocal State Visit, the first by an Irish president to Britain. Once there, gifts were distributed by way of goodwill gestures, including a first edition of Oscar Wilde's *The Happy Prince* for Prince George.

At the height of the Troubles, peering through a glass darkly, no one could have foreseen such courtesies. Yet as Tolstoy had a character say in his masterpiece *War and Peace*: 'Time and patience are the strongest warriors.'

UACHTARÁN NA hÉIREANN
PRESIDENT OF IRELAND

20/10/98

Mr. John Hume

Dear Mr. Hume M.P., M.E.P.,

I was delighted to learn that you are to be awarded the Nobel Peace Prize. I am heartened to see that the recognition you have earned here at home for your commitment and courage over so many years has now been so emphatically endorsed on the international stage.

I hope that the award of the Nobel Peace Prize to both you and David Trimble will give renewed impetus to all the parties in Northern Ireland as you work to bring the current process to a successful conclusion.

With every good wish to you and Pat,

Yours sincerely,

Mary McAleese
President

SDLP leader John Hume and the leader of the UUP, David Trimble, are congratulated in separate letters on being jointly awarded the Nobel Peace Prize in 1998 for their efforts to find a peaceful solution to the conflict in Northern Ireland.

UACHTARÁN NA hÉIREANN
PRESIDENT OF IRELAND

20/10/98

First Minister of Northern Ireland
Parliament Buildings
Stormont
Belfast BT43 ST

Dear David,

I was very pleased to learn that you are to be awarded the Nobel Peace Prize.

I want to warmly congratulate you on receiving this well deserved international recognition of
the courage and commitment you have displayed in your efforts to secure a lasting political
settlement in Northern Ireland.

I hope that the award of the Nobel Peace Prize to both you and John Hume will give renewed
impetus to all the parties in Northern Ireland as you work to bring the current process to a
successful conclusion.

Yours sincerely,

Mary McAleese
President

President McAleese
Áras an Uachtaráin
Phoenix Park
Dublin 8

'Seen by President'

19 JUN 2008

11th June 2008

Dear President McAleese

On behalf of my wife, Wendy, our Chief Executive, Clare, and all of our team here at the Peace Centre, I would like to thank you very much indeed for the exceptional nature of your recent visit to the Centre.

The warmth of the words you expressed when addressing the audience had a profound effect upon all our guests and as I remarked in thanking you, the passion you clearly feel for the whole process of peacemaking, was remarkable in its precision and power.

For the occasion to be concluded by you announcing financial support from your government for the Foundation's work was perfectly timed and extremely welcome.

On a personal note, I would like you to thank your husband, Martin, Ambassador David, his Assistant, Amanda and all of your party for the friendliness and efficiency shown to us before and during your visit and, Wendy and I also thank you for your kind invitation to let you know next time we are in Dublin...we will be sure to do so!

Thank you once more and best wishes to you all.

Colin

Fifteen years after the Warrington bombing
the Tim Parry and Jonathan Ball Foundation for
Peace thanks President Mary McAleese for her
recent visit, for her passion for peacemaking
and for the financial support of the Irish
government.

Your Excellency,

Thank you for your letter of 4th March inviting me to pay a
State Visit to Ireland.

The Duke of Edinburgh and I are both delighted to accept
your invitation.

I much appreciate your kind words and I would like to take
this opportunity to extend my warmest wishes to you and to the
people of Ireland.

Your good Friend

Elizabeth R

5th March, 2011.

HRH Queen Elizabeth II thanks President
Mary McAleese and accepts her
invitation to make the first State Visit to
Ireland by a British Monarch. The letter is
signed 'Your good friend Elizabeth R'.

Joint recipients of the Nobel Peace Prize
John Hume and David Trimble, October
1998. In April of the same year the
leaders of Northern Ireland's two largest
political parties were signatories of the
Good Friday Agreement.

Mr President/A Uachtarain

I would like to add my congratulations to the many on your
visit to the UK this week.

As an Irish person who first came to the UK in 1973, your
visit made me immensely proud to be both Irish and part of
Britain. I am always very proud to show my Irish passport when
travelling, and have also been privileged to represent British
companies while living in Sweden and Germany and travelling
around the world.

I was studying at Birmingham University in 1974 when the
Birmingham bombs happened. Directly following that I was shown
nothing but great good will by the British people I then knew.
I will always remember one event in 1975. I was hitchhiking
from Birmingham to Holyhead to catch the ferry to visit my
family in Ireland; I was given a lift by a family - the father
turned out to be a British Army officer, who was worried I
might meet some "anti-Irish" agenda and insisted on driving 70
miles out of his way to get me on the ferry.

During the Queen's visit to Ireland three years ago, I was
incredibly moved. I think Olivia O'Leary summed it up at the
Dublin concert when she spoke of the power of symbols. The
power of symbols reached another level this week, thanks to
you and Queen Elizabeth - and others, including Martin
McGuinness.

In my local pub here in Bath I am known as Irish Phil. Today I
went in, and all my English pub friends were saying how
impressed they were by the Irish President. That you got it
"just right" - just as Queen Elizabeth did in Ireland three
years ago.

I hope you can relax over a quiet weekend now after doing such
a great job representing Ireland and the Irish diaspora.

Go raibh mile maith agat

Philip O'Connor

'Your visit made me immensely proud
to be both Irish and part of Britain'.
One of the many emails and letters of
congratulations to President Higgins and
his wife Sabina Higgins following the first
State Visit to the United Kingdom by a
President of Ireland, April 2014.

Drawing by twelve-year-old, Anna Maguire
from Fermoyle National School, Co.
Longford, of President Michael D. Higgins
and Queen Elizabeth II, waving from
each others' national flags, to mark the
president's State Visit to Britain in 2014.

President Michael D. Higgins and Queen
Elizabeth II sharing a quiet moment
during the president's State Visit to the
United Kingdom in 2014. Significantly,
the photograph is on public display at the
parliament building of the Northern Ireland
Assembly (Stormont) in Belfast.

PRESIDENTIAL CORRESPONDENCE
The Official Letters

The President of Ireland has a well-practised signature; hardly a day goes by when it isn't required on some formal document. Though the role of president is largely a ceremonial one, certain constitutional responsibilities call for a presidential signature: from the appointment of the Taoiseach, government ministers and judges, to the dissolution of the Dáil (if the Taoiseach's request has the backing of the majority in the Dáil). It is the president alone who signs bills into law, and only the president can sign an order referring a bill to the Supreme Court.

Along with the title 'President of Ireland' comes 'Supreme Commander of the Irish Defence Forces'. The president appoints personnel – signing and sealing an officer's 'commission' – but has no role in deciding on defence or military policy.

However, it is the ceremonial rather than the constitutional functions of the office which generate the largest volume of official correspondence; whether between the president and other Heads of State around the world, or citizens of Ireland. Letters of credence (presented to the Head of State by a newly appointed ambassador); letters of commutation (to reduce a sentence – often a death sentence to a prison term); letters of commendation (usually stating that the holder of the letter is recommended for a particular position or job); and letters expressing congratulations or sympathy – they've all had their place in the correspondence files at Áras an Uachtaráin. And all make for fascinating reading.

Although our first president took office in June 1938, Irish ambassadors sent on postings abroad continued to have their letters of credence signed by the British monarch for another eleven years. King George VI's role in representing Ireland on the international stage ended only with the enactment of the Republic of Ireland Act in 1949, cancelling Ireland's membership of the British Commonwealth.

Letters of pardon require the president's signature in order to clear a person's name. The President of Ireland has signed a warrant granting a pardon on five occasions since 1937 — two of them posthumously. In 2018 President Michael D. Higgins signed a presidential pardon for Myles Joyce, one of three men hanged in December 1882 for the murders of five members of the same family, in what

Mary Robinson

Mary Robinson

Mary Robinson

I láthair Dia na nUile-chumhacht, táimse, MÁIRE MHIC RÓIBÍN, dá
gheallamhaint agus dá dhearbhadh go sollamanta is go fírinneach
bheith im thaca agus im dhídin do Bhunreacht Éireann, agus a
dlighthe do chaomhna, mo dhualgais do choimhlíonadh go dílis
coinsiasach do réir an Bhunreachta is an dlighidh, agus mo lán-
dícheall a dhéanamh ar son leasa is fóghnaimh mhuintir na
hÉireann. Dia dom stiúradh agus dom chumhdach.

Mary Robinson

An 3ú lá seo de Nollaig, 1990.

President Mary Robinson practises her
presidential signature before signing
her Declaration of Inauguration, 3
December 1990. Every president has
made the declaration in Irish, including
President Childers, who had never
learnt Irish but opted for the Irish
version in 1973. President Higgins, at his
second inauguration in 2018, made the
declaration in Irish and then in English.

became known as the Maamtrasna murders, on the Galway-Mayo border. It was the first pardon granted by an Irish president in a case pre-dating the foundation of the State.

But the most potent signature of all must be that signed by the president on a letter of commutation. Capital punishment in the Republic of Ireland was abolished in 1964 for most offences and in 1990 for all including capital murder. The twenty-ninth and last person to be executed was twenty-five-year-old Michael Manning from Limerick, hanged for murder in 1954. All subsequent death sentences, the final one handed down in 1985, were commuted by the president. That signing your name with the stroke of a pen, albeit on the advice of the government, commutes the death sentence of another person thereby saving them from execution, and shows the power a signature can hold.

President Seán T. O'Kelly receiving a letter of credence from the Belgian Ambassador to Ireland, Count du Chastel, in July 1949. It was the first time an ambassador to Ireland presented their credentials to the President of Ireland rather than the King of England.

To whom it may concern:-

The bearer, Christopher O'Flanagan, son of the late Christopher O'Flanagan of 30 Moore Street, Dublin, has asked the President to recommend him for employment.

The President has instructed me to say that to his knowledge the O'Flanagan family have over a long period given loyal, devoted and continued service, sometimes entailing very heavy sacrifices, to the cause of Irish independence.

The President would be happy to see the bearer secure employment suited to his talents and experience.

(M.McDunphy)
Secretary to the President.

30th May, 1952.

Letter of recommendation from President Seán T. O'Kelly for Christopher Flanagan. The practice was discontinued by the presidency in 1968.

Date 27/7/62.

Recd.
  at 4.16 p.m.

Sent st

From

To

By.

By

7303 3.59 London ZX 35
PRESIDENT DE VALERA ARASAN UACHTARAIN PHOENIX PARK DUBLIN
IRELAND =
RESPECTFULLY BUT EARNESTLY PLEAD WITH YOU FOR CLEMENCY
TOWARDS JAMES KELLY STOP KNOW WELL THAT YOU WILL GIVE
FULLEST CONSIDERATION TO HEARTBREAKING MENTAL FACTORS
INVOLVED STOP = LONGFORD

Telegram to President Éamon de Valera from the Right Honourable Earl of Longford, in which he pleads for clemency for James Kelly, sentenced to death for murder.

MARIE MURRAY

NOEL MURRAY

"It is the duty of the court therefore, to order that you be removed to the prison in which you were last confined and there to suffer death by execution in the manner prescribed by law, and to be buried within the precincts of the said prison."

A FAIR TRIAL FOR THE MURRAYS

MURRAY DEFENCE GROUP (LONDON) Box 2, RISING FREE, 142 DRUMMOND ST. NW1

Campaign poster for the commutation of the death sentences of Marie and Noel Murray, a married coupled convicted for the murder of off-duty Garda Michael Reynolds during a bank robbery in Dublin in 1975. Their sentences were eventually reduced to life in prison.

1425 6th St. S.E.
Minneapolis, Mn. 55414
October 21, 1976

President Carroll O'Daly
Phoenia Park
Dublin, Republic of Ireland

Dear President O'Daly,

I have received information from a number of sources,
including Mr. Farrell, First Secretary of the Irish Embassy in
Washington, D.C., that Noel and Marie Murray are sentenced to hang in
the Republic of Ireland. This news is totally repugnant to me,
and would seem to be very much out of character for a nation of
Christians such as the Irish. I realize that Ireland is
going through very troubled times these days, but I would hope
that this would not lead her as a nation to forget her Christian
and merciful heritage, and to become a people of revenge by con-
doning official violence.

I understand that the Murrays case will come before the Irish
Supreme Court on Nov. 1, and that if the Supreme Court upholds the
conviction, their lives can only be saved by an Act of Clemency
issued by yourself. I beg of you to remember the words of Jesus
Christ: "Blessed are the merciful, for they shall obtain mercy,"
and to do all within your power to see that Noel and Marie Murray
do not hang.

Very Sincerely Yours,

Anne Miriam Doyle

Anne Miriam Doyle

I, PÁDRAIG Ó hIRIGHILE, UACHTARÁN NA hÉIREANN,
on the advice of the Government, hereby commute to
penal servitude for forty years the sentence of death
imposed by the Special Criminal Court on the
3rd December, 1985 on

Michael McHugh

on his conviction of the capital murder of Garda
Sergeant Patrick Morrissey.

UACHTARÁN NA hÉIREANN

Letter to President Cearbhall Ó Dálaigh
from Anne Miriam Doyle, Minneapolis,
USA, pleading clemency for Marie and
Noel Murray.

Letter of commutation from President
Patrick Hillery for Michael McHugh, one
of two men sentenced to death for the
murder of Sergeant Patrick Morrisey
during a robbery in Ardee, Co. Louth, in
1985. Both sentences were commuted to
forty years' penal servitude.

Chapter 4

Rocking the
System

Women and the Presidency

Catriona Crowe

I n the eight decades since we've had Presidents of Ireland, things have changed substantially for Irish women. The publication of the Report of the Commission of Investigation into Mother and Baby Homes has reminded us just how bad things were for some women until relatively recently: Church, State and society colluding in the institutionalisation of mainly poor women in these 'homes' and in Magdalene Laundries, and children taken from their mothers, to be fostered, adopted and, if they were particularly unlucky, consigned to an industrial school. It is hard now to imagine a society so drenched with misogyny that these things could happen.

Irishwomen themselves drove the changes which improved their lives. After the first wave of feminism which resulted in certain women getting the vote in 1918, and universal suffrage in 1922, there was a sustained attack on women's rights through the 1920s and 1930s: contraception banned, the right to sit on juries effectively abolished, the marriage bar (once married = not allowed to work), restrictions

'Mná na hÉireann, who instead of rocking the cradle, rocked the system.'

In her victory speech on the night of her election, Mary Robinson thanked the women of Ireland in particular for voting for her in such numbers to become the first female President of Ireland, 7 November 1990.

PHONE 44929.

ULSTER BANK BUILDINGS,
3 LR. O'CONNELL STREET,
DUBLIN.

Personal
nnnnnnnnnnn

May 2?th 37

My Dear W.T.

      I dont know how you stand in regard to the Suffragette agitation arising out of the Constitution but I feel that it is time the wheel was reversed. From the standpoint of this country in its trials and troubles since the Anglo-Irish war it was a tremenous tragedy that women were enabled to play any part whatever. Their poisoned fangs were everywhere in evidence as you are well aware and the leaders of those days are still leading.

      In the light of experience I consider it wholly wrong to encourage women to emulate men in different spheres and very few women are found to differ from this viewpoint. In any case there is nothing to gain but much to lose by encouraging the Sheehy-Skeffingtons and notoriety-seekers of that ilk to get into the centre of the fair so that they may intrude their narrow views on the community.

      This little gang is now looking to your Party to place them on the map. I hope your memory is as long as mine.

      Dont trouble to reply.

Best Wishes.

As the Irish Constitution, which established the office of the president, was being drafted in 1937, former government minister J.J. Walsh warned the Taoiseach that: 'it is time the wheel was reversed' on the women's rights movement. Describing women's role in the foundation of the State he said: 'Their poisonous fangs were everywhere in evidence …'

on employment, and privileging women who stayed at home rather than going out to work. Maud Gonne's letter to Douglas Hyde in 1939, wishing she could have 'a chat with yourself in memory of old days', but refusing to come to his garden party because he is about to sign 'the horrid coercion act', 'a deep disgrace to Ireland', into law, is a reminder of the dwindling cohort of women who believed their work for female suffrage and for independence had been forgotten by their male comrades, now in power.

A letter from Eveleen O'Brien to President de Valera in 1967, asking for his help in putting a headstone over Helena Moloney's grave in the Republican Plot, is another reminder of that generation of women who saw the new state as a betrayal of their hopes for a more egalitarian society.

Throughout the 1930s, 1940s and 1950s, women like Hilda Tweedy and Andrée Sheehy Skeffington kept women's rights in view through organisations such as the Irish Housewives' Association and

Roebuck House,
Clonskea.

My dear Douglas Hyde,

While thanking you for your kind invitation to your Garden Party and telling you how much I appreciate a chat with yourself in memory of old days, I regret I cannot come to your party because of the horrid coercion Act/which you have or are about to have to append your signature.

We who used to dream of a Gaelic Ireland, loving justice for its beauty, know that such Acts will put that dream further than ever from reality, and is a deep disgrace to Ireland.

Greatly regretting what I know would have been a very pleasant afternoon.

I remain,
Sincerely your old friend,

Maud Gonne Mac Bride.

8th June, '39.

Maud Gonne MacBride turns down an invitation to a garden party at Áras an Uachtaráin in protest at President Douglas Hyde signing into law the Offences Against the State Act.

Dr Eveleen O'Brien writes to President Éamon de Valera about her efforts to have a gravestone erected at the republican plot in Glasnevin Cemetery to mark the burial place of her friend and feminist revolutionary, Helena Moloney.

the Joint Committee of Women's Societies and Social Workers, but it remained a deeply inhospitable country for women until the 1960s.

The second wave of Irish feminism, beginning in the 1960s, achieved many significant improvements for women: abolition of the marriage bar; the beginnings of equal pay; the right to sit on juries; allowances for unmarried mothers and deserted wives; widows' pensions; a plethora of important organisations including Cherish, AIM, Adapt, the Rape Crisis Centre, Women's Aid; the Commission and then the Council for the Status of Women. Second-wave feminism was a potent mixture of strong legislative reform – the Commission for the Status of Women; and colourful, militant action to highlight injustices against women – the Irish Women's Liberation Movement. The contraceptive train visit to Belfast in 1971 was a huge success in attracting attention to women's need for reproductive rights. Female journalists like Nell McCafferty, Mary Maher, Nuala O'Faoláin, June Levine, Mary Kenny and Máirin de Búrca, who boarded the train, played an important role in advocating for women's rights.

Mrs Rita Childers following the coffin of her husband, President Erskine H. Childers, the only President of Ireland to die in office. Supporting her are their seventeen-year-old daughter, Nessa Childers, and the president's son from his previous marriage, Erskine B. Childers.

ÁRAS AN UACHTARÁIN
PRESIDENT'S HOUSE

BAILE ÁTHA CLIATH 8
DUBLIN 8

26th November, 1974.

Dear Minister,

    I am writing on behalf of all his family and myself to express our deep appreciation of all the arrangements made by the Office of Public Works and staff for the relevant ceremonies for the late President.

    In particular we would like to thank the Officer in Charge, State Apartments, and Ushers, and all other staff throughout Dublin Castle, for the careful and very thoughtful arrangements made for and during the Lying-in-State there. Without precedent experience, this first ever Lying-in-State of a President of Ireland was at all times noble and respectful, as also were your staff's reception and care of me and my family.

    Would you be so kind as to ensure that each and every staff member of the Office of Public Works, at Dublin Castle and elsewhere, may learn of our gratitude?

        Yours sincerely,

        Mrs. Rita Childers

R. Ryan, Esq.,T.D.,
Minister for Finance.

Letter of thanks from Mrs Rita Childers to the
Minister for Finance Richie Ryan and all those who
helped to organise the first ever lying-in-state of
a President of Ireland. President Childers's funeral
saw the largest-ever gathering of Heads of State
on the island of Ireland.

Of course, there was a backlash against all of this; the 1980s saw two incredibly divisive referenda on abortion and divorce, and emphasised the fact that Irish women were not united on women's issues. Many felt that these advances had gone too far, and there was a strong Catholic Church reaction to what used to be called 'the permissive society'. Pregnant teenager Ann Lovett died in a grotto in Granard, Co. Longford in 1984; Joanne Hayes, in the Kerry Babies case, was tortured by our Kerry police force in the same year. Statues began to move all over the country in 1985, and then we got two female presidents in a row. Mary Robinson's election in 1990 was a watershed moment. What had been seen as a largely sleepy, symbolic role up to then became invested with a different kind of symbolism: the new reality that a woman could hold the highest office in the country, and could, as President Robinson did, make that office a focus for issues of social justice and equality. With her term came a light for the Irish diaspora burning in the windows of Áras an Uachtaráin and invitations to gay people, Travellers and others, never invited to the Áras before. There were strong public speeches on issues of national and international concern, and visits to places from Belfast to Somalia to the UN which highlighted conflict, famine and injustice. All of this combined to create the powerful image of a president who could be an activist without crossing the boundaries imposed by the office.

Plans were under way in Leinster House to ask Rita Childers, a former press attaché at the British Embassy, to succeed her late husband as president. However, the plan was prematurely revealed in public and Fianna Fáil withdrew its support. Mrs Childers and her husband had been vocal critics of Charles Haughey and Neil Blaney during the Arms Trial of 1970.

"Grasmere"
Greenfield Road,
Sutton,
Co. Dublin.

Nov. 30th. 74.

Dear Maureen, I was absolutely delighted to hear the news of Cearbhaill's nomination to the office of President. I would like to wish you both a very happy & successful term of office.

You, yourself, have all my sympathy & good wishes. Little did we think on the day recently when we travelled together from London of the task with which you were to be faced so soon. I'm quite sure that your mind must be in turmoil at the thought of packing up & moving again so soon.

2.

However, I always find that it is amazing what one can do when one has to, I'm sure you will find the strength & energy to do all that will be necessary now & you know that you are coming home to Ireland to a very full & interesting life.

T.G. John is at home here with me now in our flat & is making a good recovery. When we left you that morning I was not too sure of things, but T.G. all seems to be well now. He will not be fit for school until after Xmas but that is of little importance when one considers everything.

I will not be back in Brussels until Xmas or after it, but then, or in the meantime, if there is anything I can do to assist you here or over there after

my return I will be only too pleased to be of assistance.

If you are in Ireland in the near future & have time to spare (unlikely I'm sure!) perhaps we could meet.

I will finish by expressing to you & Cearbhaill every good wish for the future from all of us.

Yours sincerely,
Maeve Hillery.

Dr Maeve Hillery writes to Dr Máirín Uí Dhálaigh on the trials of relocating at short notice to support their husbands' careers, as the Ó Dálaighs moved from Luxembourg to Dublin. Less than two years later, she would pack up in Brussels as Dr Patrick Hillery became president following the resignation of President Ó Dálaigh.

The letter from Monica Barnes accepting her appointment to the Council of State by President Robinson 'with delight and enthusiasm' sees two old feminist friends moving forward into a new phase. Barnes was one of Robinson's four female appointees to the Council; up until then there had been a maximum of two women appointees. It was a long way from the early days of second-wave feminism, when neither of them could have dreamed that we would ever have a woman president.

Mary McAleese continued the traditions of her predecessor in terms of welcoming hospitality to marginalised groups. She also oversaw the enormously successful visit of Queen Elizabeth to Ireland in 2011, a big step forward in the relationship between Ireland and Britain. President Higgins returned that visit in 2014, and in his public appearances, speeches and use of the Áras as a venue for hospitality to people like survivors of Magdalene Laundries, created a vision of the presidency as a compassionate, intellectual and effective force for uniting the country. All three of our most recent presidents brought their own unique emphases to the office they held; what they have in common is a belief that the presidency should be an active force for good, both in Ireland and the wider world. That was a huge change, only for the better, and it was initiated by our first female president, Mary Robinson.

Bridget Murphy was a secretary to President Douglas Hyde, but lost her job once she married, due to the 'marriage bar'. Fifty-one years later, she was one of the first to volunteer on the election campaign of Mary Robinson, who as a lawyer had worked for the removal of the 'bar'.

To our President

Irish men who never voted now
see what our President is doing.
Yours Sincerely
Valerie Kent
House For
Autistic children

Drawing by Valerie Kent, aged ten, following a visit by President Mary Robinson to Ballymun, Dublin in October 1992 – 'now see what our President is doing'.

Letter from Monica Barnes, politician and women's rights campaigner, accepting 'with enthusiasm and delight' her appointment to the Council of State by President Mary Robinson. Appointees included five women, a disability campaigner and a voluntary sector worker from Northern Ireland.

DÁIL ÉIREANN
BAILE ÁTHA CLIATH. 2
(Dublin. 2)

15th January 1991

Ms Mary Robinson,
Uachtarán na hÉireann
Áras an Uachtaráin
Phoenix Park Dublin 8.

Dear President Robinson
It is with delight and enthusiasm that I accept your appointing me to the Council of State. I look forward to working with you and the other members of the Council in a supportive and advisory capacity.

I am privileged to be part of your exciting Presidency and appreciate the opportunity you have given me to help realise our shared vision.

All my thanks and best wishes
Sincerely
Monica Barnes

Caitlín bean uí Chléirigh

The first female Lord Mayor of Dublin,
Catherine Clarke, signs the visitors' book at
Áras an Uachtaráin in 1939. She was the 626th
holder of the office.

President Douglas Hyde's first Council of State
meeting, in January 1940. Among the all-male
gathering were two future presidents, Seán T.
O'Kelly and Éamon de Valera. The first woman
member of the Council was appointed by
President de Valera in 1964. It would be fifty
years after this photo was taken before Ireland
would have its first female president.

Dear Mrs President

I wish you the best of luck. Congratulations on your first anniversary of being President. Also for being our first Lady President. I am a great fan of yours. My name is Elaine I Live in Millstreet Town. My teachers name is Sr. Geraldine. I am nine years.

your friend
Elaine Buckley.

Nine-year-old Elaine Buckley, from
Millstreet, Co. Cork, congratulates
President Robinson on being the first
'Lady President' on the anniversary of her
first year in office.

The Capital Times   Thursday, June 6, 1996

HILLARY RODHAM CLINTON

Women learn and grow by sharing their stories

Clinton

An extraordinary woman is coming to the White House next week: Mary Robinson, the president of Ireland. She is also a mother, a human rights lawyer, a law professor, a force for reconciliation between Protestants and Catholics, and a voice for women all over the world.

I met President Robinson last year when Bill and I were in Dublin. I admire her efforts to legalize contraception and to help women win the right to sit on juries when she was a young legislator in the Irish Senate. In outlining her philosophy, she has quoted the early feminist writer Mary Wollstonecraft, who said 200 years ago: "I do not wish women to have power over men but over themselves."

President Robinson's message about women's empowerment echoes the thoughts and words of many other women I have spoken with around the world during the past 3½ years.

Whether they are scholars, poets, historians, journalists, political activists or stay-at-home mothers, women have much to teach each other about the choices and challenges we face as we try to lead integrated lives.

As the writer Deborah Tannen has pointed out in her books about communication and gender, women need to talk, and often they need to talk to each other. It is that need for conversation and direct communication that distinguishes most women from most men.

As women, talking can be our greatest friend. That's why I'm so excited that President Robinson will be in the United States, spreading her message of humanity and opportunity for the people of Ireland and for women everywhere.

It's also why I feel so fortunate to have had face-to-face discussions about women's lives with everyone from the Prime Minister of Norway, to the Empress of Japan, to a destitute mother of 10 children in a dusty village in rural Pakistan.

When the best-selling author Mary Pipher visited me recently at the White House, we talked about our lives and the pressures confronting teenage girls today.

The poet Maya Angelou teaches me about literature and life, particularly from the perspective of an African-American woman who grew up in Arkansas

Robinson

and is now a citizen of the world.

Rose Styron, the writer and human rights activist, always provokes my thinking about the obligations we owe to men and women whose names are unknown, yet who are suffering for the cause of freedom and democracy.

Historians Doris Kearns Goodwin and Blanche Wiesen Cook both have shared their thoughts about Eleanor Roosevelt, someone I wish I could have talked to in person about the role of First Lady. In fact, I occasionally have imaginary conversations with Roosevelt to try to figure out what she would do in my shoes. She usually responds by telling me to buck up or at least to grow skin as thick as a rhinoceros.

Mary Catherine Bateson, an anthropologist and the daughter of Margaret Mead, has written many books, including one called "Composing a Life." She and I have spent hours discussing the ways in which women in different societies attempt to fulfill their responsibilities to their families, jobs and communities.

Jean Houston, an expert on philosophy and mythology, has shared her views with me on everything from the ancient Greeks to the lives of women and children in Bangladesh.

I've even had the pleasure of sitting across the dinner table from Ann Landers, asking advice on matters both trivial and not so trivial.

But of all the women I've had the chance to meet, I've probably learned the most from those you've never heard of — women who have never written a book, appeared on television or been the subject of a newspaper article. From a poor barrio in Managua, Nicaragua, to a grassy field in Indonesia, I've met women who find comfort and unity in telling each other about their children, jobs, families, health, education and all the issues that touch their lives.

I don't always agree with what I hear. What's important is to have the chance to listen to women whose perspectives and ideas may differ from my own so that I can broaden my understanding of women's lives and roles today.

Whoever is doing the talking, the stories we share contribute to our history as women and our understanding of our own time.

I hope we will all make time to talk things over with each other.

Hillary Rodham Clinton is first lady of the United States.

To Mary Robinson with admiration—
Hillary Rodham Clinton

'An extraordinary woman is coming to the White House next week … a voice for women all over the world,' wrote Hillary Clinton about President Mary Robinson in an article she sent to her in June 1996.

· 5th. August. 1997.

Dear Mrs. Robinson,
Words fails to express the emotions I felt
about your while you were president.
You have Been a huge Ray of inspiration
not only for me But for alot of young
mothers.
Your gift of Communication with everybody
improved the Irish Vision., and you
Baught equality to women.

With all my Sencereity I want to Say
Ireland will not Be able to replace
you

Teresa.

'You have been a huge ray of inspiration':
message from 'Teresa' to President Mary
Robinson on her last official engagement
as president, when she officially opened
George's Hill and Stanhope Green
apartments for Focus Ireland on 12
September 1997.

Dear President Mary Robinson,

You were the only one who spoke out on Racism in Ireland.

You are brave and courageous.
You shine like a beam of light in total darkness.
You are so special the World has yet to know you.
If more people could show and practice your qualities of love, appreciation and sincerity towards one another, Ireland would be paradise on earth
I hope and pray the next President will follow in your foot steps.
GOD BLESS YOU.

Fatima M. Aadan

Letter from Fatima M. Aadan to President Mary Robinson, presented to her in a book of messages from women at the homelessness charity Focus Ireland, on her last day as President of Ireland, 12 September 1997.

UACHTARÁN NA hÉIREANN
PRESIDENT OF IRELAND

22 March 2001

Mrs. Mary Robinson
UN High Commissioner for Human Rights
Office 148
UN Palais des Nations
8-14 Ave de la Paix
1211 Geneva 10
Switzerland

Dear Mary,

Ireland is proud of the important contribution you made
to the vital work of human rights advocacy throughout the
world as UN Commissioner for Human Rights. You have faced
formidable challenges with courage and with a deep
personal commitment to the cause of the oppressed in all
parts of the world.

As you come to the end of your term of office, I know
that your voice will continue to be raised in support of
human rights throughout the world.

I would like to take this opportunity to wish you and the
family well in the future.

Mary Mc Aleese
President

President Mary McAleese congratulates
her predecessor, former President
Mary Robinson, as her role as UN High
Commissioner for Human Rights comes
to an end, 22 March 2001. They were the
first successive female Heads of State of
any country in the world.

President Mary McAleese greets former President Mary Robinson at Áras an Uachtaráin during a 'thank you' reception for members of the Council of State as the president's second term was coming to a close, November 2011.

Cuireann an tUachtarán Micheál D. Ó hUigínn
agus a bhean chéile Saidhbhín Uí Uigínn
fáilte roimh mhná a d'oibrigh i
Neachtlann Mhagdalene
chuig fáiltiú in
Áras an Uachtaráin
Dé Máirt, 5 Meitheamh, 2018

President Michael D. Higgins
and his wife Sabina Higgins
welcome former workers of the
Magdalene Laundries
to a reception in
Áras an Uachtaráin
Tuesday, 5 June, 2018

An invitation to a reception at Áras an Uachtaráin in June 2018 for women who had been forced to work in Magdalene Laundries. Two hundred and thirty women attended the event, some of whom had travelled from Australia, New Zealand, the United States and the United Kingdom. President Michael D. Higgins apologised to the women and told them: 'Ireland failed you'.

Elizabeth Ann O'Dwyer, second from right, her daughter Anne Grehan (left), and her granddaughter Vicky Quinn (right) attending the reception at Áras an Uachtaráin in 2018 for former Magdalene workers. Elizabeth had been sent from an orphanage to a Magdalene Laundry at the age of sixteen. She became pregnant, was moved to a mother and baby home, and when her son Michael was three months old he disappeared. She was told he'd been adopted and taken to America. In 2017 she traced him to Roscommon, but he had recently died. However, Elizabeth met his family, including Vicky, a granddaughter she never knew she had.

Mary Robinson

(3 December 1990–12 September 1997)

In a world full of endless forms of communication that are constantly changing, writing a letter is often dismissed as being somehow unnecessary and 'old-fashioned'. Why write a letter when you can telephone, text, zoom, email or whatever? I believe the answer is simply that we should do so because it is so much more meaningful, both for the sender and for the recipient.

Personally, my interest and belief in the importance of letters started when, as a very young child, I became aware of the excited anticipation that permeated my family home when the postman brought an oblong envelope made of a strange crinkly paper and bearing an unusual stamp with funny letters on it.

The letters were from India, from my father's sister, our Aunt Ivy, who was a member of the Sacred Heart order of nuns working in Bangalore and Bombay. Those letters brought the daily life and experiences of a far-off but much-loved family member into our home and strengthened the bonds between us. I learnt from my parents how important it was to reply to every letter and to invest time and effort in doing so; in subsequent years I realised and benefited from what was in fact an investment in a relationship. Letters can play an important role in protecting the memories of lives lived in a way that technological communication cannot, which brings me to key letters I recall from my period as president. When I was asked to identify a small number, my immediate reaction was, *This is 'mission impossible'!* I approached the task by focusing on the two key aspects of the office, the constitutional function and the representative role for *all* of the people of Ireland. And to this framework I added in my personal awareness and appreciation of how often I depended on the work of others: I choose to exemplify this by selecting a letter from Seamus Heaney. While it is a letter that is very generous about me it is, I believe, appropriate to include because all who supported my work and whose work I depended on were unstintingly generous.

Many of the letters to and from a Head of State are invariably very formal, and often drafted by others. However, there is an opportunity to personalise by adding a handwritten salutation or postscript. An example of this is shown in the letter Queen Elizabeth II wrote in response to mine in relation to a visit to Rwanda. In signing off on her letter, that by its nature had to be very formal and correct, the queen took the opportunity to show the depth of the relationship we had developed and which we both considered to be of vital importance between close neighbours.

Obviously the most critical aspect of the relationship between the United Kingdom and Ireland is Northern Ireland. In November 1987, on Remembrance Sunday, there was a bombing in Enniskillen, Co. Fermanagh which killed eleven people. One of them was a young nurse, Marie Wilson, whose injured father, Gordon Wilson, held her hand as she died in the rubble. In a TV interview hours after her death he said, 'I bear no ill will. I bear no grudges … I will pray for these men tonight and every night.' His words, reported worldwide, had a powerful, emotional impact. Gordon Wilson attended my inauguration and the letter he wrote to me afterwards had its own powerful emotional impact on me.

The power of the individual leads me to the power of communities and the resultant strength in unity. I welcomed many community groups to Áras an Uachtaráin, both to the house itself and to the annual garden parties, but one particular group stands out: the two Shankills, Belfast and Dublin, working together. They showed the meaning of true community activism.

It's impossible to 'tick every box' in a work like this so I have decided to book-end my last two choices across the age spectrum I was proud to represent. A greeting card from a senior citizen, who happened to be from my own county of Mayo, is at one end, and a wonderful drawing from a child at the other. The drawing depicts my visit to Limerick Jail and Elvis Presley in *Jailhouse Rock* was clearly being channelled! I know these two final choices show a somewhat loose interpretation of what is a letter, but the important thing is they protect the memories of lives lived.

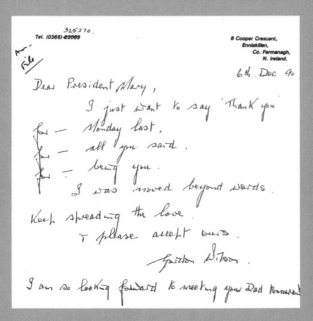

'Keep spreading the love …' Addressed simply 'Dear President, Mary', Senator Gordon Wilson thanks President Mary Robinson for inviting him to her inauguration ceremony. Senator Wilson became known internationally as a peace campaigner following the death of his daughter Marie and ten other people in the IRA bombing in Enniskillen, Co. Fermanagh, in November 1987. That night he told BBC News that he forgave his daughter's killers and called for no reprisals.

12 September 1997

President Mary Robinson
Áras an Uachtaráin

Dear Mary,

What we are feeling here is something close to grief: the full realization that you are really leaving office only dawned on us this morning. It's ridiculous, of course, to feel bereaved when we've actually been transformed by all you did and meant in the Áras. "The dance-like glory that those walls begot" was beyond expectation. And what was behind it was once again what W.B. called "a woman's powerful character." You really did set the tune and call the dance. I'll never forget the elevation I felt at being invited to the inauguration, and from that moment (and not only because of the pride I felt at being quoted by you) there was a new verity and brightness in our public life and private spirits. The

Nobel Laureate Seamus Heaney describes 'the joy and honour of being welcomed in the Áras that night in October 1995'. The poet and his wife, Marie Heaney, had been on holiday in Greece when news broke that he was to be awarded the Nobel Prize in Literature 1995. They travelled from Dublin Airport straight to Áras an Uachtaráin, where their three children and the television cameras awaited.

light in the window never went out, and
has lit new lamps all over the world.
I remember Andy Gallagher saying that
after Sean O'Riada's music swept the
country, everybody stood a little taller and
straighter. The music of what happened
during your presidency was even more
potent, more like Amphion's than O'Riada's.
I believe it was thanks to the lyre-
plucking of the bard Amphie that the
stones moved of their own accord and
raised the walls of the city of Thebes.
At any rate, you built us up and never
let us down. Everything was set on a
new footing. Your integrity and future-
seeking intelligence countered the scandals
and decays. (Great to be able to say
all this and feel no exaggeration or
plamás).
    We have many sweet memories of
events we attended where you spoke and
we met, but nobody in this house
will ever forget the joy and honour
of being welcomed in the Aras that
night in October 1995 when we got
back from Greece. Yet the truth is,

the mixture of personal delight and
trustworthy ratification that I felt then
was only a more intense form of the
gift you gave the whole country.
    Marie and I send all our love
and blessings to you and Nick and
your family, now that fata te vocant
into even harder pats in the republic
of conscience. Hold on to the golden
bough and come back rewarded. You
are part of the rhyme of those big
H's.
                le grá~
                Sean

We think you were by far the best President this country has ever had & certainly a very hard act to follow.

We wish you the best of luck in your new job.

You reached out to us all here in Ireland as well as the people all over the world.

We from Mayo are especially proud!! I was very proud to bring the senior citizens of Kildare & Dublin into the Area to meet you. God bless you & Nick & the children.

SVP Proceeds in aid of Society of St. Vincent de Paul

May the wonderful message of *Christmas* bring you lasting *Peace* and Joy.

& the very best of luck in 1998.

Rosemary Timmins & lots & lots of senior citizens.

A 1997 Christmas card from Co. Mayo tells President Mary Robinson she was the best president the country had ever had: 'You reached out to us all here in Ireland as well as the people all over the world.' It was signed 'Rosemary Timmins & lots & lots of senior citizens'.

This drawing by eight-year-old Linda McInerny, a third-class pupil at Ballyguiltenane National School, Co. Limerick, depicts President Mary Robinson during a visit to Limerick Prison in 1997.

SANDRINGHAM

2nd February 1995.

Dear President

Thank you for your letter and the attached aide-memoire of 5th December about the recent events in Rwanda.

The United Kingdom has joined the international community in responding positively to the challenge that the tragedy of the refugee camps has made. My Government have committed over £60m in humanitarian aid to the relief effort and attached a contingent of 600 British troops to the UN force in Rwanda for three months last year to support humanitarian relief efforts. I share your view that the situation in the camps remains difficult but believe that the international response has enabled the physical conditions to be improved, particularly since the time of your visit.

My Government share your Government's belief that there is an urgent need to support the efforts of the Rwandan Government to rebuild the country. We joined your Government in supporting the European Union decision in November to release over £52m for rehabilitation in Rwanda and we will continue to encourage the international community to seek imaginative and flexible ways to help. My Government have just announced further commitments of £2m for immediate rehabilitation needs in Rwanda and £4m for the Coordinated Inter Agency Appeal.

My Government also share your concern that those who have committed atrocities in Rwanda should be held accountable for them. For this reason, we co-sponsored the Security Council Resolution to which you referred and which established the International Criminal Tribunal for Rwanda. Furthermore, we will be contributing up to £200,000 in support of the Tribunal's operations.

The United Kingdom also agrees that the deployment of sufficient human rights monitors will help restore the confidence that is needed for the process of reconciliation to

- 2 -

commence. My Government have contributed £250,000 to support the costs of the operation and donated four vehicles. As you may know, the United Nations and the European Union have now come to an agreement whereby a group of EU monitors will join those already working for the United Nations. This will help to enhance the efficiency of human rights monitoring in Rwanda.

I would like to take this opportunity to recognise the work of Irish personnel and agencies working in Rwanda and in the refugee camps. I know that they have the respect of those who work with them in the difficult tasks that they undertake.

Your good friend

Elizabeth R

President Mary Robinson.

On 2 February 1995, Queen Elizabeth II replies to a letter sent by President Mary Robinson following her first of three visits to Rwanda during her presidency. The president wrote to more than eighty Heads of State calling for assistance for Rwanda following the genocide against the minority Tutsi population in 1994. The queen commended Irish aid agencies in her reply.

WILLIAM SMITH
WOODVALE RESOURCE CENTRE
33A WOODVALE ROAD
BELFAST
BT13 3BN

29th August 1995

Dear President,

As Northern Co-Ordinator of the Shankill/Belfast-Shankill/Dublin
Project, may I, on behalf of the people of the Shankill Road
express our thanks for the wonderful reception which greeted us
at your residence on Monday 14th August 1995.

The children and adults alike thoroughly enjoyed the hospitality
and kindness that was afforded to them.

Of course, Community workers on the ground have been working long
and hard over the years, while bombs and bullets were flying over
their heads, to try to bring young people from different
backgrounds and cultures together.

The Shankill/Belfast-Shankill/Dublin Project is a shining example
of what can be done between our two countries.

Now that there is peace in Northern Ireland, it is more important
that projects like this continue to flourish between both
countries in order to obliterate centuries of sectarianism,
bigotry and prejudice.

We hope that in the future we will be able to expand this project
and obtain support and backing from those who are able to do so.

Lastly, it augers well for the future to have so many good people
involved in Cross-Border Co-operation and I know that you
yourself will encourage and support such projects.

Yours gratefully

William Smith
CO-ORDINATOR.

Community activist William 'Plum' Smith
[left], a leading loyalist strategist from the
Shankill Road in Belfast, thanks President
Mary Robinson for the 'wonderful
reception' at Áras an Uachtaráin. Along
with Charlie Martin [right] from
Wicklow, he created the Shankill-Shankill
project, linking the Dublin suburb with
Belfast's Shankill community.

Chapter 5

Litreacha as Gaeilge

The Irish-language Letters

Harry McGee

I 1938 seoladh litir go dtí an Seanadóir Dubhghlas de hÍde thar cheann ceannairí Fhianna Fáil agus Fine Gael, Éamon de Valera agus Liam T Mac Cosgair. Tháinig an dá pháirtí mór le chéile chun tairiscint a dhéanamh.'Ba mhian le Fianna Fáil agus le Fine Gael go n-ainmneofaí tusa le bheith i d'Uachtarán ar Éirinn. Beimid an-bhuíoch díot má aontaíonn tú leis sin agus scéala a chur chugainn chomh luath is a bheas deis agat.'

An rud suntasach faoin eachtra sin ná gurbh é eiseamlár iontach é den 'pholaitíocht nua'. Ar ndóigh is annamh a chonacthas comhoibriú den chineál sin ina dhiaidh.

Luigh an rogha le réasún. Ba Phrotastúnach é de hÍde chomh maith le scríbheoir agus dramadóir mór le rá. Bhí sé lárnach i mbunú Conradh na Gaeilge agus i ngluaiseacht athbheochan na teanga.

Braitheann líon an chomhfhreagrais i nGaeilge le linn téarma oifige ar líofacht Ghaeilge an Uachtaráin. Ni chuirfidh sé iontas ar bith ar aon duine go bhfeicimid, as an naonúr, go bhfuil cuid mhaith comhfhreagrais ann as Gaeilge a bhaineann le cúigear acu go háirithe – Dubhglas

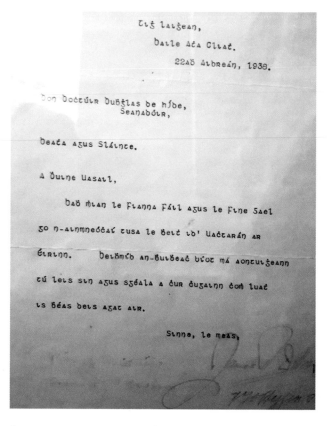

de hÍde; Seán T. Ó Ceallaigh; Éamon de Valera; Cearbhall Ó Dálaigh agus Micheál D. Ó hUigínn. Déanta na fírinne, tá na litreacha is spéisiúla ag teacht le hócáidí móra na linne sin idir stair, pholaitíocht agus chonspóidí … beag beann ar an teanga. Mar shampla nuair a fógraíodh an Phoblacht i 1949, bhí neart teileagram i nGaeilge le feiceáil sa chomhfhreagras a fuair Seán T. Ó Ceallaigh. Seo ceann ó Chumann na Gaeilge i Nua Eabhrac: 'Traoslaímid muintir na hÉireann ar an bPoblacht. Cúis áthais dúinn uilig an scéala a chloisint. Guímid chun De nach mbé i bhfad go mbeidh Éireann ó bhun go barr faoi bhrat na saoirse.'

Fuair Éamon de Valera moladh thar cuimse mar gheall ar a óráid ag cur fáilte roimh Uachtarán na Stát Aontaithe Seán Gearailteach Ó Cinnéide i 1963. Scríobh Micheál Mac Carthaigh ó Chonradh na Gaeilge chuige ag rá: 'Spreag sé chomh mór sin mé nach bhfaighim mo shásamh gan an óráid a thraoslú duit. Thug sí chun cuimhne óráidí móra stairiúla eile ins na blianta atá caite. Traoslaím duit, freisin fuinneamh, treise, agus soiléire do ghuth.'

Tá sraith fíor-spéisiúil ar an 'rás go spás' le linn na seascaidí. Scríobh Éamon de Valera i nGaeilge chuig na Rúisigh agus chuig na Meiriceánaigh maidir leis an spástaiscéalaíocht. Nuair a d'éirigh

President Douglas Hyde with participants in the Cumann Drámaídheachta na Sgol annual drama awards ceremony in Áras an Uachtaráin, 30 March 1939. Six hundred young people took part, representing the four provinces of Ireland. Irish was the only language spoken on the day.

leis na Stáit Aontaithe an chéad duine a chur ar dhromhchla na Gealaí i 1969 bhí teachtaireacht dea-mhéine ar an spáslong ó gach náisiún ar Domhan, Éire san áireamh.

Níl dabht ar bith faoin eachtra is conspóidí i stair na hUachtaránachta – sin é cinneadh Chearbhaill Uí Dhálaigh éirí as oifig tar éis don Aire Cosanta Pádraig Ó Donnagáin é féin agus a oifig a mhaslú. Mhaígh an Donnagánach gur chúis

mhór náire an t-Uachtarán mar gheall ar an seasamh a thóg sé ar reachtaíocht éigeandála. I measc na litreacha, tá a lán acu ann ó dhaoine a bhí bainteach le cúrsaí ealaíne agus cultúrtha: ina measc Liam O Murchú, Méadhbh Ní Choinmhidhe-Piskorski agus Seán Mac Réamoinn ó RTÉ; Tomás Mac Anna ó Amharclann na Mainistreach; Micheál Mac Liammóir agus Hilton Edwards ón Gate Theatre, an scannánaí Louis Marcus agus an file Seán Ó Ríordáin.

Telephone
Booking Office 44505
Secretary's Office 45412

EG/JG.

ABBEY THEATRE
DUBLIN C.8.

Date, 2nd May, 1938.

Fᵽeᴀᴣᴘᴀᴅ
-5MAY 1938

Directors W. B. YEATS, LENNOX ROBINSON
WALTER STARKIE, DR. RICHARD HAYES
ERNEST BLYTHE, F. R. HIGGINS,
FRANK O'CONNOR.
Secretary ERIC GORMAN

ar an guthán.
MW.

A Chara,

    The Directors of the Abbey Theatre hope that you will be able
to come to the first performance by the Abbey Company of your play
"Casadh an tSugain" on Monday the 9th inst., at 8.15 p.m.

                    Mise le meas,
        THE NATIONAL THEATRE SOCIETY LTD.,

                    ....
                                    Secretary.

Dr. Douglas Hyde,
Frenchpark,
CO. ROSCOMMON.

Invitation to Dr Douglas Hyde to attend the opening night of his play *Casadh an tSúgáin* at the Abbey Theatre, a month before his inauguration as president. It was sent by Eric Gorman, the secretary of the National Theatre Society, who would go on to have an acting role in John Ford's *The Quiet Man* in 1952.

Mar a bheifeá ag súil leis, d'fhógair Cearbhall Ó Dálaigh a chinneadh i nGaeilge. Mar fhocal scoir, d'fhreastail sé ar shochraid Mhic Liammóir i 1978 in éineacht lena chomarba mar Uachtarán Pádraig Ó hIrghile. Scríobh Hilton Edwards chuige: 'That you have graced Micheál's funeral with your presence, and spoken in the language which he loved – which, alas, is a closed book to me – fills me with a satisfaction which I know he would have loved.'

22adh Nollaig, 1944

A chara Síly [x]

    Seo chugat cárta beag Nollag do sgríobh mé. 'Sé an cárta beireannach a chuirfidh mé ón Árus so, óir ní beidh mé ann bliadhain eile. Tá's agam go bhfuil an ceart agam mé féin b'ainmniú chun beith im' Uachtarán arís, acht tá sé ceapaighte agam gan mé féin b'ainmniú. Tá mé in aois go ró mhór agus badh chóir fear níos óige a bheith im' áit-se.

    Tabhair mó mhíle meas dod' bean-a-tighe agus le móran meas duit féin.

Dubhglas de hÍde [x]

[x] In President's own handwriting

'I am too great an age, and there should be a younger man than I in my place.'
A Christmas card sent by President Douglas Hyde in December 1944, in which he says it's the last one he'll write from Áras an Uachtaráin as he has decided not to nominate himself for a second term in office.

Bhí tábhacht na Gaeilge le brath mar théama láidir sna horáidí insealbhaithe a thug an tUachtarán Máire Mhic Róibín agus an tUachtarán Máire Mhic Giolla Íosa. Gheall an bheirt go gcuirfeadh siad feabhas ar a gcuid Gaeilge féin le linn a dtéarmaí. Mar a tharla sé, d'fhreastal an t-Uachtarán Mhic Giolla Íosa ar chúrsaí samhraidh Gaeilge i nGleann Cholm Cille, Co. Dún na NGall, i gcaitheamh a h-ama mar uachtarán.

Tá béim nach beag curtha ag an Uachtarán Micheál D Ó hUiginn ar an nGaeilge mar theanga bheo agus tá foras saibhir dá scríbhneoireacht sa chéad teanga oifigiúil. Maidir leis na hócáidí móra, chuaigh an Chuairt Stáit go dtí an Bhreatain i 2014 go mór i bhfeidhm ar an bpobal. Ag freagairt don líon mór litreacha molta i nGaeilge a fuarthas, scríobh Rúnaí an Uachtaráin: 'Bhí gliondar ar an Uachtarán agus ar Sabina gur éirigh chomh maith leis an gCuairt Stáit agus bhí lúcháir orthu go raibh a n-óstaigh Bhriotánacha chomh croíúil agus chomh flaithiúil agus a bhí.'

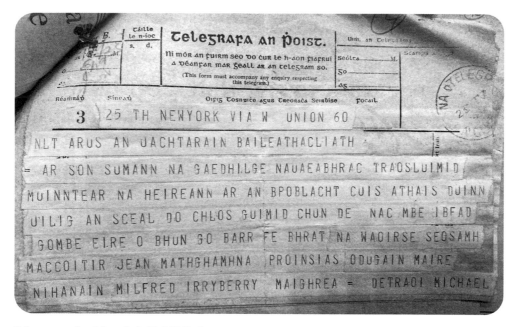

Telegram to President Seán T. O'Kelly from an Irish society of New York to congratulate him on the enactment of the Republic of Ireland Act, April 1949.

Le linn na ráige de Chovid-19, tháinig ardú mór ar an líon daoine a bhí ag scríobh litreacha chomh maith le daoine a bhí ag foghlaim, agus ag ath-fhoghlaim, na Gaeilge. Bhí an borradh seo le feiceáil i mbosca poist Uí hUiginn. As a stuaim féin, scríobh seisean i nGaeilge chuig oibrithe sláinte, chuig daoine ag déanamh obair dheonach, agus chuig páistí na hÉireann a bhí ag foghlaim ó bhaile ar feadh níos mó ná bliain.

Ba mhaith leis
an Uachtarán agus Bean de Valera

a bheith i láthair ag Fáiltiú in Áras an Uachtaráin,
ar ócáid chuairt
Uachtarán Stáit Aontaithe Mheiriceá,
Déardaoin, 27 Meitheamh, 1963, 4-6 pm.

R.S.V.P.
Rúnaí an Uachtaráin

Culaith Mhaidine nó Lae.

Invitation from President Éamon de Valera and his wife, Sinéad, to attend a reception at Áras an Uachtaráin in honour of the visit of US President John F. Kennedy, in June 1963. The dress code was morning or day wear.

CONRADH NA GAEILGE

ÁRAS THOMÁIS ÁGHAS
14 CEARNÓG PHARNELL
BAILE ÁTHA CLIATH 1
GUTHÁN 79145

Cnoc a Bhile,
Dún Droma,
Co. Thiobraid Árann.
4. 7. 63.

Dá Shoilse, Éamon de Valera,
    Uachtarán na h-Éireann,

        Beatha agus Sláinte.

Chuala ó Radio Éireann do óráid fháiltithe nuair do
thuirling Uachtarán na Stát Aontaithe, Seán Geartach Ó Cinnéide, ag
Baile Uí Chorláin an tseachtain seo caite.

Spreag sí chomh mór sin mé ná faghaim mo shásamh
gan an óráid do thraoslú duit. Thug sí chun cuimhne
ócáidí mórs stairiúla eile ins na blianta atá caite.

Traoslaim duit, freisin, guinneamh, treise, agus soiléire do ghutha.

Gura fada buan tú.

Le h-omós duit,
    Is mise,
        Micheál Mac Carthaigh.

Letter to President Éamon de Valera from Micheál MacCarthaigh of Conradh na Gaeilge (the Gaelic League) in which he compliments the president on his oration during the visit of US President John F. Kennedy in 1963.

President Éamon de Valera joins the leaders of seventy-two other countries in sending a goodwill message to be placed on the surface of the moon by the astronauts aboard Apollo 11, July 1969. The wording was engraved onto a silicone disc and carried to the moon in Buzz Aldrin's shoulder pocket.

Go ndeonaí Dia go dtabharfaidh an mheabhair agus an
misneach a chuir ar chumas an duine cos a leagan ar an
ngealach go mbeidh ar a chumas chomh maith síocháin agus
sonas a chur in áirithe ar an talamh seo agus teacht slán ó
chontúirt a léirscriosta féin.

Eamon de Valera

May God grant that the skill and courage which have
enabled man to alight upon the moon will enable him, also,
to secure peace and happiness upon the earth and avoid the
danger of self-destruction.

Eamon de Valera.

ROINN AN TAOISIGH
DEPARTMENT OF THE TAOISEACH

BAILE ÁTHA CLIATH 2
DUBLIN 2

13 Deireadh Fómhair 1971

A Uachtaráin, a chara,

Ar an ócáid shoilbhir seo, is cúis mhór-áthais dom
mo chomhghairdeas a dhéanamh leat.   Gura fada
buan thú faoi rath agus faoi shonas.

Is mise, le hárd-mheas,

Seán Ó Loinsigh

Éamon Uas. de Valera,
Uachtarán na hÉireann.

Taoiseach Jack Lynch sends his
congratulations to President Éamon de
Valera on the occasion of his ninetieth
birthday, when he became the oldest
Head of State in the world.

Star of the Sea
Tramore
Co. Waterford
3.12.71
~~Pres~~

Dear Mr. President
I am writing on behalf of fifth class
We think that the Irish people should
speak Irish as it is their native language. We can't do much Irish at home as
our parents know different Irish. A lot
of the Irish words are just English
words with an Irish flavour. If you
stop changing the Irish we are willing
to teach our children Irish when we
grow up. Most countrys have their own
Irish so why don't we. We realise we
should speak Irish because we had a
debate about it. Also we realise the
Irish language is dying out and we don't
want thee. This country might as well
be England and soon all our dances,
poems and songs will be changed for
English ones if something is not done soon.
Please Sir do something about it
            Yours sincerely Mary Balfe xxx
Julie Murphy
Monica Connolly
Susan Jackman
Carmel Brett
Catherine Kiely
Susan Cowman
Breda Whelan
Claire Murray

'Soon all our dances, poems and songs
will be changed for English ones.' Fifth-
class pupils of Star of the Sea school,
Tramore, Co. Waterford, plead with
President de Valera to 'do something'
about the decline of the Irish language.

Despite speaking no Irish, Erskine H.
Childers agreed to take his oath of office
in the Irish language on his inauguration
day, Dublin Castle, 25 June 1973.

CEARBHALL Ó DÁLAIGH

ÉIRÍ AS OIFIG MAR UACHTARÁN NA hÉIREANN

ÉIRÍMSE, Cearbhall Ó Dálaigh leis seo, as oifig mar

Uachtarán na hÉireann, le héifeacht ón a 6 chlog tráthnóna,

inniu an 22ú lá de Dheireadh Fómhair, 1976.

AR NA thabhairt
fé mo láimh agus mo Shéala,
inniu, an 22ú lá de
Dheireadh Fómhair, 1976.

CEARBHALL Ó DÁLAIGH

P S1/213(a)
(28)

THE NATIONAL THEATRE SOCIETY LIMITED

Amharclann na Mainistreach/Abbey Theatre   Peacock Theatre/An Phéacóg

Lower Abbey Street Dublin 1 Telephone 748741/2 Ticket Office 744505

Manager
David M. Liddy

Artistic Director
Tomás Mac Anna

Directors
Mícheál Ó hAodha
Chairman
Tomás Mac Anna
Charles McCarthy
Thomas Murphy

Bill Foley
Gemma Hussey
Bill Hoy

Secretary
Martin Fahy

date   your ref.   our ref.   28ú Dheire Fómhair

A Chearbhaill a chara,

Ní raibh fhios againn nuair a sheol
tú "Independent People" le Laxness thar n-ais chugainn go
mbeadh ort do dhualgas do chló-líonadh agus imeacht ó
gcodam agus féin. Is cúis díomáidh liomsa agus le
Conalín do imeacht, agus is mór a sheoill sé ar mhuintir
na hAmharclainne annso. Ach is mórú ar meas ort féin
agus ar gcodam na hUachtaránachta dá bhliana.

Sma go raibh tú agus do bhean
uasail, agus tá súil againn nach ró-fhada a bheidh sé
go bhfeicfidh muid sibh treist 'r láthair annso ag na
deanaí a bheas againn amach annso.

Le mór meas agus buannacht
do chara

Tomás Mac Anna

President Cearbhall Ó Dálaigh's official resignation document. The president conducted most of his official presidential business through Irish; he occasionally spoke Irish, English and French during the same press conference.

Letter to President Cearbhall Ó Dálaigh from Tomás Mac Anna, Artistic Director of the Abbey Theatre, Dublin, who tells the president of his disappointment over his resignation but assures him he has emerged from the debacle with great respect.

PSI/223 (63)

Hilton Edwards
4, Harcourt Terrace,
Dublin 2.   10th March, 1978.

Dear Cearbhall,

    That you should, injured as you unhappily are,
have graced Micheál's funeral with your presence, and
should have spoken in the language which he loved -
which, alas, is a closed book to me - fills me with a
satisfaction which I know he would have loved and without which the occasion would have been incomplete. To
have two presidents of his beloved country honouring
him is unique to any man.

    You have always been a good friend to us. May
I hope for your swift recovery and the continuation
of that friendship to aid me in a task to which I have
pledged to devote what years remain to me, and which,
heaven knows, will be hard without my dear partner's
help.

    Please, please, forgive this letter being typed.
I too am an old man now and am not yet steady in the
hand. May you recover soon and accept our gratitude
for adding to so much that we already owe to you.

        Yours sincerely and gratefully,

        Hilton Edwards

P.S. With my thanks go those of Micheál's relatives:
his niece, Sally Travers and his great nephew, Michael
Travers who wish to join me in gratitude.

HE:ae

Actor and producer Hilton Edwards thanks
former President Cearbhall Ó Dálaigh for
speaking in Irish at the funeral of his fellow
actor, partner and friend, Micheál Mac
Liammóir, in March 1978.

President Cearbhall Ó Dálaigh in
pensive mode at Áras an Uachtaráin in
the days leading up to his resignation,
which came into effect at 6pm on
22 October 1976.

19 Samhain 1990

26 Cearnóg Mhuirfean, Baile Átha Clia
Tell.: 01-767283. Telex: 90314. Fax: 01-767(

gael-linn

A Shoilse An Dr. Pádraig Ó hIrghile,
Uachtarán na hÉireann,
Áras an Uachtaráin,
Páirc an Fhionnuisce,
Baile Átha Cliath.

A Uachtaráin na hÉireann,

Thar ceann Gael-Linn, is mian liom an deis seo a ghlacadh agus tú
ag druidim le deireadh do thréimhse mar Uachtarán, buíochas mór an
eagrais seo a chur in iúl duit as ucht do thacaíocht fhial don
Ghaeilge agus do Ghael-Linn ó ceapadh tú id Uachtarán don chéad
uair i 1976.

I rith do thréimhse fhada mar Uachtarán, bhí tú riamh
lán-toilteanach teacht i láthair ar an iliomad ócáid chun cur le
gradam na Gaeilge i súile an phobail agus labhairt go neamhbhalbh
chun tacaíocht a thabhairt dár dteanga agus dár n-oidhreacht
dúchais, go háirithe i láthair na hóige. D'fhreastail tú ar
Bhailchríoch beagnach gach 'Slógadh' ó 1976 i leith agus bhí tú i
láthair ag mórán ceolchoirmeacha a reáchtáladh chun ceol na
hÉireann ar cheirníní Gael-Linn a chur os comhair an tsaoil. Tá
ár mbuíochas ó chroí ag dul duit féin agus do Bhean Uí Irghile as
ucht bhur dtacaíocht dhílis thar na blianta do Ghael-Linn.

Thar ceann Bhord Stiúrtha Ghael-Linn agus thar ceann na foirne
uilig, is mian linn ár ndeaghuí a chur leat-sa agus le do
nuachar. Guímid fad saoil faoi shonas agus faoi shíocháin oraibh
beirt agus go gcúití Dia bhur gcineáltas agus bhur ndílseacht libh
sna blianta romhaibh amach.

Beir beannacht agus buíochas,

BRIAN MAC AONGUSA

Gael Linn, an organisation which promotes the Irish
language, thanks President Patrick Hillery for his support.
The chief executive of the organisation, Brian Mac
Aongusa, said the president's tireless work over fourteen
years had helped to raise the profile of Irish as a living
language, particularly among young people.

President Mary Robinson at Cathaoir Synge (Synge's Chair) on the island of Inis Meáin off the west coast of Ireland. It was named after the Irish writer John Millington Synge's favourite writing spot on the island, where he wrote some of his best-known plays including *The Playboy of the Western World,* in the early 1900s.

28ú Lúnasa 1993

D' Uachtarán na h-Éireann
Mary Robinson
I gcuimhne ar do chuairt
go h- Inis Meáin, Earrach '93.

Muintir Inis Meáin.

'In memory of your visit to Inis Meáin':
a card from the people of Inis Meáin to
President Mary Robinson following her
visit to the Aran Islands in August 1993.

Uachtarán na hÉireann

Tá Uachtarán againn,
Le trí bliana
Is é an chéad bhean.
A bhí os cionn na tíre

Tá sí ag teacht,
Go dtí ar oileán
Le haghaidh an lae,
A chaith i suaimhneas.

Sí Máire Mhic Róibín,
Uachtarán na hÉireann.
Sí an bhean is fearr liom.
Faoi bhun na spéire.

- Máirín Ní Chonghaile (Rang a cúig)
  Scoil Chaomháin
  Inis Óir.

Uachtarán na hÉireann

Fáilte romhat an Uachtarán
Go dtí na scoil
Is beidh áras agad
Nos é sa tír

Cearnóg amhráin dul
Is déanfaimid cúpla dán
Is nuair a thiocfaidh gach rud déanta
Déanfaimid leat stair

A Mháire a Uachtarán
Táimid an-bhródúil asat
Lean ar aghaidh leis an dea-obair
Is nárbhfhada ar meas ort

- Gráinne Ní Chonghaile (Rang a Seacht)
  Scoil Chaomháin
  Inis Óir.

Uachtarán na hÉireann

A uachtarán na hÉireann,
A Mháire Mhic Róibín
Tá míle fáilte romhat
Anseo go hInis Óir

Tá súil agam go dtiocfaidh
An toircín leat go mór
Mar anseo in Inis Óir
Tá fáilte romhat go leor.

Táimid bródúil asat a uachtaráin
Ní dearmad sin go deo
Tá súil agam go mbeidh tú sásta
Fad is a mhairfidh tú beo.

Sorcha Ní Dhonncha
Rang a Seacht
Inis Óir.

Three poems composed for President Mary Robinson by pupils of Inis Óirr Primary School to mark her visit to the Aran Islands in 1993. Legend has it that the president invited 'the whole island' to tea at Áras an Uachtaráin.

UACHTARÁN NA hÉIREANN
PRESIDENT OF IRELAND

12th August 1998

Dear Liam,

A big thankyou from all the McAleeses for the wonderful time we had in Donegal. All your preparations are deeply appreciated and they made things so easy for us. The house was ideal, the children loved Teelin, the course at Glenn was just incredible and Glenfin was very special. All of the things which bring strangers to Ireland you protect and nurture at Oideas Gael, the warmth, vitality humour, humanity, generosity especially with their language, music, dance, soul - all of these elements you capture and offer to the newcomer. One man said it all when he said the memories would last him to the grave. We will of course be back to haunt you again good willing next year - the price of success!

I hope you had a great time in Milwaukee and a bit of a rest. Meantime of course there has been Omagh its ghastliness redeemed by the awesome goodness of the Irish people. We are good at death, our rituals keep us through the awfulness of loss, dwell, home. We hold blindly to the hardwire of faith and custom and they take us, stumbling, through - somehow.

If you are in Dublin please give us a call. We'd love to see you. Renewed thanks for everything, Mary.

UACHTARÁN NA hÉIR...
PRESIDENT OF IRELAN...

Liam Uasal Ó Cuinneagáin
Oideas Gael
Gleann Cholm Cille
Co. Dhún na nGall

2 Mean Fomhair 2011

A Liam, a chara

Ba mhaith liom féin agus Máirtín buíochas a ghabháil leat as gach rud a eagrú dúinn arís i mbliana idir chóiríocht agus rannpháirtíocht i gclár Oideas Gael.

Bíonn muid ag súil lenár gcuairt bhliantúil ar Dhún na nGall ó cheann ceann na bliana. Ar an chorruair nach mbíonn an aimsir cineálta, ní chuireann sé isteach ná amach orainn. Is iad na ranganna, an damhsa, an t-atmaisféar agus an chraic is mó a mbaineann muid sult as; agus is mó a mheallann muid ar ais bliain i ndiaidh a chéile.

Buíochas ó chroí leat, a Liam, agus sonas ort.

Is mé, le gach dea-ghuí

Máire

Máire Mhic Ghiolla Íosa
Uachtarán na hÉireann

Two letters from President Mary McAleese which are now framed and hang at Oideas Gael, the Irish language and cultural centre in the Donegal Gaeltacht. The first, written in English, followed the president's first language course there in 1998; the second letter, in Irish, came thirteen years later; she'd attended the courses annually throughout her presidency.

UACHTARÁN NA hÉIREANN
PRESIDENT OF IRELAND

Teachtaireacht ón Uachtarán Micheál D. Ó hUigínn

Ba mhaith liom mo bheannachtaí a thabhairt dóibh siúd go léir atá páirteach i Mol Scoile Baile RTÉ.

Is tionscnamh spreagúil agus samhlaíoch atá sa Mhol Scoile Baile, a thugann páistí ar fud na hÉireann le chéile i seomra ranga fíorúil mór amháin. Cuireann sé i gcuimhne dúinn, cé go bhfuilimid scartha go fisiceach óna chéile, go bhfuilimid aontaithe inár mian leanúint ag obair agus ag foghlaim chomh maith agus atá ar ár gcumas.

Tá a fhios agam gur tráth deacair atá ann don iliomad daoine óga a bhfuil géarchéim an choróinvíris tar éis cur isteach orthu. In ainneoin sin, tá páistí ar fud na tíre ag leanúint leis an bhfoghlaim sa bhaile ó dúnadh na scoileanna agus glacaim buíochas leo, lena dtuismitheoirí agus lena múinteoirí as tabhairt faoin dúshlán deacair sin.

Beidh an-chúnamh le fáil agaibh go léir ón Mol Scoile Baile, a bhfuil páistí an náisiúin á dtabhairt le chéile aige agus iad ag leanúint lena dturas oideachais le linn na laethanta deacra seo.

Ba mhaith liom buíochas a ghlacadh leo siúd go léir a rinne é seo a thionscnamh, agus molaim na páistí go léir atá tar éis teacht le chéile chun dul i ngleic leis an acmhainn fhíorluachmhar agus fhial seo.

Micheál D. Ó hUigínn
Uachtarán na hÉireann

President Michael D. Higgins tells the children of Ireland that: 'though we are separated physically during lockdown, we are all united in our desire to continue to work and learn'. The president praised RTÉ's Home School Hub for 'bringing children from around the country together in one large virtual classroom', when schools had to shut due to the Covid-19 pandemic.

Letters in Irish

In 1938 a letter was written in Irish to Senator Douglas Hyde on behalf of the leaders of Fianna Fáil and Fine Gael, Éamon de Valera and Liam T. Cosgrave. The two parties came together to make an offer to Senator Hyde: 'Fianna Fáil and Fine Gael would be honoured if you were to be named as President of Ireland. We will be very grateful if you agree to this and to reply as soon as you have an opportunity to do so.'

The notable aspect of this event is it was an early and excellent example of what is now known as 'new politics'. Of course, cooperation of this nature seldom happened between the two parties in the succeeding decades. The rationale was strong: Hyde was a Protestant as well as a renowned writer and dramatist. He was central in establishing the Gaelic League and in the language revival movement.

The volume of correspondence in Irish during the term of office of each of Ireland's presidents depends on her or his fluency in the first official language. It is no surprise that of the nine who have held office, correspondence in Irish features strongly during the term of five of the office holders – Hyde, Seán T. O'Kelly, Éamon de Valera, Cearbhall Ó Dálaigh and Michael D. Higgins.

Not surprisingly, the most interesting correspondence often relates to the major events of that era – historical, political or social controversies. For example,

when the Republic was declared in 1949, President Seán T. O'Kelly received voluminous correspondence, including telegrams, mostly congratulatory. Here is an example from an Irish language society in New York: 'We praise the Irish people on the declaration of the Republic. We are heartened to hear the news. We pray to God that it will not be long before Ireland, from top to bottom, will be flying the flag of freedom.'

Éamon de Valera won abundant praise for his oration during the visit of US President John F. Kennedy in 1963. Micheál Mac Carthaigh from Conradh na Gaeilge wrote: 'It inspired me so much that I could not resist writing to praise you for the oration. It brought to mind other historical orations in the past. We praise you too for the energy, strength and clarity of your voice.'

There is an intriguing series of letters and documents relating to the 'race to space' from the 1960s. Éamon de Valera wrote in Irish to both the Russians and the Americans about their respective space exploration programmes. When the Americans succeeded in putting the first person on the surface of the moon there was a congratulatory message from every nation, including Ireland, aboard the spacecraft. President de Valera wrote his message in Irish.

There is no doubt that the most controversial events in the history of the presidency were those surrounding the resignation of Cearbhall Ó Dálaigh in 1976, after the then-defence minister Patrick

Donegan insulted the president and his office. Mr Donegan claimed the president was 'a thundering disgrace' because of the stand he adopted on emergency legislation. Hundreds of letters and telegrams in Irish were received, expressing outrage and anger at Mr Donegan's insult and praising the president for his decision. Among the letters there are many from those involved with the arts and culture including Liam Ó Murchú, Méabh Conway-Piskorski and Seán Mac Réamoinn from RTÉ; Tomás Mac Anna from the Abbey Theatre; Micheál Mac Liammóir and Hilton Edwards from the Gate Theatre; the film-maker Louis Marcus, and the poet Séan Ó Ríordáin.

As you would expect, Ó Dálaigh announced his intention to resign in Irish. Two years later, he attended Mac Liammóir's funeral along with his successor as president, Patrick Hillery. Hilton Edwards wrote to him a few days later: 'That you have graced Micheál's funeral with your presence, and spoken in the language which he loved – which, alas, is a closed book to me – fills me with a satisfaction which I know he would have loved.'

The importance of the Irish language was a notable theme in the inaugural addresses of Mary Robinson and Mary McAleese. Both presidents also pledged to work on improving their own Irish. President McAleese went so far as to spend part of her summer holidays each year learning Irish in the south-west Donegal Gaeltacht of Glencolumcille.

Michael D. Higgins has also put a huge emphasis on Irish as a living language and there is a rich seam of Irish language writing among his correspondence. His historic State Visit to England in 2014 made a strong impact on the public and he received many letters of congratulation. To those he received in Irish, he responded in Irish: 'Bhí gliondar ar an Uachtarán agus ar Sabina gur éirigh chomh maith leis an gCuairt Stáit agus bhí lúcháir orthu go raibh a n-óstaigh Bhriotánacha chomh croíúil agus chomh flaithiúil agus a bhí.' ['The President and Sabina were delighted that the State Visit passed so successfully and we were honoured that our British hosts were so welcoming and generous during the course of our visit.']

The Covid-19 pandemic too led to a surge in letter-writing, and also a surge in people (re)learning Irish. Higgins's postbag reflected this – and he, in turn, wrote in Irish to health workers, the voluntary sector and the children of Ireland being homeschooled for more than a year.

Chapter 6

Airmail
Correspondence with the Irish Diaspora

Samantha Barry

For the last seven years, the city of New York has been the place I have worked, resided in, and built my life. It is like a country in itself, full of life, light, opportunity and communities – coming together even amidst a crisis that threatened to rip us all apart. It is the place I have grown to call my home, but it is not my home town. The pull of my roots, my identity as an Irish woman – that is the true mark of who I am.

It's unbelievably special to be a member of the Irish diaspora. We're not an exclusive club – there are more than 70 million of us. There are many more of us abroad than there are resident in Ireland, but there's something extraordinary about being a member of this particular tribe. We've found challenges and triumphs in every corner of the world, from America to Australia.

Our scale and impact have been widely documented, from the cities we helped build, the industries we excel in and our art that's celebrated globally. The scattered diaspora has always found ways to congregate through stories, songs and letters: powerful, beautiful, poignant letters in and out of the shores of Ireland. Letters to presidents, royalty and

Irish hearts at home and abroad beat a little bit faster and rejoiced at our Presidents visit to USA.

rock stars. These letters mark moments of history, like the flurry of telegrams that celebrated the fact that Ireland was to become a republic in 1948. Some authors didn't always get the name of the country right, this 'baby republic', as one called it, or 'Eireland', another interesting version.

The correspondence can capture a time or a sentiment; from the imagery put on paper by Irish children to letters that take a stance, such as when President Mary McAleese declined the invitation by the Ancient Order of Hibernians to lead the New York City St Patrick's Day Parade. The organisation has consistently excluded LGBTI+ groups from taking part in the largest annual event for Irish people in the United States.

The letters also memorialise allegiances. President Éamon de Valera, who was born in New York, made many trips to the United States, where he travelled widely, addressed the US Congress, and met numerous US Presidents. He sent telegrams on behalf of the Irish people on the death of President John F. Kennedy, and at-

'As we say over here in America "T'is another grand day for the Irish"': Charles L. Donlon of the Chrysler Corporation in Detroit congratulates President Seán T. O'Kelly on the news that Ireland can (from 18 April 1949) officially be described as 'The Republic of Ireland'.

Collage made for President Mary Robinson by Miriam Healy, aged ten, a pupil at Presentation National School, Millstreet in Cork. It was presented to the president during her visit to the school in November 1991.

tended his funeral just months after welcoming him to Áras an Uachtaráin. A year later, on a State Visit, he was reminded by President Lyndon B. Johnson: 'This will always be your home. You belong to us, Mr. President, just as in a very special way John F. Kennedy belonged to you.'

That sense of belonging underlies a century of correspondence between Ireland and the United States. However, those bonds haven't always been as strong elsewhere in the world. In a poignant speech he made in Warwick, Queensland in 2017, President Michael D. Higgins apologised to Irish people throughout Australia for letters home that went unanswered. 'I am sorry for that broken connection with all those families; they must have felt: what is happening back in Ireland, have we lost connection'. About 25,000 Irish people arrived in the town of Warwick between 1860 and 1863. Higgins added that there were practical reasons for the 'missing letters': postal services could be expensive – letters could take as long as eight months to arrive, and people didn't

Michael L. Kelly wrote from South Australia, 'As a back countryman lacking etiquette' to express his delight to President Seán T. O'Kelly on Ireland becoming a republic: 'We are no more British than the Greeks are Turkish,' he told him.

President Sean T. O'Kelly,
"Free state of Erie"
Ireland

One of the many envelopes addressed to President Seán T. O'Kelly in which the writer was confused over the name of the new republic; this one was addressed to the 'Free State of Erie'.

Calle Paysandú 854.
Apto N° 4. 3rd Floor
Montevideo P.O. del Uruguay.
South America
21-4-1949.

Mr Sean O'Kelly.
(President of Ireland.)
Dublin - Ireland.

My most fervent congratulations to you, and all my Countrymen of the Emerald Isle. on the occasion of the birth of the Irish Republic.

Long live Old Ireland.

Yours sincerly

Vivian JJ Martin
Vivian J.J. Martin

Montevideo. Uruguay.
South America

'Long Live Old Ireland' wrote Vivian J.J. Martin from Montevideo, Uruguay, to President Seán O'Kelly on 'the birth of the Irish Republic'.

NATIONAL HIBERNIAN ANTI-PARTITION COMMITTEE
407 BERGEN STREET, BROOKLYN 17, NEW YORK

Rev. Edward Lodge Curran, Ph.D.
Chairman

Vice-Chairmen:
George R. Reilly,
National President
Michael J. Dowd,
National Vice-President
Joseph Lanigan,
Canadian National Vice-President
John F. Geoghan,
National Secretary
P. J. Kelly
Charles F. Connolly

Daniel C. Culhane
Hon. Matthew J. Troy
Hon. Harold J. McLaughlin

All National Officers and Directors of
the Ancient Order of Hibernians.

All National Officers and Directors of
the Ladies' Auxiliary of the Ancient Order of
Hibernians.

All State and County Presidents of the
Ancient Order of Hibernians and Ladies'
Auxiliary.

ANCIENT ORDER OF HIBERNIANS IN AMERICA

January 16, 1952

My dear Friend:

I am enclosing copy of a protest letter in the contents
of which I believe you will be interested. The Hibernians are willing
and ready to cooperate in every way for the abolition of the artificial
and tyrannical border imposed by the British Government, in 1920, upon
the Irish Nation.

With every best wish for the New Year, I remain

Sincerely yours,

Rev. Edward Lodge Curran
Chairman

To:
His Excellency
Hon. Sean T. O'Kelly
President of Ireland
Aras an Uachtarain
Phoenix Park
Dublin, Ireland

A letter of protest from the Ancient Order of Hibernians in the United States calling for the boycott of an address by British Prime Minister Winston Churchill. In recent decades the organisation has been accused of no longer representing the vast majority of Irish Americans, and it has been criticised for refusing to allow LGBTI+ groups march in the NYC Saint Patrick's Day Parade. In March 2010 President Mary McAleese declined its invitation to lead the parade as Grand Marshall citing scheduling problems as the official reason.

NATIONAL HIBERNIAN ANTI-PARTITION COMMITTEE
407 BERGEN STREET, BROOKLYN 17, N. Y.

REV. EDWARD LODGE CURRAN, Ph.D.
Chairman

Vice-Chairmen
GEORGE K. REILLY,
National President
MICHAEL J. DOWD,
National Vice-President
JOSEPH LANIGAN,
Canadian National Vice-President
JOHN F. GEOGHAN,
National Secretary
P. J. KELLY
CHARLES F. CONNOLLY

DANIEL C. CULHANE
HON. MATTHEW J. TROY
HON. HAROLD J. McLAUGHLIN

All National Officers and Directors of
the Ancient Order of Hibernians

All National Officers and Directors of
the Ladies' Auxiliary of the Ancient
Order of Hibernians

All State and County Presidents of the
Ancient Order of Hibernians and
Ladies' Auxiliary.

ANCIENT ORDER OF HIBERNIANS IN AMERICA

Dear Congressman:

January 3, 1952

According to the Press, Winston Churchill is going to address both
houses of the American Congress.

Winston Churchill is Prime Minister of a country that has never paid a
single cent of its World War I indebtedness to the United States of America.

Winston Churchill schemed and succeeded in dragging the United States
into World War II.

Winston Churchill is Prime Minister of a Government which promises to
fight against Soviet Russia, according to the terms of the North Atlantic Pact, while
simultaneously promising not to fight against Soviet Russia, according to the terms of
the Anglo-Russian Non-Aggression Pact.

Winston Churchill is Prime Minister of a country which betrayed China
into the hands of the Reds and which prevented Chinese Nationalists, now in Formosa, from
fighting for the salvation of China.

Winston Churchill is Prime Minister of a country whose friendly military
aid for the Reds in China has prolonged the Korean War and caused the deaths of thousands
of American soldiers there.

Winston Churchill was responsible for the Black and Tan massacres in
Ireland, from 1920-1921.

Winston Churchill is Prime Minister of a Government which still holds
six counties of Ireland in political slavery, accompanied by anti-Catholic bigotry and
persecution.

Winston Churchill is here to take more money out of the pockets of
American taxpayers in order to support the shabby socialistic economy of England and to
maintain British tyranny in northeastern Ireland.

As American citizens we request you to absent yourself from the halls
of Congress during the address of Winston Churchill and to notify the presiding officer
of the reasons as well as the fact of your patriotic absence.

Sincerely your fellow-American

Edward Lodge Curran

Rev. Edward Lodge Curran
Chairman

CD   CDNVA78 6TH 1212P BOSTONMASS VIA WESTERN UNION

PRESIDENT SEAN T OKELLY IRISH REPUBLIC DUBLIN=

= DELIGHTED TO KNOW YOU WILL BE IN BOSTON DURING MARCH
WE AWAIT DEFINITE INFORMATION ON DATE OF ARRIVAL AND
LENGTH OF STAY WE SHALL ROLL OUT THE GREEN RUG

= JOHN B HYNES MAYOR OF BOSTON++

The Mayor of Boston, John B. Hynes, reacts to the news that President Seán T. O'Kelly is to make a three-week State Visit to the USA in March 1959. Along with his wife, Phyllis, he was to be a guest of President Dwight D. Eisenhower, and was invited to address both houses of Congress.

want to share 'bad news' about deaths in their families.

I first became aware at the age of eight of the concept of 'Irish diaspora' as I watched Ireland's first female president take office. In her 1990 inauguration speech, President Mary Robinson made it clear that she represented many millions more than those living in the Republic of Ireland: 'The State is not the only model of community with which Irish people can and do identify. Beyond our State, there is a vast community of Irish emigrants extending not only across our neighbouring island – which has provided a home away from home for several Irish generations – but also throughout the continents of North America, Australia and of course Europe itself.' President Robinson's symbolic light in the window at Áras an Uachtaráin shines as a welcome beacon to the Irish diaspora in every corner of the world.

I didn't know then, watching President Robinson's inauguration from my home in Ballincollig, Cork, how much being part of the Irish diaspora would become part of my adult identity. I lived it – in Papua

New Guinea and London in my twenties and early thirties and now in New York.

Working in One World Trade Center, I get glimpses of Lady Liberty and Ellis Island from my office. Both serve as a constant reminder to a modern immigrant of passages of the past. Lower Manhattan is filled with monuments to the Irish diaspora, past and present, from the brilliance of Brooklyn Bridge to the works of Irish art in the Metropolitan Museum of Art.

A short train ride away in Washington DC, 1600 Pennsylvania Avenue is home to another proud member of the Irish diaspora, President Joe 'a chara' Biden. President Biden is fond of quoting an Irish poet or two, most often Seamus Heaney. And another Irish poet, Bernard O' Donoghue, perfectly sums up the Irish diaspora experience for me: 'Neither here, nor there, and therefore home'.

```
     Your letter 2nd February.    Protocol
advises dark business suits are in order
for all daytime functions in Washington
and elsewhere.   President Eisenhower does
not wear top hat.    White tie evening
functions in Washington and black tie almost
all evening functions elsewhere.



                         Hibernia.
```

Weeks before his term as president was to end, President Seán T. O'Kelly made the first State Visit to the United States by a President of Ireland. In a protocol briefing letter, President O'Kelly was advised on the dress code for the trip: no top hats required.

Western Union telegrams to President Seán T. O'Kelly as he and his wife, Phyllis, prepared to sail for home following their hugely successful three-week State Visit to the United States in March 1959.

Bon Voyage

by WESTERN UNION

B170CC 3K PD BOSTON MASS 530PME MAR 30 1959

THE HON SEAN T KELLY, PRESIDENT OF IRELAND

     SAILING MAR 31 SS FLANDRE PIER 88 NR NYK

WARMEST GOOD WISHES TO PHYLLIS AND YOU FOR A PLEASANT AND RESTFUL

JOURNEY HOME AFTER YOUR HIGHLY SUCCESSFUL VISIT HERE. BOSTON STILL

TAKING ABOUT YOUR BRIEF VISIT HERE, AND THE WONDERFUL IMPRESSION

YOU MADE. I HOPE YOU AND PHYLLIS WILL COME BACK AGAIN SOON.

             JOE GANNON
             140 FEDERAL ST
             BOSTON

             558PM

Bon Voyage
by
WESTERN UNION

NZ081 RX BON PD=TDNK SOUTHORANGE NJER 31 925AME=

=HON AND MRS SEAN T OKELLY=

=SS FLANDRES WEST 48 ST=A   1959 MAR 31 AM 10 19

AT THE CLOSE OF YOUR HISTORICAL VISIT TO THE UNITED STATES
WE SEND YOU OUR LOVE. YOUR SAY HAS DEEPENED THE REGARD
AND RESPECT AMERICANS HAD FOR OUR RACE. WE WISH YOU BOTH A
SAFE PLEASANT AND RESTFUL TRIP HOME.MAY GOD PROTECT YOU AND
GIVE YOU MANY MORE YEARS OF HEALTH AND HAPPINESS
AFFECTIONATELY=

    ANNE AND GENE KINKEAD=

Mrs. JOHN F. KENNEDY

January 22 1964

Dear Mr President

I do wish to thank you with all my heart –
for coming to my husband's funeral – and for bringing
with you the Irish Cadets – who had moved him so
a few months before in Ireland – and who then moved
the world at his grave.

I am only grateful for one thing in these sad
days – that he did have the chance to return
to Ireland as President of the United States last
summer. That trip meant more to him than any
other in his life – He called me every night of it
and would tell me all that had passed in the day.

He would never have been President had he not been
Irish. All the history of your people is a long one of
overcoming obstacles. He felt that burden on him
as a young Irishman in Boston – and he had so many

obstacles in his path – his religion, his health, his youth. He fought against each from the time he was a boy, and by always striving, he ended as President –

He was so conscious of his heritage – and so proud of it – and Ireland can be proud that they gave the United States its greatest President. Now those words may sound the words of a bereaved wife – but in a generation that is what they will be teaching to school children.

I know your country mourned him as much as his own country did – and through you I thank them for that –

I will bring up my children to be as proud of being Irish as he was. Already our house is

named <u>Wexford</u> – and they play with those beautiful animals – the Connemara pony and the deer. Wherever they see anything beautiful or good they say "That must be Irish" – And when they are old enough I will bring them there –

Please thank Mrs de Valera for me for her most touching letter which you gave me. She taught him poetry – which he remembered and often said to me – and tried to teach his daughter –

All the most moving things I have read about his death have been Irish poetry – "Who to console us now, Sean of the Gael" – and so many others.

I send to you and to Mrs de Valera – two cards – One was how he looked during the campaign, the youngest one – and the other as President –

4) How it aged him in less than three years –

I know we were all so blessed to have him as long as we did – but I will never understand why God had to take him now –

I send you my deepest gratitude –

Sincerely

Jacqueline Kennedy

'I am only grateful for one thing in these sad days – that he did have the chance to return to Ireland as President of the United States last summer. That trip meant more to him than any other in his life.' Jacqueline Kennedy thanks President Éamon de Valera for attending her late husband's funeral and speaks of John F. Kennedy's enduring love for Ireland.

Mrs. JOHN F. KENNEDY

3)

On a State Visit to the United States in May 1964, President Éamon de Valera took time out from official engagements to pay a courtesy call on Jackie Kennedy and her children at their home in Georgetown, Washington DC.

CNT   GA001   SCL DL 34/32   OTTAWA ONTARIO   JUNE 2/64   9.11 AM

PRESIDENT DE VALERA

    CARE IRISH EMBASSY OTTAWA ONT.

FELICITATIONS FROM AN EX CORKONIAN. YOUR MAGNIFICENT VISAGE AND

BEARING SIR, AT 81, ALMOST MAKES POSSIBLE CHILDHOOD DREAMS OF

TIR-NA-HOG. GOD BLESS YOU FOR YOUR EXEMPLARY LIFE AND SERVICE

TO OUR COUNTRY.

                        MRS. MARGARET FOLEY-MOSLEY

                        2082 BLOSSOM DRIVE OTTAWA 8

            CANADIAN NATIONAL TELEGRAPHS

A very complimentary telegram to
President Éamon de Valera from Mrs
Margaret Foley-Mosley of Ottawa,
following a visit by the president to
Canada in 1964: 'Your magnificent
visage and bearing, sir, at 81, almost
makes possible childhood dreams of
Tir-na-Nog.'

The Governor of California, Ronald
Reagan, and his wife, Nancy Reagan,
are welcomed to Áras an Uachtaráin
by President Éamon de Valera, in July
1972. Mr Reagan would return to
Ireland on a State Visit as President
of the United States in 1984, and
make a visit to his ancestral home in
Ballyporeen, Co. Tipperary.

Edward M. Kennedy
Massachusetts

United States Senate
WASHINGTON, DC 20510

March 1, 1996

Her Excellency
Mary Robinson
President of Ireland
Áras an Uachtaráin
Dublin 8
Ireland

Dear President Robinson:

I'm enclosing a copy of a letter which I sent to Ambassador Madeleine Albright recommending that the United States support you for the position of Secretary General of the United Nations.

I know we haven't discussed it, but I hope you may be considering it, and I decided to join the "Draft Robinson" movement because I'm confident you'd do an excellent job.

With respect and warmest regards,

As ever,

Edward M. Kennedy

Senator Edward 'Ted' Kennedy informs President Mary Robinson that he has started a campaign for her to be elected Secretary General of the United Nations: 'I know we haven't discussed it, but I hope you may be considering it,' he tells her.

The famous light in an upstairs window at Áras an Uachtaráin, first placed there by President Mary Robinson. A symbolic beacon, it lights the way for Irish emigrants and their descendants, welcoming them to their homeland. The original light was replaced by this Tilley lamp donated to President McAleese on the day of her inauguration. President Michael D. Higgins continues the tradition and the light still shines today.

COUNCIL of IRISH GENEALOGICAL ORGANISATIONS

(Incorporating the G.R.O. Users' Group)

Cathaoirleach: Michael Merrigan
14, Rochestown Park
Dun Laoghaire
Co. Dublin
Ireland.
Tel: +353-1-285 1556
Fax:+353-1-285 4020

13. January 1995

A.S. Maire Mhic Robin
Uachtaran na hEireann
Aras an Uachtarain
Pairc an Fhionnuisce
Ath Cliath 8.

A Uachtarain, a Shoilse,

It is with great delight that the Council notes the theme of your forthcoming address to both houses of the Oireachtas as it is a subject very close to the hearts of our Constituent Members.

Indeed, in this year of the 150th Anniversaries of two very important events for those researching the history of the Irish diaspora, namely An Gorta Mor and the introduction of Civil Registration in Ireland, the eyes of the diaspora are drawn to the land of their ancestors. The Constituent Members of the Council (all voluntary bodies) are developing plans to mark these anniversaries and they have sought the advice and comments from similar organisations overseas. Two of our Constituent Members, Dun Laoghaire Genealogical Society and North of Ireland Family History Society, operate a Journal Exchange Programme with over seventy overseas societies with Irish Interest Groups. All our Constituent Members are in contact with the descendants of the Irish in their far-flung home-lands from New Zealand, Australia, Argentina, South Africa, Mexico, U.S.A. Canada, Great Britain and mainland Europe to assisting them on their arrival in Ireland to trace their roots.

The Council, established in 1994, is a croos-border, cross-community, national and international forum for the genealogical and family history organisations concerned with the Irish at home and abroad. In recent months the Council has been active in the promotion of the preservation of our genealogical heritage by the inclusion of the following definition in the Heritage Council Bill, 1994 :-

"genealogical heritage" includes records of births, baptisms, marriages, deaths and burials, census returns, testamentary and property records, biographies, family histories, heraldic devices, clan/sept and local histories, gravestones and inscriptions thereon;

Our interest in this Bill is reflected by the concerns of the Irish diaspor for the protection, preservation and accessibility of such records which embody their visable link with their Irish ancestors and therefore, provide a focus for personal research and a reason to visit Ireland. The Council has welcomed this piece of legislation and we look forward to the completic of its passage through the Oireachtas this session.

contd..

"An All-Ireland Council of Voluntary Genealogical Organisations"

2.

The Council has promoted genealogy as an open access educational research activity available to all in our community, indeed, it is proposed to co-ordinate various All-Ireland projects to be undertaken by the individual members of our Constituent Member Organisations. These projects would be aimed at increasing the research material available in our repositories and at providing a vehicle for closer co-operation between individuals from both parts of Ireland.

We believe your forthcoming address to both Houses of the Oireachtas is a very important contribution to the increasing awareness by Irish people at home of the vital contribution our diaspora can and do, make to the development of our economy and, more importantly, to the consolidation of the peace in the North through imaginative proposals for co-operation with respect for diversity in Ireland.

Therefore, a Uachtaran, on behalf of the Council, may I wish you every success and our best wishes will be with you during your address.

Mise le meas,

MICHAEL MERRIGAN
Cathaoirleach

Council of Irish Genealogical Organisations - C.I.G.O.

Irish people in New Zealand, Australia, Argentina, South Africa, Mexico, the United States, Canada, Great Britain and mainland Europe are being helped to trace their roots in Ireland, according to a letter to President Mary Robinson in 1995. The Council of Irish Genealogical Organisations wrote to wish the president well as she was about to address the joint Houses of the Oireachtas on the theme of emigration.

Drawings for President Mary Robinson by nine-year-old Katrina Murphy, a pupil at Presentation National School, Millstreet, Co. Cork, in November 1991. It reflects two of the main stories that were making the news at the time: the Gulf War and emigration from Ireland.

GOVERNOR ARNOLD SCHWARZENEGGER

December 16, 2008

Via facsimile: 011-353-1-617-1004

Her Excellency Mary McAleese
President of Ireland
Áras an Uachtaráin
Phoenix Park
Dublin 8
Ireland

Dear Madam President,

Thank you for a fascinating conversation this afternoon. It was good to see you again, and I was glad we were able to schedule some time for the four of us to sit down together because, as our talk made clear, California and Ireland face many of the same challenges and many of the same opportunities for leadership and change.

I'm especially proud of the tremendous strides we've made to develop renewable energy and green technology, but, as with most good work, we still have much to do. Green energy is the key to building a cleaner, more sustainable future for our children, but until we invent a way to pipe California sunshine to Ireland, we'll need our partners around the world to help us move the process along. I also appreciated your insight on our current economic challenges, and you're exactly right about the opportunities they bring to showcase our leadership, resilience and depth of character. You shared an inspiring message about overcoming adversity, and I look forward to working with you to build an even brighter future for the millions of people who look to us for leadership.

Maria and I were delighted to have the chance to see you and Martin, and I would love to take you up on your offer to visit Ireland again sometime soon. I hope to arrange a trip while I'm still governor, but one way or another, I guarantee I'll be back. In the meantime, thanks again for the terrific visit and for the beautiful vase. I hope your trip home was as pleasant as your stay in California.

With warm regards,

Arnold Schwarzenegger

/jh

STATE CAPITOL • SACRAMENTO, CALIFORNIA 95814 • (916) 445-2841

'I'll be back …' Arnold Schwarzenegger, the Governor of California, tells President Mary McAleese of his hopes to visit Ireland again with his wife, Maria Shriver, a niece of John F. Kennedy. President Mary McAleese met the governor during a State Visit to the United States in December 2008.

Liam Neeson waves to the camera at Áras an Uachtaráin in January 2018. The Ballymena-born actor had just been presented with the Presidential Distinguished Service Award for the Irish Abroad at a reception hosted for him by President Michael D. Higgins and his wife, Sabina Higgins, a former actress. Neeson said he was proud to be Irish and will 'continue to fly the flag for Irish artists and for UNICEF'.

President Michael D. Higgins apologised to Irish emigrants in Australia for the 'broken connection' with family at home in Ireland. Speaking during a State Visit in 2017, he said there were far fewer letters sent between Ireland and Australia than between Ireland and the United States. He renewed ties with many of his Irish-Australian cousins during the visit.

UACHTARÁN NA hÉIREANN
PRESIDENT OF IRELAND

Mr. Joseph Biden
President of the United States of America.

20 January, 2021.

Dear Mr. President, Joe, a chara,

I write to offer my most heartfelt congratulations as you assume the Office of the
President of the United States of America today.

There can be no greater honour than to be given the trust of one's fellow citizens to lead
and no greater responsibility then to vindicate that confidence by having their interests,
their welfare and their aspirations at the forefront of all that we do.

As President of the great nation that is the USA, there is so much positive change that
you can bring about over the coming years and so many challenges that we must all face
together.

There is an Irish saying which you may know: "Is ar scáth a chéile a mhaireann na
daoine". It means that we live in each other's shadow and in each other's shelter. It
reminds me that we are all interconnected, we are all interdependent, we all have an
effect on each other on this fragile planet that we share.

The US has been a true friend to Ireland in so many ways. Your own friendship and
support for so many years has been invaluable. Ireland, of course, has made its most
valuable contribution to your great land by providing so many of our daughters and
sons. The descendants of some turned out to be rather fine Presidents!

May I wish you well in all that you do. John O'Donoghue, a fine poet, puts it well in *A
New Beginning* and this might be appropriate for a man in your present position:

Though your destination is not yet clear
You can trust the promise of this opening;
Unfurl yourself into the grace of beginning
That is at one with your life's desire.
Awaken your spirit to adventure;
Hold nothing back, learn to find ease in risk;
Soon you will be home in a new rhythm,
For your soul senses the world that awaits you.

I look forward to Ireland and the US working closely and constructively together in all
that needs to be done. Recalling the warmth of your two previous visits to Áras an
Uachtaráin, Sabina and I sincerely hope that we will have the privilege and the pleasure
of welcoming you and Jill to Ireland once again, as soon as circumstances permit.

Traoslaím leat, beir bua agus gach beannacht do'n todhchaí agus leis na dúshláin atá
romhat.

Michael D. Higgins
Uachtarán na hÉireann
President of Ireland

'Dear Mr President, Joe, a chara',
President Michael D. Higgins warmly
congratulates the President of the
United States of America on his
election and says he looks forward to
Ireland and the United States 'working
closely and constructively together in
all that needs to be done'.

CENTENARIAN BOUNTY
Happy 100th Birthday!

Anne Delaney, of Patrick Street, Dublin, received a letter from Douglas Hyde in 1940. It came with the president's congratulations for 'attaining the venerable age of 100 years'. Anne couldn't have known then that her birthday greeting would go down in history, but hers was the first 'Centenarian Bounty', a tradition which continues to this day and which saw almost 500 people receive their 'bounty' from President Michael D. Higgins in 2020. Along with the award comes a cheque: Anne's was for the grand sum of £5, but over the years it has increased: it was £25 in the 1960s and by the 1970s had risen to £50. Today, a 'bounty' of €2,540 is available to all centenarians on the island of Ireland, irrespective of citizenship.

The scheme was extended in 2006 to all Irish centenarians worldwide who'd been born here; this was done in recognition of the sacrifices made by emigrants, many of whom sent money 'home' to Ireland year after year. Almost half of these awards go to the US, a quarter to Northern Ireland and Britain, with a small number dotted across the globe.

People who live on past their 100th birthday receive a silver commemorative coin engraved with a quote from a famous Irish poet or writer. As people are living longer these days, there's been a marked rise in the number of centenarians. In 1940, when Mrs Delaney reached 100, life expectancy was just fifty-nine years for men and sixty for women. With men in Ireland now living to eighty-two on average and women to eighty-four, 476 awards were made in 2020, the majority to women.

But only a tiny minority of us will get to become *super*centenarians. This title is reserved for the one in a thousand centenarians who live to at least 110: remarkable people such as Kathleen Snavely, originally from Co. Clare, who on her 113th birthday became the oldest Irish person anywhere in the world since records began. Kathleen died in New York in 2015; her family attributed her long life to hard work, the love of two good men and the odd Manhattan cocktail.

'Everybody toasted Mary': centenarians make the headlines and are celebrated by their communities.

COPY/

P.1735

1adh Deire Fomhair, 1940.

Letter issued on P.1736

A Chara,

 I am desired by the President to convey
to you his congratulations on your attaining
the venerable age of one hundred years, and
his sincere good wishes that you may enjoy
good health and happiness for many years to
come.

 It would give the President great pleasure
if you would accept the enclosed cheque for
£5 as a birthday gift from him.

    Mise, le meas,

   (Sgd.) M. McDunphy,
     SECRETARY.

Mrs. Anne Delaney,
44 Patrick St.,
Dublin.

The first Centenarian Bounty letter was sent
by the first President of Ireland, Douglas
Hyde, on the first day of October 1940 to
Anne Delaney of Patrick's Street, Dublin.
So rare was it to reach the age of 100 at
the time that Mrs Delaney was the only
recipient that year.

She wove a silk tablecloth for Queen Victoria
and remembers 'The Night of the Big Wind'.
A 'Woman Correspondent' writes a profile of
Mrs Anne Delaney in *The Irish Times*.

DUBLIN'S OLDEST WOMAN WORKED AS WEAVER AT THIRTEEN

(BY A WOMAN CORRESPONDENT.)

Dublin's oldest woman is also Dublin's oldest silk weaver. She is Mrs. Anna Delany, whom I interviewed the other day in a room overlooking St. Patrick's Cathedral at 44 Patrick street. She is 101 years of age.

"I am a real Dubliner and proud of it," said Mrs. Delany, awaking on my arrival from her afternoon slumber, with its dreams of stage coaches and crinolines. "I was born at No. 16 Brabazon row, Dublin, in September, 1840, and at the age of thirteen 5 began work in a silk factory and worked as a weaver in Kevin street."

During one of her early visits to Dublin, Queen Victoria was presented with a silk tablecloth, which was woven by Mrs. Delany, and sent to Buckingham Palace on behalf of the city's weavers. Mrs. Delany remembers stage coaches travelling along the roads of Ireland, the Fenian Rising, the Famine, the famous "Night of the Big Wind," and Daniel O'Connell's funeral. She dislikes the modern girl's make-up, her short-cut hair and the cocktail habit. But just in case you think that she is following the accepted dislikes of centenarians, remember that she likes the pictures and has on several occasions accompanied her son, William, to see a film.

Mrs. Delany's most cherished possession is a letter of congratulation sent to her on her 100th birthday by the President, Dr. Douglas Hyde.

She's 100, Still Goes Visiting

MRS. ANNE DELANEY, 44 Patrick Street, Dublin, who celebrated her hundredth birthday yesterday, attended early Mass, visited many old acquaintances, and spent the afternoon at the home of her daughter, Mrs. Daly, Lismore Road, Kimmage, who gave a reception for the occasion.

Mrs. Delaney has two sons and three daughters living: Mr. Patrick Delaney, 44 Patrick Street, who is over 70; William Delaney (66), Mrs. Lee (68), Birmingham; Mrs Daly (64), and Miss Martha Delaney, who is at business in Dublin.

Born in Brabazon Row, Dublin, in 1840.

Mrs. Delaney Mrs. Delaney is a daughter of Samuel Eves, of Fry's weaving factory, which was in Lower Kevin Street.

She is the widow of Mr. John Delaney, whom she married in 1868.

Serving her apprenticeship with her father and mother to the weaving and lace-making business, Mrs. Delaney worked for many years in England and was in Manchester during the famous Fenian prison-van rescue, as a result of which Allen, Larkin and O'Brien were executed.

Hale and hearty, Mrs. Delaney is an early riser and attends Mass almost daily.

Up to a couple of years ago, she read the newspapers without glasses.

She is keenly interested in the war situation and one of her grandchildren reads daily to her the latest developments.

She still has the war news read to her, and also listens to the broadcast war bulletins.

When an **IRISH PRESS** reporter called to her home yesterday, a grand-daughter who resides there said that she did not expect Granny back till late.

Many friends, including Very Rev. Patrick Canon Hayden, P.P., Francis Street, called on Mrs. Delaney to offer their congratulations yesterday.

'Gone visiting': in a piece in *The Irish Press*, Anne Delaney's granddaughter says she did not expect 'Granny back till late', as the Dublin woman celebrated her 100th birthday.

11 Donnellan's Bldgs
Rosbrien R⁴
Limerick
22. 9. 78

Dear Sir
Regards my mother Mary Paget while I appreciate your intentions I have to refuse such a offer
As you met my mother & asked her age which she told you was 43 I know her to be more, but no she is happy thinking she is only this age her happiness does mean a lot to me so in order to keep her as I have to refuse the President fifty Pound also to continue in keeping mother happy as she is Yours Sincerely
Thanking you (Mrs) Mary J. Flood (Daughter)

Not all Centenarian Bounty awards are welcome. On occasion, a letter has arrived to Áras an Uachtaráin explaining how the centenarian would prefer not to find out that they have reached the age of 100.

Now aged 101, Jack Martin still helps out at The Cabin ice-cream parlour, where he and Georgina Gaskin, whose family owns the business, delight in reaching the age of 110 between them.

UACHTARÁN NA hÉIREANN
PRESIDENT OF IRELAND

30 April 2020

Mr. John Phillips Martin
c/o Mr. Brian Martin
26 Willowbrook Park
Bangor
Co. Down BT19 7GY

Dear Mr. Martin,

I have learned with great pleasure that you will celebrate on 6 May, 2020 the hundredth anniversary of your birth.

What a wonderful occasion for you, your extended family and friends as you reminisce and celebrate a life great in years, and I have no doubt, rich in accomplishments. I join with your family and friends in wishing you a very happy birthday.

You have lived through remarkable times in the history of Ireland and the world. You have witnessed remarkable changes, in lifestyles and technological developments, unimaginable at the time of your birth in 1920.

May you be surrounded today by the warmth of happy memories and secure in the knowledge that you continue to make this world a better place for all who love you. I am delighted to send my warmest personal congratulations and most sincere good wishes, along with the enclosed centenarian payment.

Yours sincerely,

Michael D. Higgins
Uachtarán na hÉireann
President of Ireland

On his 100th birthday in May 2020, Jack Martin from Donaghadee in Co. Down was delighted to receive a message from Queen Elizabeth II, along with a letter and a cheque for €2,540 from President Michael D. Higgins.

Birth certificate for Kathleen Hayes, b. February 16, 1902.

Supercentenarian Kathleen Snavely (née Hayes) emigrated to the United States during the War of Independence. A successful businesswoman, she lived through two world wars, eighteen US presidencies and outlived her two husbands. On her 113th birthday she became the oldest Irish person ever on record anywhere in the world.

Anyone born on the Island of Ireland who is entitled to Irish citizenship is eligible to apply for a congratulatory payment from the president to celebrate their 100th birthday. This Centenarian Bounty is currently valued at €2,540, and is accompanied by a personally signed letter from the president. On reaching the age of 101 and subsequent birthdays, centenarians are eligible to receive a special commemorative silver coin; a new one is designed for each year.

CENTENARIAN BOUNTY AROUND THE WORLD

According to the United Nations, there are now more than half a million people worldwide aged 100 or over. Ireland is very unusual in offering its citizens a monetary gift. Below are some examples of how other countries celebrate their centenarians:

- In the UK and Commonwealth, the monarch sends greetings on the 100th birthday and on every birthday from the 105th.
- Centenarians born in Italy receive a letter of congratulations from the president.
- Swedish centenarians can look forward to a telegram from the country's king and queen.
- In the United States, centenarians traditionally receive a letter from the president.
- Japanese centenarians receive a silver cup and a certificate from their prime minister.
- In India, an award known as *Shatayu Samman* is given to those who live to at least 100, to promote awareness of good health.

Chapter 7

The Áras and the Arts

Joseph O'Connor

Ireland's first president, that scholarly man Douglas Hyde, was a poet and an intellectual, while our current president, Michael D. Higgins, is another passionate supporter of the arts. But in the years separating their terms of office, not every bardic presence in the Áras was welcomed.

In a sustained piece of wonderfully condescending and unintentionally hilarious po-facedness, Patrick Kavanagh's visit to a July 1943 presidential reception is reported by a civil servant. The poet was on the hallowed premises not for his poetry but in his role as freelance contributor to *The Irish Press*. Perhaps refreshed, perhaps bored, he pretended to an audience, perhaps including himself, that he was one of the honoured guests. Crime of the century, he wore 'a green woollen jumper' and 'sandals without socks'. (Surely sandals *with* socks would have been a far worse faux pas?) His presence and his appearance were the subject of a considerable amount of comment we are informed, before the grim sentence was delivered: 'Enter a caveat on his social card.' Readers will call to mind the classic BBC sitcom *Yes Minister* and reflect that even a republic has its Sir Humphreys.

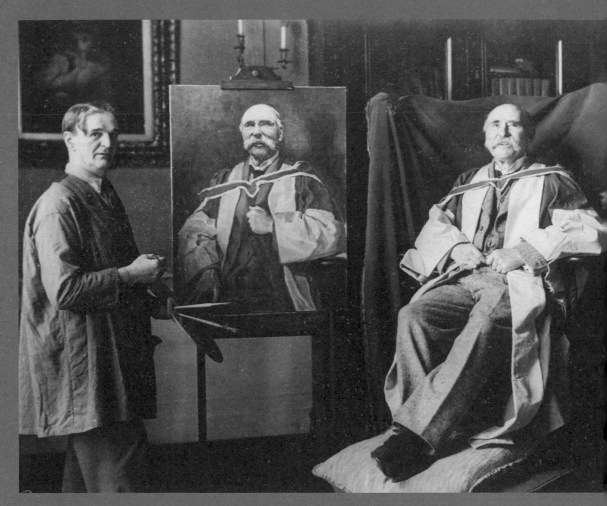

Poet, playwright and president Douglas
Hyde having his portrait painted by artist
William Conor, 8 November 1938.

World-renowned Irish tenor Count John McCormack sends a telegram from Los Angeles congratulating President Douglas Hyde on becoming the first President of Ireland.

A decade after the night of the long sandals, international literary luminaries congregated in Dublin for four days. A congress by Irish PEN, the local branch of the international organisation of writers, saw four hundred wordsmiths gather at Áras an Uachtaráin, among them Bertolt Brecht, actor Peter Ustinov and Arthur Koestler. The event was an immense success, highlighting the formal arrival on the world stage of a nation long known for its writers.

The presence of 'The great Dev', as one correspondent terms him, shines through a number of the letters. President de Valera's journey from death-cell prisoner to Head of State (there is a letter here memorialising his escape from Lincoln Jail) is so remarkable. There must surely have been mornings when he gazed out through the windows at Phoenix Park and wondered how any of this had happened. How incredible to have lived into the era when the most dangerous weapon he would face or wield that day would be a letter opener.

Ireland's nexus of relationships with the outside word, particularly the United States, is celebrated, sometimes in delightfully surprising ways. How

UIMHIR P.3112

UACHTARÁN NA hEIREANN

SGEUL .... PATRICK KAVANAGH ....

FO-SGEUL .... Piers Plowman ....

....

<u>Red Cross Reception</u>
24th July, 1943.

1.　　　Mr. Patrick Kavanagh, who writes as a free lance
journalist for the Irish Press under the pen name
"Piers Plowman", was invited with other journalists
in his professional capacity to the President's Red
Cross Reception which was held at the Árus on Saturday -
File P.3087.

2.　　　In order to give them complete liberty and to
allow them to mingle with the guests for the purpose
of their task, the Press representatives were provided
with invitation cards which gave them access everywhere.

3.　　　With the exception of Mr. Kavanagh, none of them
abused this privilege.

4.　　　Mr. Kavanagh, however, remained with the guests
in the President's drawing room and accompanied them
out of the house when the time came for the presentation
of the trophy in the garden, and generally behaved
throughout the Reception as if he were one of the
principal guests, rather than a Press representative.
In his comment on the Reception in the Irish Press of
Tuesday 27th instant he attempted to give much the
same impression - copy is attached.

5.　　　His presence and his appearance were the subject
of a considerable amount of comment.　Under his coat
he wore a green woollen jumper, and on his feet he wore
sandals without socks, and generally looked untidy and

7718).T9568.Wt.5201/4.5000.3/42.W.P.W.Ltd.20.

not/

A memo regarding poet Patrick Kavanagh's behaviour
at a reception at Áras an Uachtaráin in 1943. A decision
was taken that he would never be invited back.

UIMHIR P.3112

UACHTARÁN NA hEIREANN

SGEUL...

FO-SGEUL...

....

-2-

not altogether clean. This perhaps may be due to
the fact that he had walked the whole way from the Park to
the President's house, but I understand that he is
generally regarded as not being particular about his
appearance.

6.   The Minister for Justice told me that Mr. Kavanagh
had thrust himself on him, the Minister, at the Reception
and that he had on a number of occasions found
Mr. Kavanagh objectionable.   Mr. Kavanagh has written
some very obscene poems in English papers, and is
inclined to be truculent with Ministers.   At the
Reception referred to he engaged the Minister in
conversation, and his attitude was anything but what
it should be.

7.   It is a matter for consideration whether Mr.
Kavanagh should be included in any future invitations
to Press men.   The fact that he is a free lance
journalist makes it easy to come to a decision in this
matter.

8.   The fact that he posed as a guest coming out of the
house was commented upon to me with resentment by
another journalist - Mr.Kees Van Hoek, who thought that
I had differentiated between representatives of the
various papers.   That of course was not so.

    X Enter a caveat on his social card.

7718).T9568.Wt.5201/4.5000.3/42.W.P.W.Ltd.20.   X Déanta 8/8/43

                                    27.7.43.

wonderful to see the autographed photograph sent to President and Mrs Ó Dálaigh from Billie Holiday's pianist, James Johnson Jr, who is genuinely a part of soul and jazz history, having played on the singer's classic song 'God Bless the Child'.

Other unexpected correspondence includes letters about Chinese culture from Beijing's Dublin ambassador to President Hillery (one of them including a requested sheet of useful Chinese phrases such as 'Bottoms Up'– 'Gan Bei') and there are letters to the authorities in Tehran and Moscow. It is rather moving to witness the careful diplomacy of a state that was still very young, a state born of violence but transforming relatively rapidly to independent player on the world stage. The formalised greetings and somewhat stiffly respectful valedictions are a matter of protocol, of course, but in their own way also speak of putting dark days behind. A new language is being taken on, as well as newer modes, self-confidences. So much of a letter's meaning is in what is *not* being said. The closing lines of Robert Emmet's famous speech from the dock sometimes whisper from the space behind these letters.

But often, what is not being said has to do with the marginalised in Irish society – with women, the powerless, the victimised and voiceless. The election of President Robinson was for many citizens a moment of joyous breakthrough, both a catalyst and sign of a change that had been a long time coming. Seamus Heaney's beautiful letter to her is a highlight: '… to have you where – and what – you are'. I knew Mr Heaney only very slightly, but I hear his warm, affectionate, generous, much-loved voice in those lines as audibly as if he were twinkling them aloud from a lectern. The confession he offers about half-wanting to stand outside his house in Sandymount and ask passers-by if they'd heard the president quoting him is so endearing. His brother-in-words Patrick Kavanagh would have gone ahead and done it, sandal-soles flapping in celebration.

City Commentary

By Piers Plowman

AS I entered by the City Gate on my way to Aras an Uachtaráin on Saturday, I was the only pedestrian on the sun-flooded landscape. This was the special entrance for those who were to be received by the President. On either side of me the lawns showed acres of good wheat. The hazy air was vibrant with the wings of bees. Walking alone that avenue, that is as healthy a mile as ever I footed. I could imagine myself rambling up to a palace of the Ming dynasty. But it was better for, the first time a going to meet literary man who had become President of his country. Nothing more romantic than that in Chinese literature.

After the presentation of the trophy, at which the President spoke lovely Irish, we broke up into groups on the lawn. There was a great run on autographs. The only autograph in which I would have been interested would be that of the man who helped to secure me several cups of tea, Mr. J. J. McElligott. Incidentally, to find how he spells his name I have just searched in my pocket for a ten-shilling note.

I next found myself in argument with Mr. Boland, Minister for Justice, an intense man of sincerity. In this discussion I was supported by one of the most delightful persons, Mrs. Dr. Ryan who is, perhaps better known as Mairin Cregan. The ceremonial lowering of the flag to music that is some-what plaintive was impressive. That was the end of the Garden Party.

The poet, Patrick Kavanagh, writing in *The Irish Press* newspaper under the pseudonym Piers Plowman, describes a garden party at Áras an Uachtaráin, in 1943.

President Seán T. O'Kelly and his wife, Phyllis,
welcome hundreds of international writers to
Áras an Uachtaráin in June 1953 for a reception
to mark Ireland's hosting of the international
PEN congress.

The rich compilation here includes correspondence from great comedian and hero of the Liberties Brendan Grace, poet Brendan Kennelly and artist Louis le Brocquy, as well as presidential letters to Ken Loach and Shane MacGowan. President Higgins's letter to his fellow octogenarian poet Bob Dylan includes a fascinating reference to a complex long poem by Wordsworth. There's a sense of the Irish presidency often being in touch with artists, tuned into creative wavelengths.

One night a couple of years ago, my wife and I went along to Dublin's National Concert Hall – a place I adore – for a gig by the great Declan O'Rourke. Five minutes before showtime, a burst of affectionate cheering rang through the auditorium. An American woman beside me asked me what was going on, and I answered that, without any heralding fuss, President Higgins and Sabina had been seen taking their seats upstairs. 'Your president, like, goes to stuff?' the visitor asked me. Yes, our president goes to stuff.

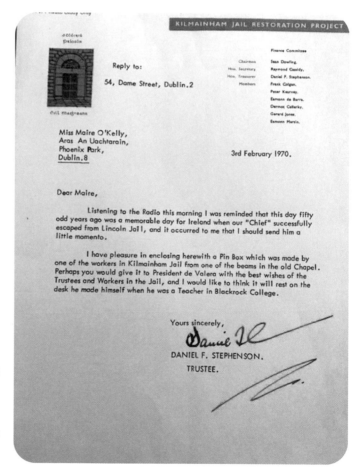

President Éamon de Valera receives a memento from Kilmainham Jail, as it is being restored and converted into a museum. As a young man he'd been held prisoner there and was due to be executed along with fourteen of his fellow leaders of the 1916 Rising.

VOGUE

The Condé Nast Publications Inc.
420 Lexington Avenue, New York 17

October 18, 1946

The President
Of Ireland
Arus An Uacparan
Phoenix Park
Dublin, Ireland

My dear Mr. President:

Under separate cover I am sending you a copy of the October 15th issue of VOGUE, in which a photograph of you and Mrs. O'Kelly appears.

We are happy to have been able to publish your photograph and wish to thank you and Mrs. O'Kelly again for your kindness in posing for our photographer.

Respectfully yours,

Allene Talmey
Allene Talmey
Feature Editor

AT:bb

A letter from the feature editor of *Vogue*, New York, to President Seán T. O'Kelly, was enclosed with the August 1946 edition of the magazine, which included a feature on Irish culture and the arts. The president and his wife, Phyllis, had hosted *Vogue* at Áras an Uachtaráin and a photograph of the occasion would appear in the October edition, which the magazine sent separately.

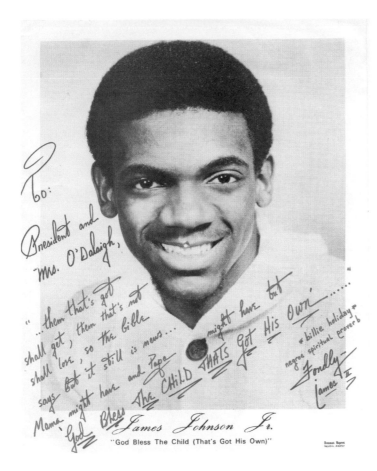

Signed photograph for 'President and Mrs O'Dalaigh' from US musician James Johnson Jr, in Ireland to take part in a production of *Joseph and the Amazing Technicolor Dreamcoat.* Johnson performed on several records by American jazz singer Billie Holiday.

I have seen President Higgins and his two immediate predecessors at concerts, plays, readings, literary festivals, giving lectures and attending lectures by others. Indeed, as a teacher – I am a professor of creative writing at the University of Limerick – I remember the great pleasure and excitement felt by participants in the 2017 UL Creative Writing Festival when President Higgins's warm letter of greeting was read to them. But my favourite memory is a more personal one, for there were no reporters or press photographers there to record it. In 2018, Francis Street Christian Brothers School in Dublin, which my father attended in the 1940s, celebrated its centenary. I felt blessed to be asked to give a reading on the occasion. The guests of honour were President Higgins and his wife, whose arrival received the only fanfare that really matters, a cloud of balloons. The couple remained at the event hours longer than had been promised, and the president's speech was so touching: about art, creativity, culture, storytelling and education, not only as means of self-

ALÞINGI

Oct. 12th 1976

Mr. President,
Friend of Iceland.

Never could I fully express my gratitude for the honour you showed me by coming to my play in Dublin and for the kindness you showed our company be inviting them to your official residence. Their description of that visit fills me and my wife with regret over not being able to accept that invitation. They were fascinated, enchanted.

As a small - very small - token of my gratitude I am sending you under seperate cover one of Halldőr Laxness´ novels.

Tomorrow I will get an audience with our President. I will report to him on our visit to Ireland and bring to him your wish for closer relations between our nations. Which is - needless to say - what we all wish very much. This message has also been brought to the nation by me and Gunnar Eyjőlfsson through the press and other media. Most Icelanders should now be aware of the interest that the President of their cousins in Ireland takes in the life and culture of the Icelandic nation.

My best wishes to you and your fine people.

Yours respectfully,

JÓNAS ÁRNASON
PARLIAMENT
ICELAND

Bronze bust of President Seán T. O'Kelly by Séamus Murphy, RHA. The renowned Cork-born, Paris-trained sculptor (1907–1975) told O'Kelly in a letter that his 'life's work is now complete'. Murphy also created the official busts of Presidents de Valera and Childers.

Icelandic playwright and politician Jónas Árnason thanks President Cearbhall Ó Dálaigh for entertaining his Icelandic theatre company during the Dublin Theatre Festival in 1976, and for his great interest in and knowledge of Icelandic culture.

expression but as forms of solidarity. He spoke individually to almost every single child in the school that day, slipping in and out of Irish if the student addressed him in Irish, addressing everyone with such respect and encouragement, from children whose ancestors had lived in the Liberties for centuries to children whose brave parents came to Ireland in recent times for new chances. It would have meant a great deal to my Francis Street grandparents to see a President of Ireland visit the school to which they sent their sons, and it meant a very great deal to me as a citizen.

Writing a letter of hope and solidarity is a fine thing to do. Living it out is another.

```
        Daily Expressions in Chinese

    Hello                            Ni Hao

    Good Morning!                    Zhao An

    Good Evening!                    Wan An

    Thank You !                      Xie Xie

    Good Bye!                        Zai Jian

    Bottoms Up!                      Gan Bei

    Friends!                         Peng You

    Good!                            Hao

    Very Good!                       Fei Chang Hao

    Beautiful!                       Piao Liang

    It'S lovely.                     Ke Ai

    China                            Zhong Guo

    Ireland                          Ai Er Lan

    I'm very glad to meet you.       Jian Dao Ni Wo Hen Gao Xing.

    We're friends.                   Wo Men Shi Peng You.

    We're good friends.              Wo Men Shi Hao Peng You.

    Welcome                          Huan Ying

    Excuse me!                       Lao Jia

    The friendship remains evergreen! You Yi Chang Qing.

    I like it very much.             Wo Hen Xi Huan.
```

'The friendship remains evergreen!' President Patrick Hillery receives a list of handy 'Chinese phrases' among cultural material sent to him by the Ambassador to Ireland of the People's Republic of China, Zhou Yang, as he prepared to become the first President of Ireland to make a State Visit to China. May 1988.

STARWOOD,
SAGGART,
CO. DUBLIN.

A Uachtáran Dhil,

19-FEB-1990

As you approach your well deserved retirement, I
feel the need to address myself to Your Excellency simply as one
of the many many Irish people who would want to wish you well
and to thank you for a most wonderful and gracious term as the
first citizen of our dear land.

For me personally, it was an even greater joy to
have had the honour of not only meeting the President but also
entertaining your goodself in my capacity as a performer. It will
remain always as a high point in my life.

May I wish you great joy, good health and
happiness now and always, particularly when you receive this
forthcoming promotion, and that is, becoming once again, Paddy
Hillery.

Thank you Mr. President agus comhgartagus !

SLAN IS GO nEIRI LEAT,

Is mise le meas,

BRENDAN GRACE.

Entertainer Brendan Grace wishes President Hillery well on his retirement from office and says performing for the president was 'a high point in my life'.

On a visit to the set of the 1978 feature film *The Great Train Robbery* in Phoenix Park, Dublin, President Patrick Hillery was delighted to pose for photographs; pictured here with (from left) unidentified woman, Seán Connery and Sheamus Smith of Ardmore Studios. The film, written and directed by Michael Crichton, also starred Donald Sutherland and Leslie-Anne Down. Former Minister for Justice Charles Flanagan had a role as an extra.

9 October 1992

President Robinson
Áras An Uachtaráin

Dear Mary,

We saw your press conference and felt that a new element had entered the world of public affairs. The transmission of personal emotional force and impersonal intellectual force, the combination of immediately felt hurt and conscience-stricken helplessness, the latent anger at indifference in the big powerplaces - it was all electrifying. We were, as ever, proud of you.

And then, to discover you had used those lines from Cure at Troy in USA, and to find they had been given such currency. I was caught between a well-behaved aw shucks and an inclination to stand out on Strand Road asking passersby if they'd heard what the President said in the States.

I had no idea, when we spoke at The Provost's house, just how fiercely exposed, both personally and representatively, you would be. It has been a magnificent thing for all of us citizens to have you where - and what - you are. Hallelujah. Get a rest. Best to Nick.

Affectionately
Seamus

'We were, as ever, proud of you.' Poet Seamus Heaney writes to President Mary Robinson in 1992, having watched on television an emotional press conference she gave on leaving famine-stricken Somalia.

Louis le Brocquy   Les Combes, Carros 06510, France. Tel. 93 29 10 61

PRESIDENT MARY ROBINSON
ARUS AN UACHTARAIN
PHOENIX PARK

2 NOVEMBER 1996

Our President,
I was much moved, not
only by the great honour you did me in
opening the exhibition, but by the words
you chose to speak with such eloquence
and feeling in respect of my work
and my concerns as an Irishman.
            I thank you from my
heart and please give my very
kindest regards to your much
respected husband, Nick.
            yours ever
            Louis

Anne says love from her to you both.

Artist Louis le Brocquy writes from
his home in France to President Mary
Robinson, thanking her for speaking
with eloquence about 'my work
and my concerns as an Irishman', in
November 1996.

President Mary Robinson

. . . . You made them speak as only you could do
Of Generosity or loneliness or love
Because, you said, all men are voices, heard
In the pure air of the imagination.
I hear you now, your rich voice deep and kind,
Rescuing a poem from time, bringing to mind
Lost centuries with a summoning word,
Lavishing on us who need much more of
What you gave, glimpses of heroic vision . . . . .

Brendan Kennelly

Brendan Kennelly wrote this poem
for President Mary Robinson when
she resigned from office, eight weeks
before the end of her term, to become
the UN High Commissioner for Human
Rights. 'You deepened and extended
Ireland. Nobody can forget that', says the
accompanying note.

UACHTARÁN NA hÉIREANN
PRESIDENT OF IRELAND

Mr Ken Loach
London

29th May 2006

Dear Mr. Loach

As Patron of the Film Institute of Ireland, may I congratulate you on your wonderful achievement winning the Golden Palm, at the Cannes Film Festival this year. "The Wind that Shakes the Barley" has been recognised as an exceptional and dramatic work richly deserving the accolade for telling an important story of the days of the War of Independence in Ireland that is refreshingly uncompromising in its commitment to telling the truth about the horrors of war.

Please convey my congratulations, also, to the rest of the crew, particularly to Cillian Murphy and to Padraic Delaney, for their contribution to this wonderful achievement.
Yours sincerely

Mary McAleese

Mary McAleese
President of Ireland

President Mary McAleese congratulates film director Ken Loach along with actors Cillian Murphy and Padraic Delaney, as *The Wind that Shakes the Barley*, based on the War of Independence, wins the coveted Palme d'Or at the Cannes Film Festival in 2006.

The official portrait of President Michael D. Higgins, by painter and sculptor Mick O'Dea, is installed in 2017 at Leinster House, where it will remain until it joins those of the first eight Presidents of Ireland in the portrait gallery at Áras an Uachtaráin once the president has left office.

President Patrick Hillery painting in the grounds of Áras an Uachtaráin weeks before leaving office in November 1990.

UACHTARÁN NA hÉIREANN
PRESIDENT OF IRELAND

Mr. Shane MacGowan
22 Simmonscourt Castle
Simmonscourt Road
Ballsbridge
Dublin
D04 CY51

4 January 2017

Dear Shane

On behalf of Sabina and I, I would like to extend my deepest condolences to you and your family
on the sudden and tragic death of your beloved mother, Therese, on New Year's Day.

I know your mother was a much loved member of the community of Silvermines,
Co. Tipperary and her tragic passing will also be keenly felt by her neighbours and friends.

You have spoken often over the years of the influence your mother has had on your own music
and creativity. You have described how, as an award winning folk singer in her own right, she
inspired you to develop your own musical talents.

The love of Irish music and traditions that she nurtured in you has resulted in the wonderful
music and lyrics you have created, that has been a source of much joy for so many people,
connecting Irish people all over the world to their culture and history, encompassing so many
human emotions in the most poetic of ways.

May I convey my sincere sympathies to you and Victoria, your sister Siobhan and your father
Maurice, as well as your wider family.

Ar dheis Dé go raibh a h-anam dílis.

Yours sincerely

Michael D. Higgins
Uachtarán na hÉireann
President of Ireland

P.S I know you will have
been also destressed at
the premature passing of
Frank Murray. I wish
you well and look
forward to meeting when
Circumstances allow

President Michael D. Higgins writes to
Shane McGowan on the death of his
mother, Therese: 'as an award-winning
folk singer in her own right, she inspired
you to develop your own musical talents'.

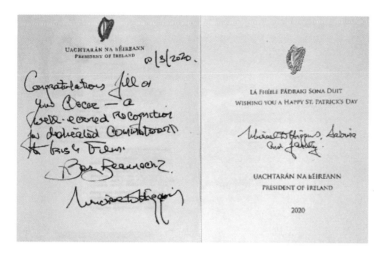

President Michael D. Higgins
congratulates Dubliner Jill
Beecher on winning the Academy
Award for Best Production Design,
2019 with her production team
for their work on the Quentin
Tarantino film *Once Upon a Time
... in Hollywood* starring Brad Pitt
Leonardo DiCaprio and Margot
Robbie. Jill has won awards for
her work on Irish and international
films.

UACHTARÁN NA hÉIREANN
PRESIDENT OF IRELAND

Mr. Bob Dylan

20 May, 2021

Dear Bob, a chara,

As one 80 year-old to another, and as one poet to another, I felt I should share
with you my view that the best poem on an 80 year-old is William Wordsworth's
poem 'Michael', which deals with the consequences of the enclosures in England
in the 18th Century, and their making of a working class of men, women and
children for the factory system at the cost of intimate rural life. I feel it's a
beautiful work and would love sometime to talk to you about it.

In 2016, I said of you: 'Bob Dylan's linking of the American folk tradition to
moral, economic and political challenges has been a significant achievement, and
the appeal of his music has been inter-generational. His lyrics, with their
rhythms, have linked followers of country, jazz and rock to counter-cultural and
politically engaged movements. In doing this, he has narrowed the space between
the poetic, the musical and the political.'

My opinion hasn't changed.

Keep going. Good luck with everything. Traoslaim leat (I congratulate you).

Beir bua (May victory be yours).

Michael D. Higgins
Uachtarán na hÉireann
President of Ireland

'As one 80 year-old to another,
and as one poet to another.'
President Michael D. Higgins
sends birthday wishes to Bob
Dylan, who turned eighty one
month after the president.

Chapter 8

Church and State
A Presidency in Progress

Justine McCarthy

Evolution is forever a work in progress and sometimes it can feel tediously slow. For most of the twentieth century, Ireland was marooned in a time warp of insularity and conformity. In twenty-six of the island's thirty-two counties, the revolutionary period gave way to entrenched, dogmatic conservatism in the fledgling decades after achieving self-determination. It was a dour land where few dared eat meat on Fridays and public kissing was barely tolerated. Home Rule was often indistinguishable from Rome rule.

It was not until January 1973 that the constitutional recognition of the Catholic Church's 'special position' enshrined in article 44 of Bunreacht na hÉireann was repealed following a referendum carried by 84.38 per cent of the voters. In Áras an Uachtaráin, the amendment was signed into law by President Éamon de Valera who, as Taoiseach, had composed the 1937 Constitution, resisting demands that it should explicitly uphold Catholicism as the official religion of the State. But it most assuredly was, in all but name. Ireland wallowed in its self-coined sobriquet as the Best Catholic Country in the World.

The Church ran the state's schools and hospitals as well as most of its orphanages, adoption agencies, Magdalene laundries for unmarried

Saint Patrick's Cathedral, Dublin, 14 July 1949. Participation in Protestant ceremonies is a 'reserved sin' under Catholic Church doctrine. Noël Browne was the sole member of the cabinet to attend the funeral service of Douglas Hyde.

Among the hundreds of telegrams to President Seán T. O'Kelly on the enactment of the Republic of Ireland Act in 1949, many came from religious leaders. Others, such as this one, invoked several saints.

mothers, industrial schools and mother and baby institutions. For multitudes of citizens, especially women and children, the Vatican's influence on Irish life was oppressive and repressive. The extent to which the country was shaped by the bang of a bishop's crozier was exemplified in 1950 by the controversy over the Mother and Child Scheme, proposed by Noël Browne, the Minister for Health. The Catholic hierarchy objected to the planned provision of free gynaecological care, deeming it anathema to the Church's moral teaching and fearing it would pave the way for the introduction of birth control and abortion services. John Charles McQuaid, the formidable archbishop of Dublin, summoned Browne to his palace in

Drumcondra for an episcopal earwigging but the politician refused to bend. Ultimately, Browne resigned from the cabinet and his proposed modernisation of public healthcare perished on the rock of stagnation.

On reading the presidents' letters in this collection, it is difficult to imagine how anybody could have surpassed Dev's Catholic obsequiousness. It was with 'profound homage and filial devotion' that he wrote thanking Pope John XXIII for his 'felicitations on assuming office'.

The practical prohibitions created by a body politic bent in perpetual genuflection to Rome were illustrated when the first president, Douglas Hyde, died in 1949. His successor, Seán T. O'Kelly, sat in

Translation.

Mr President:

The Irish people have again helped the people of Germany, especially the inhabitants of the East zone, with liberal gifts of food and clothing.

Permit me in the name of the recipients and in my own name to offer you my heartiest thanks for these generous gifts which have relieved thousands, and in many cases have actually saved their lives.

May God richly reward you and your people.

Conditions with us are still very serious and every gift which comes from outside is most welcome and helps a serious need.

Be assured, Mr President, that we are profoundly grateful.

With the expression of my highest esteem

I am, Mr President,

Yours very truly,

(Sgd)   Konrad Cardinal von Preysing,

Bishop of Berlin.

The Bishop of Berlin writes in 1948 that people in the German capital are 'profoundly grateful' for food and clothing donated from Ireland. He says, 'conditions with us are still very serious'.

Dear Monsignor Flaherty,

      I would like to send you just a few words of warm thanks for your courtesy and kindness to me during my recent visit to Rome.

      I was glad when I saw your smiling face at the Aerodrome on my arrival, and more than pleased to see you on a good many occasions again at the various functions I attended during my few days visit in the Eternal City.

      Again you were gracious enough to come to the Aerodrome to see me off, and I know what trouble that meant to you and to the other friends who assembled to greet me and to salute me and send me on my way home happy.

      I enjoyed my brief stay very much indeed. I would have loved to have stayed longer but public duties at home called for my early return. I must add, however, that I was delighted to find you looking so fit and well despite all the troubles and tribulations you must have been through, especially during the period of the war years.

      With warmest personal regards and best wishes.

      Yours very sincerely,

Right Rev. Monsignor Flaherty,
Congregation of the Holy Office,
Vatican City,
Italy.

In the first State Visit by a President of Ireland, President Seán T. O'Kelly was hosted at the Vatican by Msgr Hugh O'Flaherty, known as the 'Irish Schindler' who had helped more than 5,000 people escape Nazi persecution.

his car outside Saint Patrick's Cathedral during the funeral service, as did most of the cabinet, because Catholics were forbidden by their religion to attend Protestant church services.

O'Kelly was so personally religious that, when he was a government minister, de Valera had asked him to resign from the Knights of Saint Columbanus due to cabinet leaks wending their way to the men-only lay Catholic order.

The taboo on presidential inter-faith participation continued until November 1993 when Mary Robinson became the first president to attend an ecumenical service at Saint Patrick's. Four years later her successor, Mary McAleese, was roundly condemned for receiving communion in Dublin's other Protestant cathedral, Christchurch. Cardinal Desmond Connell called it 'a sham'. Mary Robinson, Ireland's first woman president, had a knack for nettling conservative Catholicism. During a visit to Pope John Paul II in 1997, she eschewed the standard black costume required of women by Vatican protocol in favour of a green dress. A Meath diocesan priest, Fr David O'Hanlon, wrote to *The Irish Times* calling her 'cheap' and memorably dubbing those who defended her 'Áras-lickers'.

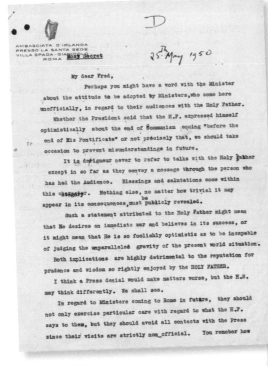

Despite the predominance of the Catholic Church, two of Ireland's nine presidents to date have been Protestants: Douglas Hyde and Erskine Childers. In fact, there have been as many Protestant presidents as women presidents.

As Ireland grew more confident, prosperous and outward-looking, the State had little choice but to shed some of its church complaisance. The papal tour of Ireland in 1979 saw more than 2.5 million people turn out to attend events, a high point for the popularity of the Catholic Church here. But the 1990 election of Mary Robinson, a feminist and lawyer with a quiver of court victories vindicating women's rights, was a seismic reflection of how society was changing. There was a political rationale too for dispensing with the State's Catholic pomp and ceremony: as the sectarian-driven Troubles wore on in Northern Ireland, the architects of the nascent peace process acknowledged that religious inclusivity was a prerequisite for success. This is illustrated in Cardinal Cathal Daly's letter to Robinson, dated 30 September 1996, commending her 'courage in meeting diverse groups in

But what a long letter I am writing ! Please give me a penance for breaking in on you with an epistle of such length. But if you only knew what a joy it is to be writing to you as I recall, among so many other things, that night at your residence in the Park when the President of Ireland, and the Apostolic Delegate sang a duet "The West's Awake" and promised ourselves that we would repeat the performance one day in Moscow !   Pardon me, but I don't think either of us would have won a prize in some singing contest for that extraordinary performance.   Certainly I wouldn't, and, frankly, I seriously doubt that Your Excellency would.   How the Bishop of Galway enjoyed that performance.

But it's ten-thirty.   Time for all self-respecting Apostolic Delegates to be in bed.   So I'll say good-night, assuring you once again what a joy it is to be writing to you.

With a blessing,

Devotedly yours in Our Lord

+Gerald P. O'Hara

Apostolic Delegate

On the second page of a letter to Seán T. O'Kelly, former Apostolic Nuncio to Ireland Msgr Gerald P. O'Hara reminds the president of the night they sang 'The West's Awake' together at Áras an Uachtaráin.

Northern Ireland' and her 'significant contribution to the long and arduous search for peace'.

Because the Catholic Church has been the dominant faith in Irish public life, other religions have tended to get overlooked in the narrative of Church and State relations. The Jewish community had an active engagement with Áras an Uachtaráin in the State's early years, and particularly after World War II, when an Éamon de Valera memorial forest was planted near Galilee. There is a marked contrast between the warm correspondence that flowed between Tel Aviv and Phoenix Park in the mid-twentieth century and Ireland's currently tense political relationship with Israel. 'I see in this planting of trees in President de Valera's distinguished name a fitting expression of the traditional friendship between the Irish and the Jewish peoples,' wrote the Israeli Prime Minister, Levi Eshkol, in August 1966.

One of the most fascinating missives of all exploded from the pen of Colonel Muammar Gaddafi. Boy, was he angry. He was incensed! In a two-page cable, the

Libyan leader berated President Patrick Hillery for not acknowledging the Koran, 'which you do not read and you do not believe in because of misleading Israeli propaganda'. Calling for a Christian cultural revolution, Libya's dictator, who was supplying arms to the IRA, bizarrely fulminated that 'it is you who threaten peace ... hatred is embodied in you'. A note dated 7 January 1986 from Anne Barrington in the Middle East section at the Department of Foreign Affairs delicately advised Hillery not to reply.

As can be true in life generally, sometimes what is not said is as illuminating as what is said in this treasure trove of letters.

Eamon de Valera,
President of Ireland
to
His Holiness Pope John XXIII

Most Holy Father,

Having received the letter of the 27th of June by which Your Holiness was so good as to send me greetings and felicitations on the occasion of my entering upon office as President of Ireland, I desire to express to Your Holiness, with profound homage and filial devotion, my sincere thanks for this most gracious message.

It is my earnest prayer that in carrying out the duties of the high office to which I have been called, I shall be guided and inspired by the eternal truths of Faith and that I shall be fortified at all times in my task by the ~~manifold~~ blessings of Divine Providence.

I share Your Holiness's hope that Ireland may enjoy peace and prosperity, and I humbly pray that she may remain steadfast in the pursuit of the great ideals of truth, justice and charity which are, as Your Holiness has said, an integral part of her treasured Christian heritage.

In conveying heartfelt appreciation on my own behalf and on behalf of the Irish people at home and overseas for the gracious bestowal by Your Holiness of your special Apostolic Blessing, I beg Your Holiness to accept the assurances of my profound homage and of my attachment to the person of Your Holiness.

I am, Most Holy Father,

Your Holiness's most devoted son,

DUBLIN, this 12th day of October, 1959.

EAMON DE VALERA.

On his inauguration in 1959, President Éamon de Valera tells Pope John XXIII that he is 'Your Holiness's most devoted son'.

משרד ראש הממשלה
PRIME MINISTER'S OFFICE

Jerusalem, 18 August 1966.

Professor Mervyn L. Abrahamson,
Jerusalem.

Dear Professor Abrahamson,

      The name of Eamon De Valera is not only enshrined for all time on the tablets of Irish independence. His name is a by-word across the world as one of the pioneers of the present epoch in human history, a central theme of which is the emergence of small countries to independence, their assertion of their freedom and right to pursue their national destiny without external interference and to make their contribution on the international scene in equality. Eamon De Valera's leadership, integrity, deep humanity and sense of purpose have for many decades now left their imprint on the international community. In Israel it is not forgotten that in the crucial years of struggle for independence, he evinced understanding and sympathy towards the restoration of Israel in the land of its fathers. The forest which will rise in his name in the Galilee will, I have no doubt, be a lasting symbol of friendship between Ireland and Israel.

- 2 -

      If I may be permitted to end on a personal note, may I say that my memories of this great figure and all he stands for go back to my childhood in Dublin. As I recall the words of appreciation which I heard so many years ago from my late father, of blessed memory, about the personality of Eamon De Valera, I feel privileged indeed to add to-day my humble tribute to that of his countless admirers in Ireland, in Israel and throughout the world. In meetings with President De Valera over the past few years, I have been deeply moved by his understanding of the spiritual motive of Israel reborn.

      May I ask you, on your return to Dublin, to convey to President Eamon De Valera my warm greetings and deep respect.

Sincerely yours,

Yaacov Herzog
Yaacov Herzog
Political Advisor and
Director-General

'If I may be permitted to end on a personal note … memories of this great figure and all he stands for go back to my childhood in Dublin' – Israeli diplomat Yaacov Herzog, brother of Chaim Herzog, later to become President of Israel, recounts his memories of President Éamon de Valera on the official opening of a forest in Israel dedicated to the President of Ireland.

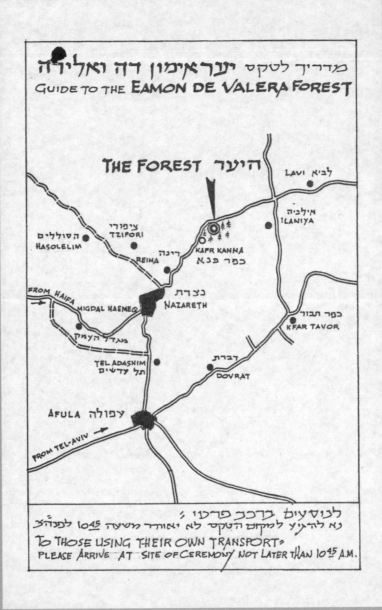

מדריך לטקס יער אימון דה ואלירה
GUIDE TO THE **EAMON DE VALERA FOREST**

THE FOREST היער

Lavi לביא

ציפורי
TZIPORI
הסוללים
HASOLELIM
רינה
REINA

אילניה
ILANIYA

KAFR KANNA
כפר כנא

FROM HAIFA

נצרת
NAZARETH

MIGDAL HAEMEG
מגדל העמק

כפר תבור
KFAR TAVOR

TEL ADASHIM
תל עדשים

דברת
DOVRAT

AFULA עפולה

FROM TEL-AVIV

לנוסעים ברכב פרטי :
נא להגיע למקום הטקס לא יאוחר משעה 10.45 לפנה"צ
To THOSE USING THEIR OWN TRANSPORT:
PLEASE ARRIVE AT SITE OF CEREMONY NOT LATER THAN 10.45 A.M.

Ten thousand trees were planted in the Éamon de Valera Forest on a hillside in Galilee in the 1960s. The forest was one of a series to honour world statesmen including Winston Churchill and John F. Kennedy. Six pine trees were transferred to Áras an Uachtaráin in 1973.

PS1|151   (89)

Dublin Islamic Society

Registered under the Friendly Societies Act of 1896, for Muslims in Ireland

P.O. Box 548,
Rathmines Post Office,
Upper Rathmines Road,
Dublin 6.

28th. December,1974.

Mr President and Lady O'Dálaigh,

Aras an Uachtaráin,

Phoenix Park,

Dublin 8.

Dear Mr President and Lady O'Dálaigh,

On behalf of the Muslims in Ireland ,
I wish to extend our congratulations to your election as President and
First Lady of Ireland.We wish you an eventful term of office and we pray
to GOD ALMIGHTY to give you strength to fulfill your endeavours.
The Dublin Islamic Society has a membership of about 250 Muslims, and of
these 90% are undergraduate university students from various parts of the
world. Because of our predominant student population, we have very recently
been invited to membership of the Irish Council for Overseas Students. It
is indeed an honour to have you as Life President of I.C.O.S.
I will be representing our Society on the Council and am looking forward
to meeting you in the near future.
Wishing you and Lady O'Dalaigh a Happy New Year,

I remain,

Sincerely Yours,

Ahmed.G.M.Adam.
Assistant Secretary.

The Dublin Islamic Society tells newly
elected President Cearbhall Ó Dálaigh
details about its membership and wishes
the president an 'eventful term of office'.

Text of Cable

His Excellency Patrick J. Hillery
President of the Republic of Ireland

Excellency,

I felicitate you on the coming of a new Christ year and the end
of 1985 years since Jesus Christ's birth (Peace be upon him). We would
have never known about Him, Except through the revelation descended upon
Prophet Mohamed (Peace upon him), in which God told us the complete story
of Jesus and His mother Mary, daughter of Omran.

We Moslems do believe, according to the Koran which you regret-
fully do not acknowledge, in the miracle of Jesus' birth and his Prophethood. We also do not have a clear vision, neither from the old nor the
new testament, because both have been falsified and changed. The mention-
ing of the Prophet Mohamed, besides other things, has been intentionally
ommitted from them as well. Jesus says in the original Bible, while
addressing the children of Israel, who denied him and attempted to kill
him (Oh you children of Israel, I am God's messenger to you, making credible
of what I have at hand from the Torah and the Bible, forseeing a prophet
coming after me, whose name is Ahmed).

On this holy occasion, I invite the new generations of the Christian
world to read the Koran to know the facts about Jesus (Peace upon Him),
his mother Mary, and her brother Haroun; and how Gabriel came to him
announcing Jesus' birth from Mary, the virgin, and how God offered her
out of his bounty: drink and food from the palm tree; how people attacked
her and how the infant Jesus spoke in the cradle and convinced them that
he was a prophet, blessed and illustrious and Mohamed was the prophet to
come after him; and how children of Israel disbelieved him, and attempted
to kill him, and crucified him, but God rose him up; how Jesus healed the
blind, the leper, and rose the dead alive.

All the details which made us Moslems, believe in the miracles of
Jesus' birth, prophethood, his start and his end, the war of Israelis
against Him, and the disciples support to him: We learned all of this

Libyan leader Colonel Muammar
Gaddafi tells President Patrick Hillery:
'it is you who threaten peace' and
'hatred is embodied in you'.

Text of Cable
page two

only from the Koran, which you do not read and you do not believe in, because of misleading Israeli propaganda against the Moslem world, and the ignorance which made you unaware of the prophet Mohamed's reality to whom God told Jesus' story in details and other prophets' stories as well.

Therefore, I direct my call to all new generations of the Christian world to initiate a cultural revolution in the concepts and beliefs of the Christian world, which has already lagged behind, and started to decay and become in need of Sofo Morola, Martin Luther and Calvin.

Once again, I do not want to speak ironically about peace in 1985 because it is you who threaten peace, and without you peace is in peace. Also I do not want to be ironic about love, because hatred is embodied in you to the extent that you made the most trecherous means of mass killing to destroy others; others whom Jesus told you about (who slaps you on your right cheek, give him your left cheek, and who asks you for a piece of your dress, give him the whole dress, and told you I do not kill, and do not kill and do not get made for whoever gets mad at others, will deserve to be burnt in hell.)

Peace upon those who follow guidance.

COLONEL MUAMMAR QATHAFI

Telefón Phone   (01) 780822

Telex 25300

Tagairt
Reference

AN ROINN GNÓTHAÍ EACHTRACHA
Department of Foreign Affairs

BAILE ÁTHA CLIATH, 2.
Dublin 2.

7 January 1986

Secretary
Department of the Taoiseach
Government Buildings
Dublin 2

Attention: Mr. B. Collinge

Please find enclosed a transcription of a cable received through our Permanent Mission to the U.N., New York, addressed to the President. The Libyan Permanent Mission to the U.N. asked that the cable be conveyed to the Head of State. We would not advise that the President reply directly to this communication. We understand that the usual New Year's greetings have been despatched already.

Anne Barrington
Anne Barrington
Middle East Section

The Department of Foreign Affairs advises President Patrick Hillery not to reply to Colonel Gaddafi, stating: 'New Year's greetings have been despatched already'.

To His Excellency
Patrick J. Hillery
President of Ireland

The many kindnesses that you showed to me when
I visited Ireland last year are treasured in my
memory. I thank Your Excellency for them and with
this letter I express my gratitude in particular
for the thoughtful gift of early eighteenth-century
Dublin silverwork that you gave to me on that occasion. It is a much appreciated reminder of our
meetings.

I renew my prayers for Your Excellency's welfare
and for the peace and prosperity of your country.

From the Vatican, 13 June 1980

Joannes Paulus PP. II

Pope John Paul II tells President Patrick
Hillery that his 'many kindnesses' during
the papal visit to Ireland are 'treasured in
my memory'.

APOSTOLIC NUNCIATURE
IN IRELAND

Dublin, May 13, 1981

N.2950

Your Excellency,

    I am sorry to inform Your Excellency that
the Holy Father at the beginning of the General Audience,
while meeting the faithful, as usual, in St. Peter's
Square in Rome before approaching the papal throne has been
wounded by a projected bullet. He was immediately carried
to the Gemelli Hospital and submitted to surgical
intervention. His condition which gives concern allows
founded hope.

    Please accept Excellency the renewed
assurance of my highest consideration and esteem.

Apostolic Nuncio

His Excellency
Dr. Patrick HILLERY
President of Ireland
Aras an Uachtarain
Phoenix Park, DUBLIN 8

The Apostolic Nuncio in Ireland,
The Most Rev. Gaetano Alibrandi,
informs President Patrick Hillery
that Pope John Paul II has been
shot and wounded during a
public gathering in Saint Peter's
Square, May 1981.

In a letter to *The Irish Times* in April
1997, an Irish priest based in Rome
criticised President Mary Robinson
for not dressing in black as was
customary during State Visits to the
Vatican. However, the president's
visit had been a private one. The
Vatican rejected the claim that there
had been a breach of protocol and
Catholic Church leaders in Ireland
strongly defended the president who
received many letters of support.

Ara Coeli, Armagh BT61 7QY
Telephone 01861 522045
Fax 01861 526182

September 30, 1996

Your Excellency,

My retirement as Archbishop of Armagh will be announced on Tuesday, 1st October which is my 79th birthday. I wanted you in courtesy to be among the first to know.

I intended to write to you anyhow following a recent trip to London and after your recent visit to the North, to say two things. Firstly, I wish to say how greatly your visits to Britain have enhanced the confidence and pride of the Irish community in Britain and how greatly they have helped to transform attitudes towards Ireland of political and public opinion in Britain.

Secondly, I wish to say how much I personally, with so many others, admire your courage in meeting diverse groups in Northern Ireland, and both pleading for reconciliation and giving concrete examples of reconciliation in the planning and conducting of your visits. This is making a significant contribution to the long and arduous search for peace in Northern Ireland.

I shall send you separately a copy of some remarks I myself made to a recent Conference of European Methodist Churches, held in Belfast. I think that the words of John Wesley are as relevant today as when they were spoken. I hope that more and more people will listen to them. I enclose also a copy of a statement I will make at a Press Conference to mark my retirement.

I wish to thank you for your courtesy and kindness to me at all times and to assure you of my good wishes and prayers in the future.

Yours sincerely,

+ Cahal B. Card Daly

Archbishop of Armagh

Her Excellency,
Mrs Mary ROBINSON,
President of Ireland,
Aras an Uachtarain,
Phoenix Park,
DUBLIN 8.

In advance of announcing his retirement, Cardinal Cathal Daly, the Catholic Primate of All Ireland, tells President Mary Robinson: 'I wanted you in courtesy to be among the first to know.'

UACHTARÁN NA hÉIREANN
PRESIDENT OF IRELAND

23rd March 2007

President meets with Pope Benedict XVI

President McAleese has this morning met with His Holiness Pope Benedict XVI at the Vatican.

During a 35-minute meeting, the President and Pope Benedict discussed a range of issues. The Pope indicated that the Irish bishops had invited him to visit Ireland to which he responded, 'We must see what is possible.'. The President replied, 'I, the Irish people and the government would welcome this visit and support it in every way possible.'.

The peace process in Northern Ireland was also discussed and the Pope said that the world needed this process to work and emphasised the importance of Christians working together, demonstrating that reconciliation can work.

Pope Benedict, in particular, made reference to the structured, inter-church dialogue that the Irish churches have initiated and which he hopes will become a model for other countries. He also complimented Ireland on its White Paper on development aid and expressed his hope that this aid would continue in partnership with Irish missionaries whose work has been so well-recognised throughout the decades.

President McAleese will address the Commission of the Bishops' Conferences of the European Community Congress in Rome before returning to Dublin tonight.

President Mary McAleese visits Pope Benedict XVI at the Vatican to discuss a papal visit, the Northern Ireland peace process and inter-church dialogue.

UACHTARÁN NA hÉIREANN
PRESIDENT OF IRELAND

13th July 2011

Statement by President McAleese on the Cloyne Diocese Report

The Commission of Investigation Report into the Catholic Diocese of Cloyne shows that many lessons still have to be learned in relation to the welfare and protection of our children. Clearly, an immediate priority today must be the abused victims, ensuring that they receive all necessary support and reassurance in the wake of the publication of this distressing and damning report.

It is a matter of grave concern that the report's findings show that, up to 2008, the Cloyne Diocese failed in large measure to comply with the Catholic Church's own 1996 guidelines on clerical child sex abuse. Had these guidelines been fully honoured and rigorously adhered to (as the public had been led to believe they would), this report would never have been necessary and children need not have been rendered so vulnerable. Allowing for the efforts that the Church has made to date to address child protection issues, nonetheless the narrative set out in the Cloyne report indicates that the leadership of the Catholic Church needs to urgently reflect on how, by coherent and effective action, it can restore public trust and confidence in its stated objective of putting children first.

The painstaking, authoritative work of Judge Yvonne Murphy and the Commission is to be commended. The chastening truth revealed in the Cloyne Report about such recent facts and events must compel the strictest future adherence by church, state and citizens to all laws and best practice protocols around child protection, and further steps in this regard are being taken by the Government. Every effort must be expended so that we can firmly consign this shameful period to history and be sure that our children do in fact come first.

Statement from President Mary McAleese describing as 'distressing and damning' the findings of a report into clerical child sex abuse in the Diocese of Cloyne.

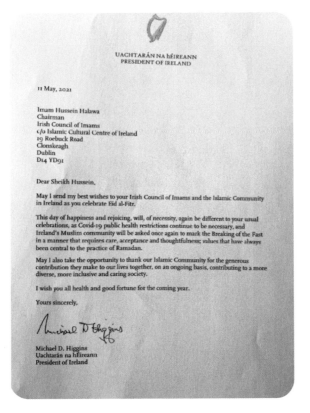

UACHTARÁN NA hÉIREANN
PRESIDENT OF IRELAND

11 May, 2021

Imam Hussein Halawa
Chairman
Irish Council of Imams
c/o Islamic Cultural Centre of Ireland
19 Roebuck Road
Clonskeagh
Dublin
D14 YD91

Dear Sheikh Hussein,

May I send my best wishes to your Irish Council of Imams and the Islamic Community in Ireland as you celebrate Eid al-Fitr.

This day of happiness and rejoicing, will, of necessity, again be different to your usual celebrations, as Covid-19 public health restrictions continue to be necessary, and Ireland's Muslim community will be asked once again to mark the Breaking of the Fast in a manner that requires care, acceptance and thoughtfulness; values that have always been central to the practice of Ramadan.

May I also take the opportunity to thank our Islamic Community for the generous contribution they make to our lives together, on an ongoing basis, contributing to a more diverse, more inclusive and caring society.

I wish you all health and good fortune for the coming year.

Yours sincerely,

Michael D. Higgins
Uachtarán na hÉireann
President of Ireland

To mark the Muslim festival of Eid al-Fitr in May 2021, President Michael D. Higgins thanks the Islamic Community in Ireland for 'contributing to a more diverse, more inclusive and caring society'.

Mary McAleese

(11 November 1997–10 November 2011)

When I was president I sent and received a lot of letters. The sending was often to congratulate on occasions of great joy but it was just as often to commiserate in the face of awful tragedy.

I used to imagine what it would be like to receive a letter from the president's office, to read it and to realise that your triumph or pain was something that mattered at the very heart of Ireland. So each letter sent had to be carefully worded to convey our nation's care. Often people would tell me how much that letter they received mattered and how it created a connection that stayed long in their memories, sometimes framed as a family memento. I especially loved the letters sent to schoolchildren and centenarians and the letters received back from them.

For it is the same with letters the president receives. Usually they lift the heart with their encouragement and create connections of kindness that help us to keep going. That was particularly true of thank-you letters from visitors to the Áras whose experience of its hospitality and the welcome from its great team energised the staff time and again.

Sometimes the letters were heartbreaking in the personal stories they told. Always they revealed the importance of the letter, the connecting with one another through words carefully chosen. How awful it was to meet men and women for whom letter-writing was impossible, for school and life had failed them as youngsters, leaving them with literacy problems which dogged their lives. How miraculous it was, though, to meet men and women who had overcome their literacy problems and had entered the world of letter-writing with a surging joy and wonder that was a reminder of just how much we give and receive from the written word.

UACHTARÁN NA hÉIREANN
PRESIDENT OF IRELAND

Mr. Peter & Mrs. Rose Scanlon
Co. Meath

31st May 2005

Dear Peter & Rose

It was my privilege to meet you both, your daughter Caitríona and Deirdre's Granny when I visited your home yesterday.

I was so very saddened to learn of your daughter Deirdre's death in such tragic circumstances. Please accept my sincere condolences to you and your family as you try to come to terms with this terrible tragedy. To lose a child is a most cruel blow for parents and my heart goes out to you on the loss of such a promising young life.

You spoke so proudly about Deirdre's talents and how much joy she had brought to you both. I pray that you may draw comfort from your family and friends and your happy memories of Deirdre.

It was good to briefly meet Rose's two brothers, including the legendary Mattie McCabe.

Many thanks for your hospitality - the lovely tea and scones.

Yours sincerely

Mary McAleese

Mary McAleese
President of Ireland

Letter to the Scanlon family, Co. Meath,
from President Mary McAleese following
her visit to sympathise with them on
the loss of their daughter Deirdre in the
Navan bus crash in which five people were
killed, May 2005.

HRH Queen Elizbeth II at the State Dinner hosted in her honour by President Mary McAleese, Dublin Castle, 18 May 2011.

A uachtaráin agus a chairde

phonetically A ook tar (oin eyen) aug us a hardje.

President and friends

Orange and green – it doesn't matter
Until now
Don't shatter our dream
Scatter the seeds of peace over
our land
So we can travel
Hand in hand across the
bridge of Hope.

In June 1998, twelve-year-old Shaun McLaughlin was one of six pupils from Scoil Iosagáin in Buncrana, Co. Donegal chosen to make a school trip to Áras an Uachtaráin. There he presented President Mary McAleese with a poem that he and his classmates had written. Two months later she attended his funeral. Shaun was one of thirty-one people, including unborn twins, killed in the Omagh bombing by the Real IRA on 15 August 1998.

In advance of her State Visit to Ireland, a high-level planning meeting had vetoed a suggestion that HRH Queen Elizabeth II would say a few words in Irish. 'Too risky', it was decided. However, the queen had other ideas. Using this envelope on which President Mary McAleese had some weeks earlier written out a phonetic version of the greeting, she astonished all those present in Dublin Castle, not least the president, by opening her historic speech with the words: 'A Uachtaráin agus a Chairde' (President and Friends).

UACHTARÁN NA hÉIREANN
PRESIDENT OF IRELAND

9 March, 2005

Ms. Mary Davis
Director
Special Olympics Ireland
4th Floor
Park House
North Circular Road
Dublin 7

Dear Mary,

I was delighted to learn of the wonderful achievements of the Irish team in the Special Olympics World Winter Games in Japan. Please convey my heartiest congratulations to each member of the team on their success.

Everyone in Ireland is very proud of their dedication, courage and, most of all, their commitment. I look forward to welcoming the team to the Áras on the 11 April next to celebrate their great achievements.

With every good wish.

Yours sincerely

Mary McAleese

Mary McAleese
President

President Mary McAleese congratulates Team Ireland on its success at the Special Olympic Winter Games in Japan in 2005. Two years earlier, the president had officially opened the Special Olympic Summer Games which saw more than 7,000 athletes from 150 countries travel to Ireland, where they were welcomed by host families.

President Mary McAleese welcomes the Special Olympic Flame of Hope at a ceremony at Áras an Uachtaráin in June 2003.

Former President of South Africa, Nelson Mandela, at the Special Olympic Summer Games in Dublin, summer 2003, where he said that Special Olympic athletes are proof of 'our capacity to overcome hardships and obstacles'.

16th July 2011.

Dear Madam President,

Just a brief word of thanks to you and to Dr. McAleese for the very gracious Invitation for _____ and me to be present at the Reception on the 12th and to partake of your lavish hospitality.

It was a great pleasure and honour to meet you both again and to have been included in such an extensive and prestigious Guest List.

We enjoyed ourselves immensely and I can assure you it was certainly a different 12th July to any I have previously experienced.

Again sincerest appreciation

(Belfast)

'Seen by President'

Just a simple 'thank you very much.'

'. . . it was certainly a different 12th of July.' A card sent to President Mary McAleese to thank her and her husband, Dr Martin McAleese, for hosting their final 12th July Garden Party at Áras an Uachtaráin, in the summer of 2011. The annual event was inaugurated by the president thirteen years previously to fulfill her promise of 'building bridges' between communities.

Drawing by twelve-year-old Ciaran
Smyth from Dunshaughlin, Co. Meath, to
celebrate President Mary McAleese's first
visit as president to the area where her
family had lived when her three children
were born. It references the poem 'Come
to the Edge' by Christopher Logue, which
she quoted in her inauguration address
in November 1997, and was used as the
cover of the president's Christmas card
that year.

Chapter 9

Visitors to the Park

Lise Hand

As the open-topped limousine passed the last phalanx of well-wishers lined up outside the gates of Áras an Uachtaráin on the soggy summer afternoon of 26 June 1963, the standing figure of President John F. Kennedy resumed his seat beside President de Valera and briefly put on his hat. Under its brim, and despite the murky light, the famous megawatt smile seemed as wide as the Atlantic Ocean.

At the entrance, the two leaders posed for the scrum of photographers before disappearing inside for a private meeting. It was to be a brief respite from the tumultuous throngs, the waving forest of outstretched hands, the ceaseless click of cameras and cheerful chaos which greeted President Kennedy's every step during this four-day visit to his ancestral home. His return to the Áras the following day for a garden party in his honour would spark a well-heeled scrum on the elegant lawns.

On 23 July, in response to a warm thank-you letter from the White House, an avuncular Éamon de Valera wrote back: 'I was somewhat relieved to see by the newspapers that you are being mobbed in the White House gardens as you were here!'

US President John F. Kennedy arrives in Dublin on his much-anticipated four-day State Visit to Ireland. Record crowds lined the route and cheered as he was accompanied by President Éamon de Valera to Áras an Uachtaráin on 26 June 1963.

The Honorable John F. Kennedy,
President of the United States of America,
Shannon Airport.

Mr. President:

Your visit has been a source of joy and pride to all
the people of Ireland and to all their kin throughout the world.
We wish you long life, health and happiness and pray God's
blessing upon you and upon the people of the United States.

Beannacht leat.

Eamon de Valera
President of Ireland.

President Éamon de Valera wishes the
departing US President John F. Kennedy
'long life, health and happiness'.

Kennedy was not the only distinguished recipient of kindly gestures from this president. In June 1961 thousands had lined the streets of Dublin for the first official visit of Prince Rainier and Princess Grace of Monaco, who sprinkled Hollywood stardust over the capital. 'I feel very inadequate in trying to express the love and emotion I feel for the Irish people,' Princess Grace told de Valera in a handwritten letter dated 2 October 1961. She wrote again in January 1962, enclosing a thank-you note from her four-year-old daughter, Caroline. The little princess had just received a present from de Valera – a pony from the Irish National Stud, named Babbling Brook.

Over the years a long procession of royalty, presidents, prime ministers, popes, politicians, diplomats, poets, actors, activists and revolutionaries have signed the bound visitors' books upon arrival at Áras an Uachtaráin. The building's surrounding lawns are dotted with trees planted by a panoply of powerful people whose presence in the Phoenix Park residence traces the arc of history as Ireland found its feet as a sovereign

The White House,
Washington.

July 25, 1963

Dear Mr. President,

Mrs. Kennedy was particularly delighted with the
beautiful antique silver dish ring that you presented to me
on my recent trip, and which I took directly to Hyannis Port
where she and the children are staying for the summer. It
truly brought "a little bit of Ireland" to the Cape, and
somewhat alleviated her disappointment in not being able to
visit with you and Mrs. de Valera also. Please accept our
warm thanks for this very handsome gift, and for the books,
so graciously inscribed, that I am most pleased with.

I shall never forget the wonderful reception given to me
in Ireland - it will always be one of my most pleasant
memories and a reminder of the close relations our two
countries have had for many years.

Mrs. Kennedy joins me in extending best wishes to you
and your family and to the people of Ireland.

Sincerely,

His Excellency,
Eamon de Valera,
President of Ireland,
Dublin.

US President John F. Kennedy writes
to President Éamon de Valera to say
he 'shall never forget the wonderful
reception' he received in Ireland.

THE WHITE HOUSE
WASHINGTON

August 16, 1963

Dear Mr. President:

I send you many thanks for your generous
message of sympathy. You were very kind to
think of us at this difficult time, and your message was a comfort to us. Mrs. Kennedy and I
are very grateful to you.

Sincerely,

[signature]

His Excellency
Eamon de Valera
President of Ireland
Dublin, Ireland

Re death of baby Patrick Kennedy – died a few days after birth (swR)

Letter to President Éamon de Valera from US President John F. Kennedy thanking him for his sympathy on the death of the Kennedys' third child, Patrick, August 1963.

nation. In 1969 an international press frenzy was sparked when newly resigned French President Charles de Gaulle chose to holiday in Ireland. The day he visited the Áras, 18 June, marked the twenty-ninth anniversary of his famous wartime speech made in exile from London, and throughout the day telegrams of con-gratulations arrived at the Áras for the general. More than four decades later im-ages were beamed around the world of a smiling Queen Elizabeth II being ushered by President Mary McAleese into what was formerly British Crown property, the Viceregal Lodge, as a military guard of honour stood to attention for 'Banríon Eilís a Dó'.

Our presidents have welcomed a diverse range of famous faces. The long list includes British Prime Minister Margaret Thatcher; Pope John Paul II; President of Israel Chaim Herzog; King Juan Carlos of Spain; President of South Africa Nelson Mandela; leading missionary Mother Teresa; Zimbabwean Prime Minister Robert Mugabe; Palestinian leader Yasser

Irish gifts for Kennedy children

Aer Lingus hostesses Miss Geraldine Hoban and Miss Marie McCarthy make friends with two " passengers " awaiting their flight to America. The two deer are gifts from the President, Mr. de Valera, to President Kennedy's two children. Now 18 months old, the deer were born wild in the Phoenix Park.

Aer Lingus 'hostesses' pose with Blossom and Bambi, two deer who were about to be flown to New York as a gift from President Éamon de Valera to Caroline and John Jr, the children of US President John F. Kennedy.

Arafat; Chinese President Xi Jinping (then vice-president); Indian Prime Minister Narendra Modi; and Pope Francis.

Each visit has doubtless played its part in forging links and strengthening political relationships between Ireland and other countries. However, the stacks of visitors' books offer tantalising glimpses into not only the delicate diplomacy, but also the relaxed entertaining that took place behind the closed doors by a succession of hospitable hosts. We can enjoy speculating, for instance, if famed American aviator Douglas 'Wrong Way' Corrigan regaled the room with tales of

his 'accidental' transatlantic solo flight from New York to Ireland when an extra leg of his journey brought him to the Áras in July 1938. We wonder if world-renowned tenor Count John McCormack answered a Noble Call when he visited a few months later in October and thrilled the president with a song.

Other signatures, particularly from the earliest days of the presidency, open small windows on Ireland's progress as a fully fledged republic, even at a time when World War II dominated the political landscape. One page from 25 March 1938 holds the signatures from Douglas Hyde's

Mrs. John F. Kennedy,

The White House,

Washington D.C.

The whole Irish people mourn in sympathy with you stop

Their hearts go out to you, and we pray that the soul of your

husband who had become so dear to us here may now be with

God in Heaven and that the Holy Spirit may give you His consolation

in this hour of terrible sorrow for you.

Eamon de Valera.

'The whole Irish people mourn in sympathy with you …' Telegram from President Éamon de Valera to Jacqueline Kennedy on the assassination of her husband, US President John F. Kennedy, 22 November 1963.

installation as first president. It was an event carried in headlines around the world, including Germany, where Hitler ordered the story onto the front pages of Berlin's newspapers.

The visitors' books also have multiple entries for Eduard Hempel, the German Minister to Ireland who was a regular guest at the Áras between 1938 and 1945. What tension surely must have crackled through the gracious room when Herr Hempel entered on 9 May 1945 – the day after Winston Churchill had announced the unconditional surrender of Germany and the end of the war in Europe?

Not everyone was made welcome at the Áras. One of the more intriguing documents from these early days is a de facto 'blacklist'. The document goes to some length to explain that a person placed on this 'caveat' list may have been included by their own request 'and [this] is not necessarily to the discredit of the person concerned'. Such was the case with the first name on the list, 'Madame Maud Gonne McBride'. The revolutionary and suffragist was a friend of Douglas Hyde who in 1888 described her in his diary as 'the most beautiful woman I have ever seen'. Her elegant signature in the visitors'

Kennedy had pledged to return to Ireland 'one day soon' with his family. That opportunity never came, but Jacqueline visited with their two children, Caroline and John Jr, in the summer of 1967. They were welcomed by cheering crowds on arrival at Shannon Airport.

In 1961 Prince Rainier and Princess Grace made the first official visit by any Head of State to Ireland. They travelled to the Kelly ancestral home in Co. Mayo and called on the de Valera family, with whom they enjoyed an enduring friendship. The photo shows them with their children Princess Caroline and Prince Albert at Áras an Uachtaráin, in July 1963.

book attests that she visited him at his new address in 1938, but in June 1939 she refused an invitation to a garden party and her name was added to a caveat list, where it remained for the next seven years.

The second recipient of a 'caveat' is far more unexpected – that of English entertainer, the 'Ukulele King' George Formby, who had a string of hits in the 1930s and 1940s. 'Music Hall Comedian' sniffs the entry on 1 April 1942. The reason for his exclusion is given in one terse sentence: 'Alleged offensive references to Ireland.'

But throughout its existence, Áras an Uachtaráin has predominantly been a place of warm welcome to the high powered and high profile. John F. Kennedy was only the first sitting American president to visit Áras an Uachtaráin; he was followed by Richard Nixon in October 1970, Ronald Reagan in June 1984, Bill

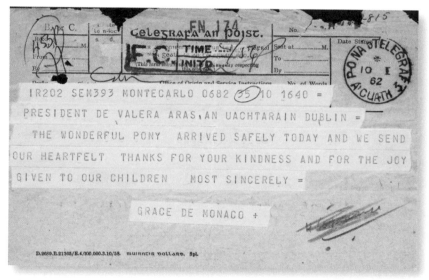

Telegram from Princess Grace to President Éamon de Valera announcing the safe arrival in Monaco of an Irish pony, a gift from the president to Princess Caroline.

Clinton in December 1995 and December 2000, and Barack Obama in May 2011. Each one acknowledged his Irish roots. Current US president Joe Biden quoted from Kennedy's speech to Dáil Éireann when he signed the book as vice president during his visit in June 2016. 'Our two nations, divided by distance, have been united by our people,' he wrote.

Going back to where we started, a special poignancy shines through in the correspondence between Éamon de Valera and John F. Kennedy, revealing a genuine warmth between Ireland's elder statesman and America's charismatic president. On 29 June 1963, as President Kennedy departed his ancestral home, he received a farewell telegram from Éamon de Valera. 'We wish you', he wrote, 'long life, health and happiness.' Little did he know how short a time was left for Kennedy.

Princess Caroline and her brother, Prince Albert, meeting their new pony Babbling Brook for the first time in the courtyard of the Royal Palace, Monte Carlo. With them are their parents Princess Grace and Prince Rainier, along with James Maher, the groom from the Irish National Stud who accompanied the six-year-old pony on its sea and rail trip to Monaco, January 1962.

January 30th
1965

Dear Sir,

Our daughter
Caroline is enchanted
with the pony you
so kindly sent for
her. She has in-
sisted on writing to
you herself to ex-
press her gratitude.
I am enclosing her
letter.

Babbling Brook
seems very happy
in her new sur —

Letter from Princess Grace of Monaco
to President Éamon de Valera to thank
him for the gift of an Irish pony to her
daughter Princess Caroline.

roundings and Caroline is learning very quickly to ride her. We are all delighted to have this lovely Irish pony and send our deepest thanks.

The Prince joins me in sending our warmest regards and best wishes.

Most Sincerely

Grace de Monaco

DEAR SIR THANK YOU.

LOVE CAROLINE

Caroline

Thank-You card from four-year-old Princess Caroline of Monaco to seventy-nine-year-old President Éamon de Valera.

President Éamon de Valera writes to Princess Caroline of Monaco with some equestrian tips. Touchingly, he signs off 'slán leat' and 'with love'.

23rd February, 1962.

My dear Princess,

     Your very nice letter has come to me.

     I am delighted that you like Babbling Brook. As you are fond of her she will grow very fond of you. When you get more used to her and have more practice, you can ride her over jumps. That will be great fun for you. But it can't be just yet, I think; your Mammy and Daddy will tell you. Sometime, when you are grown up, you may ride across our country here and jump our great big fences.

     Slán leat - this is the Irish for 'good bye'.

     Le cion - with love.

Eamon de Valera

Princess Caroline.

UIMHIR   P.940

UACHTARÁN NA hEIREANN

SGEUL......Social Functions

FO-SGEUL......Caveats

GENERAL NOTE

1.   Wherever a case arises where, for any reason,
it is considered that a particular person should
not be invited to a Presidential function of any
type, either at all, or subject to certain limitations, a personal file is opened for that person,
if one does not already exist. An appropriate
note is made on it and any documents bearing on
the matter are attached thereto.

2.   The reasons underlying a decision of this
nature need not necessarily be to the discredit
of the person concerned. In some cases it may
be the personal wish of the person himself due
to family or other circumstances. In others
the person concerned may be in mourning and the
caveat is therefore limited in tone.

3.   For this reason, the appearance of a caveat
note on a card is not to be taken as implying
anything unfavourable. It simply means that
no invitation is to be issued to the person concerned without a positive instruction from the
Secretary.

4.   In each case, a specific direction is given
by the Secretary on the file of the person concerned.

-2-

A record of all caveats should be on the
present file P.940.

Wherever a caveat decision is made by the
Secretary, the word "caveat" should be entered
on the social card of the individual concerned,
this word being followed by the number of the
relevant file. In addition, the card should be
marked on the front and back with a single red
line running diagonally from the right-hand top
corner to the bottom lefthand corner. This
will help to draw attention to the caveat and
prevent inadvertent issue of an invitation.

7.   The single line will distinguish it from
the cases of a person who is dead, the card in
that case being marked by a double red line
similarly drawn (See File P.964).

22/6/1939.

Unwelcome visitors: when your
social card is marked.

```
NAME:              Madame Maud Gonne MacBride

ADDRESS:      Roebuck House, Clonskea, Dublin.

RANK OR STATUS:   A Friend of President Hyde

FILE NO:      P.299

DATE OF DECISION:   20/6/1939

NATURE OF DECISION:      Not to be invited to any
                         future Function.

REASONS:      She said she would not come to first
              Presidential Garden Party on account of
              the "Coercion" Act which the President
              was about to sign.
```

The caveat on the file of Madame Maud
Gonne MacBride, revolutionary, suffragist
and actress.

UIMHIR ....P.499.......

UACHTARÁN NA hÉIREANN

Madame Gonne McBride ....

....

....

PRESIDENTIAL GARDEN PARTY

25th June, 1946.

————

I discussed with the President the case of
Madame Gonne McBride in connection with the Garden Party
arranged for the 25th June next (file P.2771).

He agreed that the Cavet of 20.6.39
entered against her might be withdrawn in the present case.
An invitation is accordingly being sent her.

An invitation however is not been sent to
her son, Seán McBride for reasons recorded on his personal
file P. 2791.

3.6.46

MW

Caveat Withdrawn.

President Seán T. O'Kelly has the caveat
lifted from Maud Gonne MacBride's file.
However, a caveat was to be added for
her son, Seán MacBride, who had just
founded the republican socialist party
Clann na Poblachta, which he hoped
would replace Fianna Fáil.

The leather-bound Áras an Uachtaráin visitors'
books, which date from June 1938.

Walt Disney, along with Sean Connery, Janet Munro and other cast members meet President Seán T. O'Kelly and his wife Phyllis before the world premiere of Disney's feature film *Darby O'Gill and the Little People* in Dublin, June 1959. It was the president's final official engagement. © 1959 Disney.

Along with correspondence, the files at the National Archives of Ireland hold additional material relating to State Visits to Ireland, such as this collection of speeches made by US President John F. Kennedy during his visit here in 1963.

Douglas 'Wrong Way' Corrigan poses beside *Sunshine*, the Curtiss Robin J-1 in which he made the first solo flight from New York to Dublin. Corrigan had been denied permission to cross the Atlantic but was cleared to fly to California. He took off in fog from Brooklyn's Floyd Bennett airfield, flew out over the Atlantic and twenty-eight hours later, on 18 July 1938, touched down in Baldonnel Airport. Corrigan signed autographs on O'Connell Street, met the Taoiseach and was welcomed at Áras an Uachtaráin by President Douglas Hyde.

Banner headlines in reverse, a ticker-tape parade on 5th Avenue, and crowds of more than one million people awaited Douglas 'Wrong Way' Corrigan on his return to the US aboard the liner *Manhattan*. He starred as himself in the film *The Flying Irishman* and always stuck to his story that he'd 'got mixed up in the clouds and must have flown the wrong way.'

NAME: George Formby.

ADDRESS:

RANK OR STATUS: Music Hall Comedian.

FILE NO: P.2211.

DATE OF DECISION: 1/4/42.

NATURE OF DECISION:

REASONS: Alleged offensive references to Ireland.

The caveat on the file of English musical
entertainer George Formby, who was
alleged to have made anti-Irish remarks
about Ireland's neutral stance during
World War II.

Poster for the 1938 film *Trouble Brewing*,
starring George Formby as an amateur
sleuth who takes on the horseracing
industry. The highest-paid entertainer in
England in the 1940s, Formby had spent
three years during World War I working
as a jockey in Ireland and later owned a
house in Galloping Green, Dublin.

UNWELCOME VISITORS: EMERGENCY AT THE ÁRAS

Ireland may have remained officially neutral throughout World War II, but the country didn't remain completely unscathed by its violence. In the early hours of 31 May 1941, German war planes brought the Blitz to Dublin, dropping a succession of bombs on the capital, including on the North Strand area, which left twenty-eight people dead and hundreds wounded.

Ireland's first citizen had a narrow escape on that tragic night. A 4 June memo from Michael McDunphy, President Hyde's secretary, noted that a bomb had dropped 'beside the Dog Pond in the Phoenix Park which is only about half a mile in direct line from the Áras' and had smashed a number of windows in the residence. 'One of the windows in the President's bedroom in which he was at the time sleeping was broken and a portion of the mantel-piece dislodged,' he wrote. Such was the consternation of the Taoiseach who visited the Áras

some hours after this close call, that he recommended the construction of a 'blast proof shelter' within the house, and plans for such a structure were subsequently drawn up.

Following this event, real and not-unfounded fears of a German invasion prompted the Irish government to devise a plan to protect the president if this should come to pass. A February 1942 memo by Maurice Moynihan, Secretary to the Government, outlined the Taoiseach's view that President Hyde should be moved from the Áras as secretly as possible. 'In order to achieve this, it would be necessary that he should assimilate his way of living as much as possible to that of a private citizen,' he explained. 'It is desirable that the number of servants to be employed should be reduced to a minimum and that the residence chosen should be on the small side and that elaborate furnishings shall be avoided.'

In the event, President Hyde was not obliged to quit Áras an Uachtaráin during the war – but had that Dog Pond bomb instead scored a direct hit on his bedroom that fateful night, to what extent would it have changed the course of Irish history?

A tractor ploughs the land at Áras an Uachtaráin. The introduction of rationing during the Emergency led to parts of the parklands around the main house being farmed to boost food production. Photograph dated 31 December 1942.

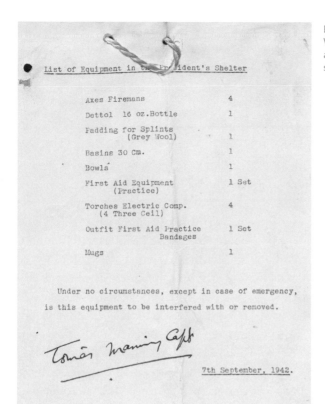

List of contents for the proposed World War II air raid shelter at Áras an Uachtaráin, including padding for splints, Dettol, and one mug.

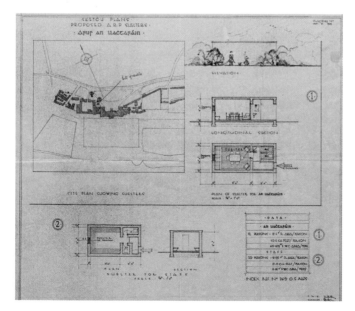

Architectural plans for a proposed air raid shelter at Áras an Uachtaráin, dated 6 June 1941.

THE PRESIDENT'S POSTBAG

From Pen and Ink to Social Media

In June 1946 a letter from Áras an Uachtaráin to the government brought attention to the flood of correspondence arriving for the president from across war-torn Europe: 'We have received here quite a number of letters', wrote Michael McDunphy, Secretary to the President, 'particularly from schoolchildren in Italy, France and elsewhere, expressing thanks for the gifts of sugar and other food ...' McDunphy suggested that the letters should get a wider audience: 'perhaps consideration could be given to the possibility of publishing these letters'.

It's taken seventy-five years, but the power of these heartfelt letters hasn't dimmed, and McDunphy was right; they deserve to be read, slowly and with respect.

Letters written in French, German, Italian, Hungarian and Serbo-Croat were delivered to President Seán T. O'Kelly, who was asked by some of the correspondents to pass their letter on to Irish families who might be willing to send aid, with entreaties such as: 'Dear Irish Sisters, I beg you to help us ... my house was bombed on 13th October 1944 and utterly destroyed with all our belongings ... please send us clothes, overcoats, underwear, stockings, hats, shoes ...'

Graphologists would point to the style of the handwriting: many of these wartime

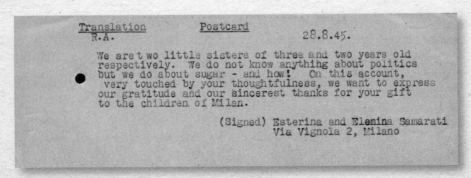

<u>Translation</u>   Postcard
R.A.　　　　　　　　　　28.8.45.

We are two little sisters of three and two years old
respectively. We do not know anything about politics
but we do about sugar - and how! On this account,
very touched by your thoughtfulness, we want to express
our gratitude and our sincerest thanks for your gift
to the children of Milan.

(Signed) Esterina and Elemina Samarati
Via Vignola 2, Milano

Translation of a postcard from children in Italy thanking President Seán T. O'Kelly for aid from Ireland, August 1945.

P.2665

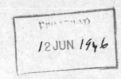
12 JUN 1946

12 Meitheamh, 1946

Rúnaí don Rialtas.

A chara,

     We have received here quite a number of letters of thanks
from Corporations, individuals, and particularly from school
children in Italy, France and elsewhere, expressing thanks for
the gifts of sugar and other food sent by the Irish Government
for the relief of suffering in Europe.

     It seems a pity that this widespread appreciation of the
generosity of the Irish Government is not widely known, and
perhaps consideration could be given to the possibility of
publishing these letters, or extracts from them, either in the
original or in the form of translations.

     Many of them are written in childish handwriting, and the
question of the publishing of fac similes might also be
considered.

     The material here can be made available at any time. We
have letters in Italian, English, French and German.

        Mise, le meas,

          (Sgd.) M. McDUNPHY

MW   Rúnaí.

A suggestion to publish some of the
letters received by the President of
Ireland during World War II is being
followed up, seventy-five years later.

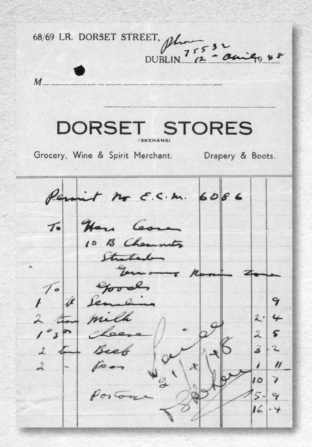

Receipt for foodstuffs including semolina, cheese and meat to the value of 16s 4d sent by D. Skehan, proprietor of Dorset Stores, Dublin to an address in the 'Russian Zone', Germany in 1948.

letters were written in desperation, a plea for help to the President of Ireland, a country neutral in the war and out on the edge of the continent. Sometimes the correspondents were sent aid directly; others were helped through the Red Cross (of which the president is patron); many never received a reply, but at least we can read their stories now, however late.

The language used to address the president in these and other letters from the 1930s and 1940s is almost always formal, and the letters are often written in pen and ink on personalised stationery, starting with salutations such as, 'Your Most Esteemed Excellency' or 'Most Honourable Sir'. But as the decades passed, these conventions relaxed. By the 1960s the influence of news stories from the US had an effect, with correspondence addressed simply to 'Mr President'.

The pared-back 'Uachtaráin' and 'Dear President' became the favourite forms of address in the 1970s and 80s, and in recent years, with the influence of online communication, roughly 50 per cent of 'letters' to the president now arrive by email, some with text-speak abbreviations, such as 'Hey Prez'.

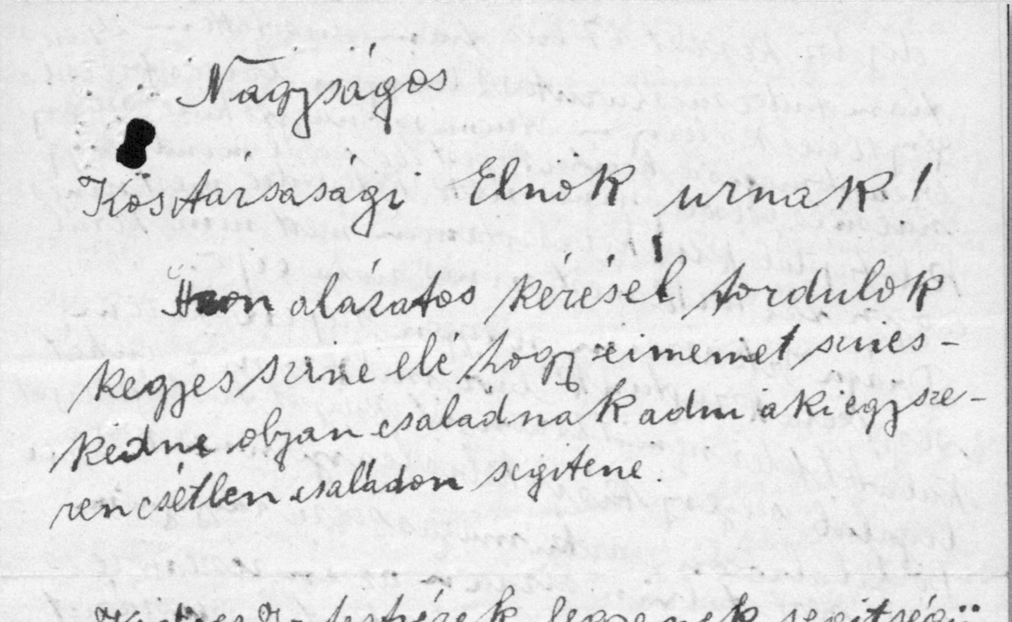
Nagyságos

Köztársasági Elnök urnak!

Azon alázatos kérésel fordulok
kegyes szine elé hogy szivemet szives-
kedne olyan családnak adni aki egy sze-
rencsétlen családon segitene.

Kedves Ir testvérek legyenek segitségünkre 6 gyermek anya vagyok házam 944 okt 13 án
teljesen tönkre ment a bombazás által teljes beren-
dezésel és ruházattal együtt mind bomba károsult
ami segélyt kaptam azt meg elvitte a front mert saj-
nos két tüz közé kerültünk, férjem már
nyugdijas trobózisban szenved olyesek-é ja a
nyugdija hogy megélhetésre sem elég és borzasztó
hogy akinek mindene odalett semmi kedvezménye
nincs borzasztó lakbért fizetünk a nyug-

Original letter (handwritten) and its translation (typed) sent from Hungary to President Seán T. O'Kelly, in April 1947. The writer, whose name and address couldn't be deciphered, sought urgent help from her 'Irish Sisters'.

Copy.

Most honoured President,

    I respectfully request you to forward this letter
to any families who would be willing to help us.

    Dear Irish Sisters,
    Be good enough to help us. I am the mother of
six children, my house was bombed on 13th October
1944 and utterly destroyed with all our belongings,
etc. The help we received after the bombing is all
gone, my husband is an invalid and we have no means
of livelihood. I lost my 17 year old son, I have
a son 24 years old, 2 girls and a little girl 12
years, all suffer very much from the cold as we
have no clothes and no shoes. Dear Irish Sisters
I beg of you to help us, please send us clothes,
overcoats, underwear, stockings, hats, shoes, at
least for my poor little school girl, low heeled
shoes or rubber shoes for myself please send low
heeled shoes size 5 or 5½ as I have to walk a lot,
also please send something for my six year old son,
overcoat, clothes, shoes and men's clothes for my
husband or son, anything will be most welcome and
we beg God's blessing on those Irish Sisters who
will help a poor needy family. We are desperate,
please help us to prove to my family that there are
still kind hearted and good people in the world, to
prove also that there really is a God who heps those
who believe in him. Dear good Irish sisters, if
you could spare a little (word illegible) we have
none and it is impossible to get any it is so very
dear. Please put it inside the lining of a coat
in case the parcel is opened they might take it
away. Dear Irish Sisters in God's name I beg of
you who can help us to please do so and accept
our most grateful thanks and may the good God bless
you all and your families.

```
                              Translation.

Emma Mechler.                        Berlin-Steglitz,

                                     Schildhornstr. 55 I Tr.r.

                                     (American Sector).

                                     29th January, 1947.

To the President of the
  Irish Free State,
      Dublin.


   Most honoured President,

              To our pleasant surprise we old people,
   over 70 years of age, have received, through the
   city of Berlin, a special ration of sugar which has
   been donated by the Irish people.

              I have found this gift particularly
   beneficial especially as our rations, not only of sugar,
   are really inadequate.  I am an 80 year old refugee
   from Sorau in Lausitz, have lost house and home and
   now live with my son.

              I should not like to fail to express to
   you, most honoured President, and to the whole Irish
   people, my deepest thanks for this generous action.

                        Respectfully,

                          Emma Mechler (Sgd.)
```

Translation of a letter to 'the President of the Irish Free State' from Emma Mechler, in the 'American Sector', Berlin in January 1947, with deepest thanks to the president 'and to the whole Irish people'.

The presidency of Michael D. Higgins is the first to fully embrace social media, with @PresidentIrl accounts on Twitter, Instagram, Facebook and TikTok. President Higgins's Bernese Mountain Dogs, Bród, Misneach and the late Síoda, have their own unofficial Twitter account, with close to 30,000 followers. And though these communications are one-way – it would be impossible to reply to every message – it is further evidence of people's wish to correspond with their president.

This need to engage is never truer than in times of crisis, and letters have been again flooding into Áras an Uachtaráin since the Covid-19 pandemic arrived in early 2020. Postcards have replaced the telegrams, headed notepaper is rarely seen, but these 'letters from lockdown' are no less heartfelt and the volume has never been greater.

Thx a mil Prez. U did us all so v v proud.

Im proud to call myself Irish on account of the really powerful job u did for us all in the UK this last week.

Maith thu.

'U are a great man Sir 'was written in an email to President Michael D. Higgins after his historic State Visit to the United Kingdom in 2014. Half of all correspondence to Áras an Uachtaráin now comes via email.

All the president's dogs: Bród (meaning 'Pride' in Irish) with Misneach ('Courage') in the background at Áras an Uachtaráin. The Higgins family's favourite breed, the Bernese Mountain Dogs appear prominently in photographs with visiting world leaders, royalty and members of the public. When Síoda ('Silk') died in late 2020, hundreds of letters of sympathy were sent to the president. Misneach, who arrived as a puppy in March 2021, was named to reflect the times we are in.

The 'Céad Madraí' ('First Dogs') have their own unofficial Twitter account with almost 30,000 followers. In contrast to the president's official social media accounts, Bród agus Misneach engage with their followers, often about social issues, news from their daily lives and requests for photos of other dogs (and the occasional cat).

Bród agus Misneach 🐾 🦴
11.2K Tweets

Bród agus Misneach 🐾 🦴
@BrodHiggins

The official unofficial account for the céad madraí na hÉireann. Maybe Jedi. Black Lives Matter. Wear a mask. We miss Síoda 😢

📍 Áras an Uachtaráin   🔗 president.ie/awesomedogs   📅 Joined October 2018

140 Following   **26.6K** Followers

Follow

UACHTARÁN NA hÉIREANN
PRESIDENT OF IRELAND

Mr. Shane Gillen
https://www.bigandbright.ie/contact-us

15th April 2020

Dear Shane

I was most interested to learn of your work, and in particular how your creativity has
come to much to the fore at this difficult time.

It is so important that we stay engaged with each other in these special circumstances.
I am very grateful to citizens like you who use your talent and skills to bring light and joy
into the lives of others as we undertake, together this unprecedented journey.

I send you my warmest regards and look forward to seeing more of your innovative work.

Beir Beannacht

Yours sincerely

Michael D. Higgins
Uachtarán na hÉireann
President of Ireland

An unsolicited letter of thanks to artist
Shane Gillen, who tried his hand at a
portrait of the president during the
first lockdown in Ireland, in April 2020,
and posted it online. Shane has since
been commissioned to draw dozens of
portraits for clients in Ireland and abroad.

The state dining table at Áras an Uachtaráin covered in 'letters from lockdown' as citizens at home and abroad wrote to President Michael D. Higgins in their thousands in the early weeks of the COVID-19 pandemic.

Chapter 10

Club and Country

Letters about Sport

Paul Rouse

From the very first year of Douglas Hyde's presidency through to Michael D. Higgins's second term in office, the sporting life of Ireland is reflected in the presidential letters. This sporting life extends from the high politics of national and international controversies down to the quotidian efforts of small clubs and the personal enjoyment of sport.

Sport and the presidency were intertwined even as Áras an Uachtaráin was being made ready for the first incumbent of the office in 1938. Plans were made to set out a grass tennis court, and also to build a golf course in the grounds. Douglas Hyde was a keen golfer and the ambition was to create a course that would 'enable His Excellency to take exercise and recreation without leaving the precincts of An Áras'.

The view was that only a small amount of work would be needed to adapt the existing grounds (some rolling, the use of natural obstacles and the construction of some bunkers). It was recalled at that time that there had previously been a private course at the Áras, when it was home to the Lord Lieutenant of Ireland. That course had been built in 1902 and had been used by the elite of Irish society until the outbreak of the Great War in 1914. It was estimated that making the new golf course for the president would cost £44 and its maintenance would not exceed £20 per annum. In the end, the course was not built and Hyde had the grave misfortune of suffering a massive stroke in early 1940.

Modern sport means much more than playing a game, of course. In an Irish context, the Irish presidency was on the bitter fault line of politics and identity that has always run through Irish sport. The idea that the Gaelic Athletic Association (GAA) could be used to draw a distinction between 'Irish Ireland' and those portrayed as 'West British' had

P.333

Fi
23 MAR 19..

20adh Márta, 1939

Rúnaí,
    Oifig na nOibreacha Puiblí.

        The President would like that a tennis court should be made available for him in the Árus.

        In the time of the Governor General there were six hard Courts in use but these, it is understood, have been allowed to fall into disrepair and their repair would probably be costly.

        In these circumstances the President would be satisfied with a grass court which could be utilised in the summer. For the moment there is no necessity to put up a permanent court; a portion of the lawn could be utilised for that purpose, the nets etc. being removed whenever necessary.

                        (Sgd.) M. Mc DUNPHY
                            Rúnaí.

MW.

A letter from the office of President Douglas Hyde to the Office of Public Works requesting the construction of a tennis court at Áras an Uachtaráin.

brought the establishment of a set of rules which redefined membership of the GAA in the early years of the twentieth century. By the 1930s these rules banned from its membership anyone who played rugby, soccer, cricket or hockey.

They also banned anyone who attended these 'foreign games', and all members of the police, the British Army, the Navy and the prison service. There was also a rule which banned membership for anyone who attended dances run by the British armed forces or by 'foreign' games clubs. On top of that, vigilance committees were established to attend 'foreign games' matches and to report if any GAA members attended. Although there was a certain idealism which underpinned these

Price tag for a hardwood croquet set from Elverys Sports Goods, sent to Áras an Uachtaráin in 1949.

rules, they did manage to expose the GAA to popular ridicule. In 1938 President Douglas Hyde attended an international soccer match in Dublin in the course of the duties of his office. Hyde had been for many years a patron of the GAA, a titular role which recognised his contribution as a founding father of modern Ireland, a distinguished Gaelic scholar and the creator of the Gaelic League. When the matter was raised by a Connacht delegate at a Central Council meeting of the GAA, the president of the Association, Pádraig MacNamee, ruled that because of Hyde's actions, he had 'ceased to be a patron of the Association'. To deploy the ban rules against a man who had helped to invent the very ideal of an 'Irish Ireland', which

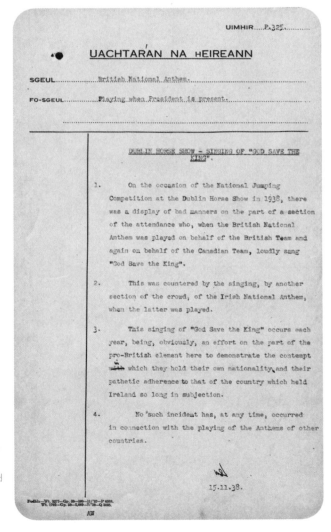

The singing of 'God Save the King' by part of the crowd at Dublin Horse Show in 1938 was described as 'bad manners' on the part of a 'pro-British element' in a memo to President Douglas Hyde.

President Douglas Hyde greeting the teams ahead of the Ireland versus Poland soccer international at Dalymount Park, Dublin in November 1938. His attendance led to him being dropped as patron of the GAA.

the rules were supposed to help establish, was a perversion of common sense. The echoes of this controversy continued through the presidency of Seán T. O'Kelly right up to the late 1950s.

Áras an Uachtaráin wasn't immune from international controversy over sport either. The US President Jimmy Carter wrote to President Patrick Hillery in 1980, seeking support for his campaign to boycott the Summer Olympic Games in Moscow 'unless the Soviet Union withdraws its troops from Afghanistan'. Hillery replied to Carter that he had forwarded the letter to the government. As the campaign gained momentum, sixty-six countries boycotted the games, but eighty-eight participated, including Ireland. Lord Killanin, the Irish president of the International Olympic Committee, spoke from the famous Bolshoi Theatre in Moscow on the eve of the games: 'I deeply regret that many athletes, either through political dictation or the dictates of their own consciences, are not with us at the Games,' he said. 'Let me stress again ... I believe the athlete is frequently the victim of sports administrators.'

Luckily, successive presidents have not been placed in such controversial dilemmas. Instead, their engagement with sport is usually one which involves unproblematic attendance at a range of sporting events and the hosting of successful teams and individuals as recognition of achievement. Individual presidents have loved sport in ways that have emphasised the diversity of Irish sporting experience.

Wexford G.A.A. Not to Welcome President

Wexford Co. Board G.A.A. at a meeting in Enniscorthy decided by 17 votes to six not to be represented at the official welcome to the President when he visits Wexford on June 9 to open the Feis.

The Feis Committee had requested the County Board to associate themselves with the official welcome.

When Mr. S. Roche, the Secretary, mentioned the request, Mr. Sean O'Kennedy proposed that they proceed to next business and Mr. M. Kehoe, N.T., seconded, saying they had no official invitation before them.

Mr. J. Goodison—I propose we do not agree to the President throwing in the ball at the Feis match. Anybody else attending foreign games would not be allowed to throw it in. If any of us attended a soccer match we would be suspended for five years.

Mr. J. Reid—I think we should take no action. The G.A.A. is supposed to be a non-political association.

Mr. S. Browne said it was not a question of politics. The President of the State was entitled to a welcome. Extraneous matters should not be introduced.

Mr. M. Kehoe—This is not an extraneous matter. What Mr. Goodison said is quite to the point.

Mr. Browne—Nobody said he was to throw in the ball.

Mr. Goodison—It is rumoured he is.

Mr. D. Doyle—A man threw in a ball for Galway - Wexford match in Enniscorthy a few Sundays ago, and although he was a Rugby official the County Board did nothing about it.

Mr. Browne—That man gave £150 to pay the expenses of that match to help the Christian Brothers build a school in Enniscorthy for training of boys of the town who will be playing Gaelic games only.

Rev. W. Mernagh, C.C. (Chairman)— The fact that he threw in the ball does not mean that he took an official part in the match.

Mr. V. Boggan—Didn't the Association suspend the last President for throwing in the ball at a Soccer match? Why don't we do the same with his successor?

Mr. J. J. Whelan said that the last President, Dr. Hyde, was Patron of the G.A.A., and President O'Kelly was not.

Mr. S. O'Kennedy said that for the benefit of the Association it would have been better not to have had this discussion

An amendment proposed by Mr. Browne and seconded by Mr. Colfer that the Board be represented at the official welcome was defeated.

A newspaper report describes the Wexford County Board of the GAA in consternation over an impending visit by President Seán T. O'Kelly, who had attended a rugby match weeks earlier.

Ronnie Delany reliving the moment he won gold in the men's 1,500m at the Melbourne Summer Olympic Games in 1956, setting a new Olympic record of 3.41.2. Delany says presidents were not in the habit of writing letters to athletes in those days but he was delighted to attend a reception hosted for him by President Mary McAleese to mark the 50th anniversary of his Olympic win at Áras an Uachtaráin, December 2006.

US President Jimmy Carter urges President Patrick Hillery to join his boycott of the 1980 Summer Olympic Games 'unless the Soviet Union withdraws its troops from Afghanistan'.

Michael D. Higgins has long been associated with soccer and was president of Galway United Football Club long before he was elected President of Ireland; Mary McAleese loved Gaelic football; Mary Robinson enjoyed rugby internationals; and Patrick Hillery was an enthusiastic golfer, said to possess at one point the lowest golf handicap of any world leader. Although there were occasional diplomatic challenges, notably in respect of anti-apartheid protests and the Olympic boycotts, it was the symbolic engagement of the presidential office in the sporting life of the country that became utterly dominant. Indeed, the presence of the Irish president at All-Ireland Finals, and at soccer and rugby internationals – all of which must be understood as significant public events – is at once commonplace and highly evocative of the important place of sport in modern Ireland.

January 20, 1980

His Excellency
Patrick J. Hillery
President of Ireland
Áras an Uachtaráin
Phoenix Park
Dublin 8

Dear Mr. President:

On January 20, I am sending the attached letter to
the President of the United States Olympic Committee
informing him that I cannot support United States participation in the summer Olympic Games in Moscow, the capital
city of a nation whose invading military forces are occupy-
ing Afghanistan. I am requesting that the Committee work
with other national Olympic Committees to seek the transfer
or cancellation of the 1980 Moscow Olympic Games unless
the Soviet Union withdraws its troops from Afghanistan
within the next month. If the Soviets do not withdraw and
the games are not transferred or cancelled, I am asking
that the United States Olympic Committee not participate
in the games in Moscow, and instead, work with other nations
to organize alternative games.

I hope that you will urge your own Olympic Committee
to take similar action. I believe that such action is
necessary to support the position of the United Nations
General Assembly, to convince the Soviet government and
people of the world's outrage at Soviet aggression in
Afghanistan and to deter future aggression.

Please hold my action in confidence until after 1:00
PM, Washington time, January 20.

Sincerely,

/s/

Jimmy Carter

Enclosure:
  As stated

His Excellency
Mr. J. Carter
President of the United States of America

Dear Mr. President

Thank you for your letter of 20 January setting out your
views in relation to the Summer Olympic Games in the
light of the invasion of Afghanistan by the Soviet Union.

Because of the nature of my office I am precluded from
undertaking the type of intervention which you request
but I have forwarded your letter and its enclosure to
the Government who, I understand, have these issues
under consideration.

In sending this reply I should like to avail of the
opportunity of conveying my warmest wishes to you and
to Mrs Carter.

Yours sincerely

Partick J. Hillery
President of Ireland

President Patrick Hillery tells the US
President Jimmy Carter that he has
forwarded his letter to the government,
and conveys his 'warmest wishes'.

In a statement sent to President Patrick
Hillery, the USSR accuses the USA of 'foul
play, arm-twisting tactics and blackmail'
with the aim of disrupting the Moscow
Summer Olympic Games.

OPS5/v 24610

WELCOME, OLYMPICS!

Trud Leader

The Soviet capital, a hero-city, a city of labour and a city of sport, is giving its welcome today to the sacred Olympic flame. Within less than 24 hours the fire of the Moscow Games will be lit in the golden "lotus" of the eastern stands of the V.I. Lenin Central Stadium in Luzhniki. That will be a stirring moment for the world's athletic movement.

Moscow as well as her Olympic sisters--Leningrad, Kiev, Minsk and Tallinn--are giving wholehearted and warm welcome to the Olympic family--athletes, coaches, umpires, world sport managers, representatives of the planet's sporting press as well as numerous foreign and Soviet tourists. Everything is ready for the opening of what is the major sporting event of every four years.

Unique sportsbuildings, giant stadiums seating hundreds of thousands, modern snug hotels and restaurants, top-class press centres, everything that has been constructed by the Soviet people with the utmost industry and inexhaustible enthusiasm, has been put in service for the Olympics.

It is necessary to emphasize, besides, that all preparations for the 22nd Games have been made in Moscow and other cities in full accord with the rules of the Olympic Charter, the requirements of the International Olympic Committee and traditions of the Olympic movement. The IOC President Lord Killanin made a special point of it in his opening address at the 83rd session of this representative organisation in Moscow. He said at the session that many athletes are not with us at these Games through political dictation or that of their own minds. To put it bluntly: the foul play of the White House, "arm-twisting" tactics, blackmail and outright bribery of certain sports leaders with the aim of disrupting the Moscow Olympics have robbed the athletes of certain countries, notably the United States, the Federal Republic of Germany, Japan and Canada, of an opportunity to join their friends and sportmates in these Games.

Yet the Olympic caravan is going its way and, as Paese Sera, a Rome newspaper, wrote: "The United States has not managed to wreck this festival of youth and sport which is to begin very soon and which we are approaching with open hearts. It is impossible to kill the Olympic movement. There will be none among the athletes forced to stay away from the Moscow Olympics that would not regret it."

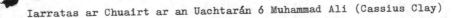

Iarratas ar Chuairt ar an Uachtarán ó Muhammad Ali (Cassius Clay)

1.   Le linn do Muhammad Ali a bheith anseo le haghaidh coimhlint
dornálaíochta le déanaí, dúirt an Teachta ó Conchubhair, (Ciarraí
Theas) leis an Rúnaí Pearsanta ar an teileafón gur mhian le
tionscnóirí na hócáide a mbeidh Al ('Blue') Lewis ag dornálaíocht
leis go bhfaighfeadh Muhammad Ali deis cuairt a thabhairt ar an
Uachtarán.   Mhol mé don Rúnaí Pearsanta a rá leo nárbh fhéidir
a shocrú.

        Cé go bhfuil dea-chuspóir leis an taispeántas i bPáirc an
Chrócaigh, .i. cabhair airgid a sholáthar do chás leanaí a bhfuil
ceataí meabhrach orthu, ní shílim gur chóir fear bladhmannach
mar Ali a bheith ag teacht chun an Uachtaráin go háirithe tar
éis a ndúirt sé faoina chuairt agus go háirithe a chuairt ar
an Taoiseach (cf sleachta as na páipéir nuachta faoi dhátaí
12/7/'72 agus 13/7/'72 leis seo).

2.   Cúpla lá ina dhiaidh sin bhlaoigh an Teachta Clinton,
Co. Áth Cliath, ag iarraidh an rud céanna ach dúirt an Rúnaí
Pearsanta leis "that an tUachtarán would be unable to receive
Mr. Ali within the dates on which the latter would be in Ireland
and on which it is understood he would be available".

3.   Ní dheachthas níos faide leis an scéal, ach má bhíonn
Muhammad Ali ag iarraidh coinne arís, níor mhór a bheith cúramach
faoi ghéilleadh dó.

mōf
24. 7. '72

Memo (in Irish) from the Office of the
President on a request from heavyweight
boxing champion Muhammad Ali for
a meeting with President de Valera,
during his trip to Dublin in July 1972.
Translation: 'I don't think it is appropriate
for a boastful man such as Ali to be
visiting the president'.

Irish Independent, Thursday, July 13, 1972   3

Muhammad takes the Dail by storm

By RAYMOND SMITH

"IF you wish, Mr. Premier, I can get this fight over in a hurry," cracked Muhammad Ali in Leinster House yesterday when he met the Taoiseach in his room. And Mr. Lynch told the boxing star he would be taking time off from the mid-Cork by-election campaign to attend the big fight in Croke Park on Wednesday night.

Muhammad took Leinster House by storm. Not since President Kennedy addressed both Houses of the Oireachtas has the visit of one celebrity engendered such spontaneous excitement. Protocol was forgotten more than once during this whirlwig visit—and it seemed to me that Muhammad must have shaken the hand of every member of the Cabinet as he made his way down the corridor to the Taoiseach's room, and later the hand of every leading member of the Opposition as he went through two steaks in the restaurant ("this is my first meal since morning and I will not eat again until this time tomorrow evenin," he told me) .

He had a coke with his meal—he never takes alcholic drinks and never eats chips with a steak. "Steak and plenty of vegetables," that is his essential diet, according to trainer Angelo Dundee.

Muhammad was in serious mood for most of the time he spent with Mr. Lynch. He said it was a great honour for him to be received by the Prime Minister of the Country. Ireland was the first European country to pay him this honour. "I have been to Britain, Germany and Switzerland, but they did not honour me like this," said Muhammad.

He told the Taoiseach he wanted to publicly compliment the Irish people "on their proud history of struggle." The Irish were a people who had shown they were prepared to stand up and fight for civil rights and justice and he knew what their struggle meant because "my people, too, have been underdogs for a long time."

He grew very serious as he pointed out that every day in the U.S. he was reading about trouble in Belfast and in the North, generally. He had one question to put to Mr. Lynch: "What is this struggle all about?"

The Taoiseach gave the ex-world champion a potted history. Then Ali gave an insight into how he had come to identify himself with the struggle of his people.

"I can never forget how when I was a little black boy in Kentucky, thinking of civil rights, the mayor of the city was a giant figure to me. Now here I am today sitting beside the Prime Minister of this country. I am just an athlete and a boxer."

Then Muhammad added simply: "I would love to be a leader of people some day — helping people."

The Taoiseach told Ali he had a fight ahead on his hands in Mid-Cork adding jocosely: "Perhaps you would come down and be a candidate for us."

Later someone suggested to Ali in another room that if he stayed around long enough he might even be invited to be President!

Before he signed the Visitor's Book and looked in for a while at the Dail proceedings from the Distinguished Visitors' gallery, Muhammad sat down to his meal in the restaurant with his party.

He signed autographs for the restaurant staff and when someone rang home to say he would be delayed, and put his wife on to Ali, the former champion said on the line: "Your husband is with the greatest boxer in the world. Now you just don't go whippin' him tonight, cause he's with the champion . . ."

"Muhammad loves people," said Angelo Dundee in between sips of his Gaelic coffee. "This Irish coffee is good—you have something goin' for you in this," he added.

Angelo's wife (nee Helen Bolton) and his daughter, Terri, are arriving for the fight. "I believe you have a Bolton Street in Dublin," Angelo said. "My wife will be pleased to hear that. She is of Irish descent on both sides of her family."

Muhammad Ali receives a warm welcome at Leinster House, where he signs autographs, meets the Taoiseach, Jack Lynch, and dines on steak and Coca-Cola.

Muhammad Ali, world heavyweight boxing champion, known as The Greatest, entertains with his famous one-liners at a press conference at Dublin Airport in July 1972. Ali would train at Croke Park, and go on to beat rival Al 'Blue' Lewis in a comeback match following Ali's controversial refusal to enlist for the Vietnam War. In 2009 Muhammad Ali was made the first Freeman of Ennis, from where his great-grandfather Abe Grady had emigrated in the 1860s.

Austin Slattery, Secretary

Lahinch Golf Club
Lahinch, Co. Clare, Telephone Lahinch 3

8-12-83.

Dear Paddy,

Your invitation to the celebration in the Park was much appreciated. I enjoyed myself immensely. It was a very pleasant as well as an historic night. Please convey to Maeve my thanks for her gracious reception of all of us.

Finally here's to seven more great and glorious years in office.

Yours sincerely.

Paddy.

Paddy Hillery

The Secretary of Lahinch Golf Club, Co. Clare thanks fellow club member President Patrick Hillery for the 'historic night' at Áras an Uachtaráin celebrating the president's inauguration for a second term in December 1983.

President Patrick Hillery, the only president to play competitive sport while in office, chipping from a bunker during the first round of the Foxrock Scotch foursomes in Dublin, April 1990. Dr Hillery had at one time a golf handicap of seven, said to be the lowest of any Head of State in the world.

The first time any president had attended the Camogie Final: President Mary Robinson looks on as Angela Downey, captain of the winning Kilkenny team, embraces Biddy O' Sullivan, her full back, Croke Park, September 1991.

Under the Constitution, the President of Ireland must seek the permission of the government in order to leave the State and here President Mary Robinson is granted permission to leave for twenty-four hours to attend an Ireland vs Scotland Six Nations rugby match in January 1993. The president would attend as many international matches as her schedule allowed.

S.21075B

ROINN AN TAOISIGH
Department of the Taoiseach

BAILE ÁTHA CLIATH
Dublin 2

17 Nollaig, 1992.

Rúnaí an Uachtaráin

I am to inform you that, at a meeting held today, the Government, in accordance with Article 12.9 of the Constitution, approved the President's leaving of the State from 16 January, 1993 to 17 January, 1993, inclusive, for the purpose of attending the international rugby match and social functions in Scotland.

Dermot Nally

Rúnaí an Rialtais

CLAUDE MONET
(1840-1926)
Spring (detail)
THE FITZWILLIAM MUSEUM CAMBRIDGE

©FITZWILLIAM MUSEUM

29/8/96

Dear Mary,

Thank you so much for all of your faxe's and letters of support and encouragement, also the kind and strong words you have expressed towards me in recent times.

Atlanta was more than dissappointing for me, however I am moving forward and leaving the past where it belongs in the past.

Best Wishes, Sonia O'Sullivan

Sonia O'Sullivan thanks President Mary Robinson for her encouragement and admits to being disappointed at winning a silver and not a gold medal at the 1996 Summer Olympic Games in Atlanta. She had won gold for Ireland in the 5,000m at the 1995 World Championships.

UACHTARÁN NA hÉIREANN
PRESIDENT OF IRELAND

28 January, 2009

Uachtarán,
San Francisco GAA,

Dear

On behalf of Martin and myself, I would like to thank you,
and your Board for the great welcome you gave us during our
recent visit to San Francisco and for allowing us the honour of unveiling the playing
pitches at Pairc na nÓg.

We attach great importance to preserving our culture and heritage and what your
Board have done not only preserves our sporting heritage but allows us to bring it to
the many generations of young Irish Americans who will exercise a crucial role on
your playing fields in taking forward that dúchas. I am sure that both San Franciscans
and the many Irish men, women and children who are drawn to the Bay Area will
benefit from and enjoy, for decades to come, what you have created at Treasure
Island.

It was truly a pleasure to unveil that magnificent corner stone. I know how much
work it takes to bring such a project to fruition and taking it from concept to reality is
a feat which all on the Board can be proud of.

It was wonderful also to see all the children from the local schools in their county and
club colours enjoying the magnificent sunny morning. It was truly a joyous and
festive occasion and we will long remember it.

I know that many people were involved in organising the opening of the Park, so
please pass on my warmest thanks to them all.

Yours sincerely,

Mary McAleese
President of Ireland

President Mary McAleese writes to San
Francisco GAA following her official
opening of its new playing pitches
during a visit to the US in 2009.

MESSAGE FROM PRESIDENT MICHAEL D. HIGGINS

I am delighted to send my congratulations and best wishes to the members of Bagenalstown Cricket Club as you celebrate your 175th anniversary.

As Ireland's oldest parochial club, the Bagenalstown cricket club is deeply embedded in our Irish sporting culture. The club has played a significant role in the lives of generations of cricket enthusiasts, while also becoming an established part of the general Bagenalstown community. It has also continued to evolve and adapt through many seismic events of Irish history, enabling successive generations of young people to continue to carry forward a love of the game through their membership of Bagenalstown Cricket Club.

May I wish you all a most enjoyable year of celebration, and every success in your future endeavours.

Michael D. Higgins
Uachtarán na hÉireann
President of Ireland

President Michael D. Higgins congratulates 'Ireland's oldest parochial club', Bagenalstown Cricket Club, Co. Carlow, as it celebrates its 175th anniversary in 2018.

Following a superb performance at the 2018 Women's Hockey World Cup in London, the Irish team is hosted by President Michael D. Higgins and his wife, Sabina Higgins. The amateur team came second, beaten in the final by a team of full-time professional players from the Netherlands.

OIFIG ARD RÚNAÍ AN UACHTARÁIN
OFFICE OF THE SECRETARY GENERAL TO THE PRESIDENT

President Michael D. Higgins
& Sabina Higgins
are pleased to invite

Mr. Jerome Pels

to a Reception to celebrate
the achievements of the Women's Irish Hockey Team

at Áras an Uachtaráin
on Friday, 7th September, 2018
3.00 p.m. - 5.00 p.m.

President Michael D. Higgins joined
sports fans of all ages and codes on
a commemorative walk with his club,
Galway United Football Club, in 2019.
'Reclaiming the Dyke' drew huge
crowds to commemorate the era when
supporters would walk to matches.

UACHTARÁN NA hÉIREANN
PRESIDENT OF IRELAND

Mrs. Pat Charlton

27ᵗʰ November 2020

Dear Pat

I am delighted to formally let you know that your late husband Jack, a great friend of Ireland and its people, has been selected to be given posthumously the Presidential Distinguished Service Award for the Irish Abroad.

This Award was established in 2012 to recognise the distinguished and sustained contribution to Ireland, Irish communities abroad and Ireland's international reputation by people living abroad. The full list of this year's recipients of the Award is attached for your information.

Jack was selected to receive the Award under the category of Arts, Culture and Sport. The Irish people took Jack into their hearts as he brought us to some of our most celebrated moments in Irish sporting history. His contribution is greatly appreciated by me and by the Government.

Under normal circumstances, you would have been invited to travel to Ireland for an awards ceremony at Áras an Uachtaráin. However, given the global impact of the Covid-19 pandemic and restrictions on international travel, unfortunately this will not be possible in 2020. I look forward to welcoming you to Áras an Uachtaráin in person during 2021, at a time when it will be safe to do so, when we will honour Jack and his fellow recipients of this year's Presidential Distinguished Service Award. The Embassy in London will remain in contact with you on arrangements, as restrictions ease and travel resumes.

Yours sincerely

Michael D. Higgins
Uachtarán na hÉireann
President of Ireland

President Michael D. Higgins tells Pat Charlton that her late husband has been given the 2020 Presidential Distinguished Service Award for the Irish Abroad. Marking Jack Charlton's 85th birthday six months earlier, the president had told the former manager of the Republic of Ireland football team: 'Under your leadership, Irish soccer fans were allowed to dream.' 'Big Jack' led Ireland to the quarter-finals of the World Cup in Italy in 1990. It was the most-watched television event in Irish sporting history.

Chapter 11

'I Know I'm Only a Child, But …'

Letters from Children

Terri Kearney

O ver the decades, children have put pen (or pencil, or crayon) to
paper to write to the presidents of Ireland about every topic under
the sun: from letters on Irish politics and geopolitics to letters pleading
the abolition of the death penalty and the abolition of homework. All
are written with the inimitable insight and candour of childhood. There
are letters chastising the president, commiserating with the president on
their resignation from office, offering fashion advice and sympathising
over the death of the president's dog. There is correspondence about
world peace, human rights and the role of the presidency itself. 'I
know I'm only a child, but it's my point of view,' is how one letter
concludes, but it's clear that the children never hold back in expressing
their opinions to their president. And their letters have been taken
no less seriously than those from other sections of society, and duly
responded to.

Carefully filed in the presidential archives are wartime letters posted
in 1946, in which children addressed their thanks to the President

President Mary Robinson welcomes Heads of State to Áras an Uachtaráin in a drawing by nine-year-old Katrina Murphy. Visits to schools have formed a significant part of the engagement diaries of each president of Ireland. President Robinson visited Katrina's school, Presentation National School, Millstreet, Co. Cork, in November 1991.

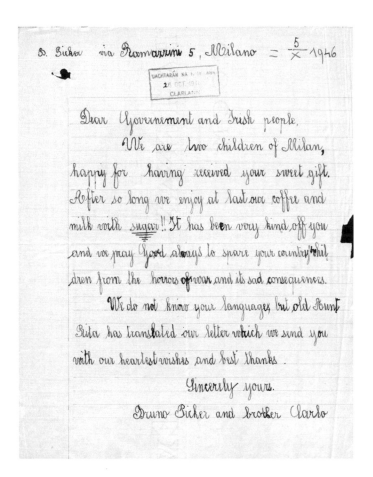

A wartime letter of thanks from children in Milan to President Seán T. O'Kelly in 1946 for the donation of sugar. The siblings say they pray Ireland will be spared 'the horrors of war'.

of Ireland in Italian, French, German and English, 'for the gifts of food sent by the Irish Government for the relief of the suffering in Europe'. Two Milanese children went so far as to ask their 'old aunt Rita' to translate a letter of thanks on their behalf, expressing their joy at being able to 'enjoy at last our coffee and milk with sugar'.

Children were not reticent in expressing their political opinions either: 'Donegan is a Thundering Disgust, as muck is on a football pitch after a week of rain,' is one boy's vehement response to the controversy surrounding the resignation of Cearbhall Ó Dálaigh, which arose when the Minister for Defence described him as a 'thundering disgrace'. A letter from a six-year-old said: 'We are sorry here at home that you are not our president. I like you and your mummy' (the 'mummy' in question being Ó Dálaigh's wife).

The children have addressed weighty human rights issues too. One eleven-year-

7 Gilbert St,
Glasgow C3,
Scotland
24/8/49.

Dear Mr O'Kelly.
Once again we both share the same Birthday I am now 8 yrs old, and for a present my mammy is sending me to Ireland for a holidays I am going to Cork where my Daddy and mammy was born and I know I will have a

lovely time with my Gran I wish you a happy Birthday and I will pray that on our next Birthday Ireland will be united

Yours Truly
Thomas O'Mahony.

I am sailing for Ireland on Tuesday 30th

In a letter written in 1949, eight-year-old Thomas O'Mahony from Glasgow reminds President Seán T. O'Kelly that they share the same birthday, and says he will pray that on their next birthday 'Ireland will be united'.

P 51/154

Phone: 065-21985

9

Highfield Park,
Ennis,
Co. Clare.

18 - 12 - '74.

Dear Mr. O'Dalaigh,

On the onset, I would like to take this opportunity to wish you many years of happiness and success in your new and honerous office.

On seeing you on various television appearances, I wish to express an opinion regarding which I trust you will not be offended. I, together with some of my friends, feel that you might consider the suggestion that perhaps a darker tie might be more suitable, due to the distinguished high office which you now hold.

Wishing you and Mrs. O'Dalaigh a very happy and peaceful christmas and new year.

I remain,
Yours sincerely,
Regina Mannion (16)

P.S. No offence meant, of course.

'No offence meant'; a group of teenagers offers sartorial advice to President Cearbhall Ó Dálaigh.

old pleaded with Hillery to intervene on behalf of two people sentenced to death in Saudi Arabia: 'They might have done it but I don't think they should be killed. Please try to stop it all.' Students from Hiroshima implored Ireland in 1985 to 'avoid the Nuclear War' by urging support for the 'Nuclear Arms limitations talk'. They invited President Hillery to 'see the evidence of the effect of the first Atomic Bomb explosion on our lives'.

Immediate concerns in children's own daily lives also feature: 'Would you please outlaw school … the worst time of your life.' Hillery's response: 'I felt the same … write to me again and tell me how you are getting on.' Children love to compose poetry for the president, especially on their reactions to big televised events they have watched. The historic State Visit to the United Kingdom by Higgins inspired a book of poems by schoolchildren from

A strongly worded letter from a nine-year-old boy on the resignation of President Cearbhall Ó Dálaigh. He brands the Minister for Defence a 'Thundering Disgust'. He also mentions his well-known grandfather, the writer and poet Séamus Ó Grianna.

Longford, one of the poems boasting the unique title 'History is Yummy'.

Typically, many of the letters are accompanied by artwork, particularly portraits, of the first citizen, or the first dog: a letter of sympathy to Higgins explained: 'I am sorry to hear about Síoda ... I was sad when my cat died. So I know that you are too.'

President Cearbhall Ó Dálaigh is surrounded by young fans on a visit to Our Lady of Lourdes School, Rutland St, Dublin 1, in October 1976. Within days, the president had resigned from office and was sent this photograph by teacher Peigí Piogóid along with messages of goodwill from the pupils, many of whom said they hoped he would 'apply for the job again'.

PS1|213①.

(68)

Dear mr o Dalaigh;
We are very sorry here at home that you are not our President.
I like you and your Mummy. I am 6 years old.

love
Cian o carroll
x x x

A six-year-old sends a supportive letter to President Cearbhall Ó Dálaigh and his 'Mummy'.

Jane

Dear President Hillary
My name is Michelle and I am
11 years of age. My cousin
Lisa is writing to you as
well. I'm writing to you to
tell that the couple that
have been accused of the
murder of Helen Feeney should
not be sentenced to death.
They might have done it
But I don't think they
Should be killed. Please try
to stop it all. They could be
innocent people really. But it
would not be right for
them to die.

Yours sincerely

Michelle Burke

XXXXX

P.S. I know I'm
a child. But it is only my
point of view.

An appeal from eleven-year-old
Michelle Burke for President Patrick
Hillery to help a couple facing capital
punishment in Saudi Arabia for the
murder of an Irish nurse. They were
ultimately released.

●*Dear*

President Hillery:

We are eagerly anticipating the 40th
Anniversary of the United Nations.   At
present throughout the world there is
a lot of talk about a Nuclear Winter.

We, highschool students in Hiroshima,
have tried to write a newspaper which
simply expresses the worst effect of a
Nuclear War.   We would like to request
that you read our newspaper.

Moreover we have read in the
newspapers that the main issue of the
November Top Summit between President
Reagan and General Secretary Gorbachev
will be a Nuclear Arms limitation talk, We
welcome such a noble step.

We sincerely hope that both them will
be able to reach an agreement which can
completely save the world from the curse
of a Nuclear explossion.

In connection with this, we also hope
the representatives of all nations to the
United Nations in the General Assenbly
will also find a way to completely avoid
the Nuclear War.

We are very much interested in meet
you and would like to invite you to come
to Hiroshima to visit the Atomic Bomb Dome
and Peace Memorial Museum, where you can
see the evidence of the effect of the
first Atomic Bomb explosion on our lives.

                                 Sincerely,

                        October 24, 1985

c/o United Nations Youth Friendship Center
802 Grace Bldg., Hatchobori 6-10, Naka-ku,
Hiroshima-730, JAPAN

Yukiko Asada	(15 years old)
Kyoko Nagao	(16 years old)
Mutsuko Hori	(16 years old)
Chizuko Ueda	(16 years old)
Yumiko Yuasa	(16 years old)
Saori Koshiro	(15 years old)

A group of teenage Japanese students
beseeches President Hillery, on the
fortieth anniversary of the United
Nations, to help the world avoid a
'Nuclear Winter'.

Dear Mister President,
Would you please outlaw school (if not for ever just for a year or two) I say school is the worst time of youn life every friend I have does'nt like school. Our school, Gael scoil Inse chór, is getting very strict you need a doctors letter if you are not allowed do sports, or if you can't go out in the yard.
 Hope you can do something about it.
  Yours hopefully
   Shane Doyle

An exchange of letters between President Hillery and schoolboy Shane Doyle on the possibility of outlawing school.

13, Feabhra, 1985

Dear Shane,

It has taken me a while to reply to your letter as I have been very busy. At the same time it is not easy to answer as I cannot grant your request to outlaw school and I know that this will be a disappointment for you.

I do not like causing you disappointment as when I was your age I felt the same about school as you do now.

I do not know any way to console a person who hates school and still has to go there every day but I hope that you will find it less hard as you get older. And you can look forward to the Easter holidays soon and then the long summer break later.

Please write to me again and tell me more about how you are getting on.

        Yours sincerely.

Master Shane Doyle.

Our President Mary Robinson
By Georgina Brennan age 11 years

President Robinson
Lisa Lawrence Age 11 years

President Mary Robinson
Margaret King Age 12 years

Our President Mary Robinson
By Christine Berigan age 11 years

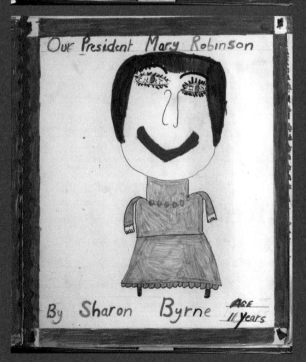

Our President Mary Robinson
By Sharon Byrne Age 11 years

President Mary Robinson

By Lisa Mountaine age 13 years

President Mary Robinson?

Jennifer Lawless Age 10 years

Our President Mary Robinson

Angelina Flanagan age 8 years

Our President Mary Robinson

Lisa Connolly Age 11 years

Our President Mary Robinson

Martina Smyth Age 12 Years

Portraits of President Mary Robinson
following her visit to Ballymun. All but
one child depict her wearing 'her lovely
green suit'; Jennifer, the exception,
opts instead for a red and purple
ballgown.

President-elect Mary Robinson chose to
give her first in-studio television interview
following her election to RTÉ's children's
programme *The Den* in November 1990.
She joined presenter Ray D'Arcy and
puppets Zig, Zag and Dustin the Turkey,
with whom she joked that she was looking
forward to Christmas.

Other artwork shows the working life of the president: welcoming Heads of State to Ireland; representing us abroad; working with minority groups.

The letters to female presidents often refer to their appearance: 'Our President is Mary Robinson / She is like a Princess / In her lovely green suit,' and hair being 'nicely styled'. But male presidents didn't escape such attention, with one group of sixteen-year-olds offering sartorial advice to Ó Dálaigh: 'My friends and I think a dark tie would be more appropriate to the office … No offence meant.'

Correspondence from more recent times reflects children's concerns about climate change and homelessness. One young girl's letter to Higgins about her family's experience is a truly heartbreaking read: 'I live in a bedroom with my mom two brothers and two sisters … we can't be a family not like this … and no one seems to be helping.'

'I will never forget the day you came to Ballymun'. Thirteen-year-old Lisa Mountaine describes the excitement of President Mary Robinson's visit to Ballymun, Dublin in December 1991.

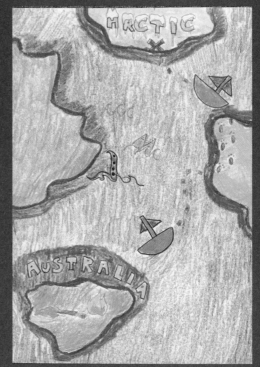

Seven-year-old Margaret Hill, from Ballyguiltenane National School, Co. Limerick, drew this picture of President Mary Robinson on a working visit to Rwanda.

Portraits of a dapper-looking President Michael D. Higgins by Nathan Pritchard and Dinovic Nkodia, second class, Sacred Heart National School, Huntstown, Dublin, November 2020. A drawing of the presidential car by Lisa O'Mahony, Presentation Convent Millstreet, Co. Cork, November 1991. And an Arctic illustration by Annika Ward from a book on global warming, by Ms Costigan's sixth class, Duleek GNS, Co. Meath, February 2020.

Every Irish president has welcomed and responded to the children's letters: 'It gives me great pleasure to reply to your letter in which you raised important questions concerning the future of mankind,' wrote Hillery, in a detailed letter about world peace, nuclear disarmament, and famine in Africa. But even the simplest acknowledgments of messages and gifts addressed the young letter-writers with humanity and respect.

The children's letters to the presidents are of immense historical value, giving voice to a cohort of citizens whose rights were not always to the fore, and offering a unique perspective on the social history of our State. But they are also proof that Ireland is a country in which children have the power to address the highest office in the land. And, what's more, they can sign off their letters with 'love' and 'xxxxx'.

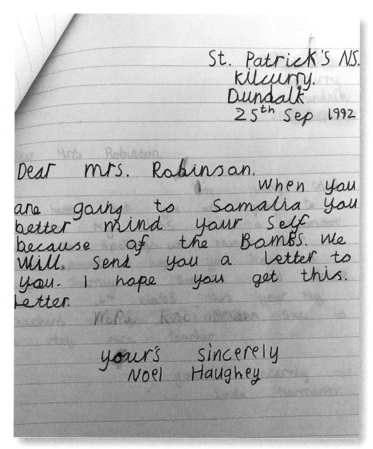

Noel Haughey, from Saint Patrick's National School, Kilcurry, Co. Louth, advises President Mary Robinson to 'mind herself' while visiting Somalia.

This is the Day -

As the jet flew away
Michael D. Higgins thinks of the day ahead.

As the connons fire
Michael D. is so proud after eight hundred years.

Sitting at the long table in Windsor Castle
emotions are flowing as the Queen raises a glass.

The castle was built over a thousand years ago
by William The Conqueror without a draught.

The beef was well hung
cooked with a secret Windsor twist.
The ice cream was as soft as Highland mist.

Ronan Rooney
Fermoyle N.S. Longford

History is Yummy

Dinner at the table
meeting new people everyday.
Could have talked forever
wishing he could stay.

Eating turkey and chicken
ham and steak filling up,
having fun talking to theQueen
dringing a sup of tea.

Eating lamb that came from English sheep
that makes your heart skip a beat.
There's no money to send
all the fun must come to an end.

Children from Fermoyle National School,
Co. Longford, write poetry about the
State Visit of President Michael D.
Higgins to the United Kingdom.

Zach Hanlon
Fermoyle N.S. Longford

'We're Allowed to Like the British'

Some might agree, some might not but, eight hundred years later and after much bloodshed this epic story in 2014 collides in peace. When the President of Ireland and Queen of England shook hands.

Ryan Docherty
Fermoyle N.S. Longford

Dear Mr Presidnt
I want to ask you for your help
I Live in a bedroom with my mom
Two Brothers and Two sisters thats six
of us in a bedroom We cant be
a family not like this my Mom is
Trying really hard and No one seem's
To be helping her nine months and
Wear still here
So Mr. Presidnt Iam asking for your
help To help my family.
Christmas is Coming and i would like
for us To be in a House Call friends over
little thinks like that mean alot when
your a ChilD
Thanks for takeing the time to
read This If you can Call someone
To help us I Would be very gratfull
for your help
Regrads Louise

President Michael D. Higgins is asked to help
a family who are homeless and in emergency
accommodation: 'six of us in a bedroom …
my Mom is trying really hard,' she writes. In
the following letter, the president replies,
having met the family.

UACHTARÁN NA hÉIREANN
PRESIDENT OF IRELAND

c/o   B & B

Dublin 1

11th September 2014

Dear Louise

I want to firstly say that I was very happy to meet you and your family at Focus Ireland earlier this week and to hear at first hand of your circumstances. Your mother, Rosemarie, is a fine mother of great and practical courage and ability. She reared a great daughter in yourself in being able to draw attention to what you are hoping to achieve.

Meeting and listening to you and other families was of immense assistance to me in getting a clear and first hand insight into the very serious issues affecting people who are homeless. I was very taken by the different stories I heard and I will do what I can to assist, and in particular, by highlighting the issue of homelessness.

You have shown a lot of initiative and courage in writing this letter on behalf of your brothers, sisters and parents, and I sincerely hope that this very difficult situation in which you, as a family, find yourselves will be resolved in the near future.

One of my staff has spoken to your mother and she has given permission, on your behalf, for me to pass your letter on to Cllr. Christy Burke, The Lord Mayor of Dublin, Mr. Owen Keegan, CEO, Dublin County Council and Mr. Gerry Danaher, Chair of Focus Ireland, who I know will continue to assist you and your family.

Best wishes to you and your family, Béir Beannacht

Yours sincerely

Michael D. Higgins
Uachtarán na hÉireann
President of Ireland

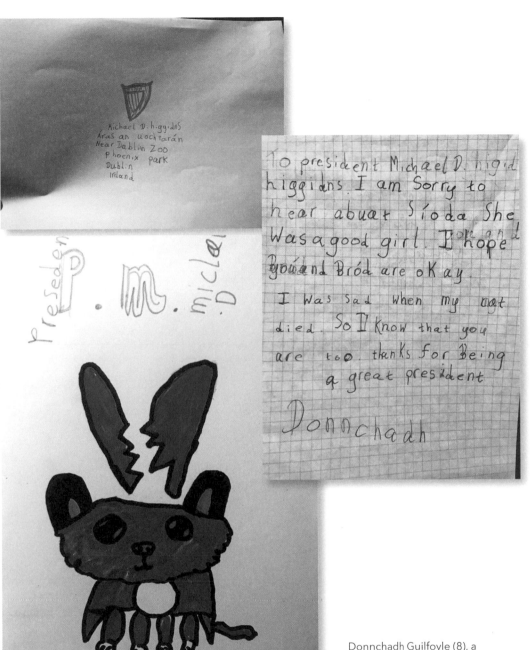

To president Michael D. higid higgidns. I am sorry to hear abuat Síoda She Was a good girl. I hope and you and Bród are okay.

I was sad when my cat died. So I know that you are too. thanks for being a great president

Donnchadh

Donnchadh Guilfoyle (8), a pupil at Kilcornan National School in Co. Limerick, writes to commiserate with President Michael D. Higgins on the death of his Bernese Mountain Dog Síoda: 'She was a good girl.'

Chapter 12

Postscript
Editor's Selection

Flor MacCarthy

The Space Race of the 1960s; a note passed to the captain of an aeroplane; a blessing for Ireland from the Native American Choctaw Nation; a woman's request for her ten-year-old son to be crowned 'King of Ireland's Eye'. If the selection in this book is subjective, this chapter is even more so: these letters I squirrelled away for myself. There is no common thread running through them; no connection between them – except that each, in its own way, has a story worth telling.

10 June, 1966.

Excellency,

I am grateful for your Excellency's letter of 1st March, 1966, with which you were so kind as to send photographs of the Moon surface taken by the Soviet automatic space station "LUNA - 9" which in an historic achievement of great scientific merit made the first soft landing on the Moon on 3rd February, 1966.

In accepting these photographs and the accompanying emblems, which mark an important step in man's exploration of space, may I congratulate you and join with you in the hope that science will always be employed for the progress and betterment of mankind, and not for destruction.

Accept, Excellency, the assurance of my highest consideration.

Eamon de Valera
President of Ireland.

His Excellency N. V. Podgorny,
Chairman of the Presidium of the Supreme Soviet,
Union of Soviet Socialist Republics.

President de Valera thanks His Excellency
N.V. Podgorny, Chairman of the
Presidium of the Supreme Soviet, USSR,
for sending him images taken by Luna 9,
the first spacecraft to make a soft landing
on the moon, 10 June 1966.

THE WHITE HOUSE

WASHINGTON

June 10, 1966

Dear Mr. President:

I thought you might want these copies of photographs
of the surface of the moon taken by the Surveyor I
spacecraft.

These and other photographs will be distributed to
the scientific community of the world in the hope
that they will contribute to our combined knowledge
of the lunar surface.

I have the strong feeling that if we are wise and
earnest, what is happening in outer space can help
us live better together on earth.

Sincerely,

His Excellency
Eamon de Valera
President of Ireland
Dublin

Letter to President Éamon de Valera
from US President Lyndon B. Johnson,
about Surveyor 1, NASA's first lunar
soft-lander: 'if we are wise and earnest,
what is happening in outer space can
help us live better together on earth'.
10 June 1966.

THE SPACE RACE

Throughout the 1960s Ireland was kept informed about, and was very interested in, the Space Race. Successive US presidents, Kennedy, Johnson and Nixon, all wrote to President de Valera, sending him pieces of moon rock, lunar photographs, and an Irish flag which had been carried to the moon and back by their astronauts. But in a wonderful bit of Cold War diplomacy, de Valera was also in touch with the USSR about its space programme. In fact, on one occasion in June 1966, letters about the lunar missions were sent between Áras an Uachtaráin and both superpowers on the same day.

'Here Men from the Planet Earth …' A cutting from *The Irish Press* shows the plaque that would be placed on the moon, signed by astronauts Neil Armstrong, Michael Collins, Buzz Aldrin and also by Richard Nixon, President of the United States of America.

His Excellency Richard M. Nixon,
President of the United States of America,
Washington, D.C.

Mr. President,

On behalf of the people of Ireland I send you our
sincerest congratulations and our unbounded admiration
for the courage and skill of astronauts Armstrong, Aldrin,
and Collins, and for the wonderful team work of all the
others who made the landing possible.

May God grant that the astronauts will return safely
home and that this great achievement will contribute to the
peace and happiness of mankind in the era which has been
opened.

Eamon de Valera
President of Ireland.

A message to US President Richard
Nixon from President Éamon de Valera
congratulating the 'courage and skill of
astronauts Armstrong, Aldrin and Collins' on
the moon landing of Apollo 11, July 1969.

Christmas 73.
E deV. Man in
the moon

'Man in the moon' doodles by President
Éamon de Valera, Christmas 1973.

At the Cawston Ostrich Farm, South Pasadena, Cal.
Nái neas an capall é seo! Connaic mé
féin é. Tá man jo mór y mé
féin, buidéacay le Dia. Tá súil ajam
jo bfuil sib-re jo mait. An Craoibín

Ireland's first three presidents had strong
links to the US, having travelled there
extensively early in their careers. This
postcard was sent by Douglas Hyde and
his wife to their children in Roscommon
from California before he was president.
Hyde writes drolly, 'Nach deas an capaill
é seo!' ['Isn't this a nice horse!'].

THE FRIENDLY SONS OF SAINT PATRICK

THESE are to Certify that Hon. Sean. T. O'Kelly has been admitted a Member of The Society of The Friendly Sons of Saint Patrick for the Relief of Emigrants from Ireland established in WASHINGTON, D.C. and incorporated agreeably to Law and he having paid the sums required by the Rules and Regulations of the Said Society, is entitled to Membership during Life.

Witness the Hand of the President, the seventeenth Day of March, 1959. *James Francis Reilly* Pres.t

Attest: Secy. *Sean F. McHugh*

Certificate admitting President Seán T. O'Kelly as a member of the society of the Friendly Sons of Saint Patrick in Washington D.C. on 17 March 1959. The organisation was founded in 1771 as an all-male charity to aid Irish emigrants. The Philadelphia branch admitted women in 2016.

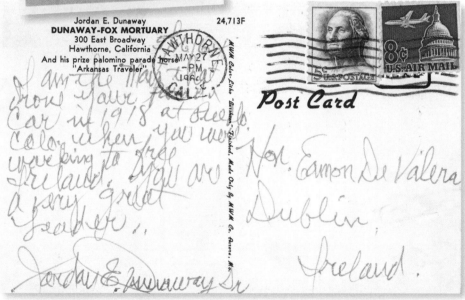

Jordan E. Dunaway
DUNAWAY-FOX MORTUARY
300 East Broadway
Hawthorne, California
And his prize palomino parade horse
"Arkansas Traveler"

24,713F

Post Card

Postcard from Californian undertaker
Jordan E. Dunaway Sr dated May 1964,
telling President Éamon de Valera that
he'd met him during de Valera's year-
long tour of the United States in 1919
'when you were working to free Ireland.
You are a very great leader'.

UACHTARÁN NA hÉIREANN
PRESIDENT OF IRELAND

9th July, 2021

Ms. Maureen Sweeney
Sonas Nursing Home
Tallagh
Belmullet
County Mayo,
F26 HW71

Dear Ms. Sweeney,

May I take this opportunity to acknowledge the key role you played during a critical moment in world history. Your story is a most inspiring one, reminding us of the many quiet but greatly influential acts that can so profoundly impact on our shared lives and those of generations to come.

As we continue, in this country, to engage in a decade of commemoration we have become deeply aware of the network of narratives that comprise decisive chapters of our history. So many of those narratives are centred on ordinary lives touched by the extraordinary, and the deep and lasting impact of unsung actors whose deeds are compelled by a great spirit of good citizenship.

Yours is such a story and your legacy a most important and enduring one. Your actions so long ago in Blacksod Bay have had a significant influence on the journey that has brought the world to this contemporary moment. That is an extraordinary legacy and one I am so glad has been acknowledged, including most recently by the US House of Representatives.

Guím gach rath agus sonas ortsa, Maureen, agus ar do chlann uilig.

Yours sincerely,

Michael D. Higgins
Uachtarán na hÉireann
President of Ireland

'Your legacy is an important and enduring one'. President Michael D. Higgins writes to ninety-eight-year-old Maureen Sweeney about the key role she played in the D-Day landings. Her weather readings at Blacksod Lighthouse, Co. Mayo, on 3 June 1944 delayed the Normandy invasion and changed the course of World War II. Maureen (née Flavin), who turned twenty-one on the night, went on to marry lighthouse keeper, the late Ted Sweeney. In June 2021 she received a US House of Representatives award.

WASHINGTON

Date	Item	$	Sterling equivalent.
19. Feb. 17	Invitation cards President's Reception Washington	51.31	
20. Feb. 20	Place cards President's Luncheon Washington	19.50	
21. Feb. 26	Invitation cards President's Reception Washington	110.48	
22. March 3	Invitation cards President's Luncheon Washington	55.70	
23. March 13	Rail tickets Mrs.Hearne Washington-New York	17.42	
24. March 24	Stenographic services Statler Hotel re President	30.00	
25.	Tickets New York-Washington 31st March Ambassador and Mrs. Hearne	37.87	
26. March 31	Liquor President's entertainment	162.10	
27. March 31	Liquor President's entertainment	82.20	
28. March 31	Liquor President's entertainment	898.60	
29. March 31	Admission cards to President's reception Washington	34.44	
30. March 31	Liquor President's entertainment	60.75	
31. March 31	Liquor President's entertainment	191.82	
32. March 31	Liquor President's entertainment	54.20	
33. March 31	President's reception Press, Radio and TV Correspondents Wash.	751.92	
34. March 31	Printing of menus for President's Luncheon Washington	72.80	
35. March 31	President's Luncheon Washington March 19	1,738.45	

Extract from an answer to a Dáil question posed by Deputy Oliver J. Flanagan TD, regarding the 'Cost to the Exchequer of journeys outside the State' made by President Seán T. O'Kelly in March 1959.

THE DREAM

Sean T he dreamt an awful dream
It filled him with dismay
He thought he had arrived in Rome
And heard The Pontiff say -
Kneel down 'til I give you the Pledge
As this is Holy Year,
For Ireland's sake you must abstain
From whiskey wine and beer.
The Uachtaráin was much upset
His knees they knocked and knocked
If he could but express his thoughts
The Pope would have been shocked.
No Sun nor Moon could give him light
His vision grew quite dark
And thought of what a fool he was
To ever leave The Park.
He put his blackest curse on Dev.
Believing 't was his fault
Then said I'll see them all in Hell
Before I chuck the malt.
But then he thought of those at home
On whose behalf he came,
And said if I refuse The Pope
I'll ne'er live down the shame.
So just as he agreed to all
The terms great and small
Was he not glad to wake and find,
He had not gone at all.

Shortfellow

Poem teasing President Seán T. O'Kelly
on his reputation for being 'fond of the
drop'. It followed his hugely successful
State Visit to the United States in 1959,
and was written by an American comedy
group, the Banshees.

UACHTARÁN NA hÉIREANN
PRESIDENT OF IRELAND

Dr. Ida Milne
Carlow College
College Street
Carlow

5th June 2019

Dear Ida

I would like to thank you most sincerely for speaking at the seminar that I hosted at
Áras an Uachtaráin last week reflecting on the impact and legacy of the Great Flu
Pandemic of 1918 – 1919.

The presentation of your research on the oral history of the pandemic in Ireland was
fascinating. It brought to our attention, in such an engaging way, the tragic implications
of the flu for tens of thousands of individuals and families in Ireland. I was particularly
pleased that some of the descendants of those that died, or of those who were involved in
treating the sick, were present for the event and your help in arranging this is much
appreciated.

As President of Ireland, I would like to commend you for your ongoing efforts in helping
us all to remember the Pandemic and to thank you for your support in helping me to
mark its centenary. I believe it imperative for us to recall this seismic event in our
relatively recent history, and Friday's seminar was such a welcome event, as part of our
decade of commemorations, to enable us to gain a more complete understanding of the
Ireland of a century ago, in order, perhaps, to gain a better understanding of the Ireland
of today.

Yours sincerely

Michael D. Higgins
Uachtarán na hÉireann
President of Ireland

President Michael D. Higgins thanks historian Dr
Ida Milne for her 'ongoing efforts in helping us
all to remember the Pandemic'. It was June 2019,
and she had just spoken at a seminar at Áras an
Uachtaráin to mark the centenary of the Great Flu
Pandemic of 1918-1919. Within months a new
pandemic was making headlines.

BIAĊLÁR

Corn seaḃóıġe

Anraıċ Duḃáın

Maonáıs Ḃraḋáın

Sıcín: Lıaṁás

Píse: Cabáıste

Prácáí

Suḃ caṁan: Uaċcar

Uaċcar Reóıóċe: Merınġues

Caıfe

Luncheon

Creamed Vichyssoise

* * * *

Coquilles St. Jacques

* * * *

Beef Bourguignonne
Broccoli Spears with Butter
Parisienne Potatoes

* * * *

Cheese Board

* * * *

Fresh Strawberries au Kirsch & Cream

* * * *

Coffee

———

Puligny Montrachet "Les Combettes" - 1970
Ch. Leoville Lascases, St. Julien - 1967

Menus for the inaugural dinner and
luncheon at Áras an Uachtaráin for
President Éamon de Valera in June 1959,
and President Erskine H. Childers in June
1973. The first, written in Irish, offered
typical Irish dishes of the time; the
second, more classic French cuisine.

SHELBURNE CO-OP. AGRICULTURAL SOCIETY Ltd.

Branches:
New Ross,
Duncannon, Haggard
Boro. Old Ross.
Foulksmills.
Ballywilliam.

Railway Station:
Campile
and Ballywilliam Stn.
for Boro. Branch.

Ports:
Duncannon and
Waterford.

Telegraphic Address:
" Co-op. Campile."

Campile 2 & 6.
New Ross 54.
'Phones: { Killanne   3.
Duncannon 3.
Ballywilliam 4.

CAMPILE, Co. Wexford.

Via Waterford.

2nd Septr 1940.

His Excellency,
Dr. Douglas Hyde,
President of Eire,
Arus an Tuactharain,
<u>DUBLIN.</u>

Your Excellency,

   I have been instructed by the
Chairman & Committee of the above Society to
convey to your Excellency their deep appreciation
of the message of condolence with them on
 their recent sad bereavement and loss.

   We feel that your Excellency voices
the sentiments of the country and this universal
sympathy is a source of the greatest encouragement to
us in our frightfully difficult task of re-constructing
our enterprise from ruins and continuing our task
of peace, prosperity and benefit to our countryside.

   I have the honour to ask your
Excellency to accept the expression of my highest
appreciation.

       Yours sincerely,

       SHELBURNE CO-OPERATIVE
       AGRI   SOCIETY LTD.

          General Manager & Secretary

Letter to President Douglas Hyde thanking him
for voicing 'the sentiments of the country' on
the deaths of three women when a German
warplane destroyed a creamery in Co. Wexford
in August 1940.

AIRMEN WRECK IRISH CREAMERY

GERMAN BOMBS KILL THREE IN CO. WEXFORD

Government Protest To Berlin: Demand For Reparation

"A BOMBER aircraft of German nationality flew over the area of Campile, Ballynitty, Bannow and Duncormick, Co. Wexford, between 2 o'clock and 3 o'clock this afternoon," says a statement issued by the Government Information Bureau last evening.

"Bombs were dropped at each of these points," the statement adds. "The Co-operative Creamery at Campile was wrecked. Three girls were killed and one injured by falling masonry.

"The Irish Charge d'Affaires in Berlin has been instructed to make a protest to the German Government and to claim full reparation."

The dead girls are **Mary Ellen Kent** (35), who was in charge of the restaurant attached to the premises, and her sister, **Catherine Kent** (25), an assistant in the drapery portion of the premises, both of Terreragh: and **Kathleen Hurley** (25), an assistant in the restaurant, of Garryduff,

The three local women who were killed in the bombing were named by *The Irish Press* newspaper as Mary Ellen Kent (35), her sister, Catherine Kent (25), and Kathleen Hurley (25).

Three's company: President Erskine
H. Childers spent his only Christmas
Day at Áras an Uachtaráin enjoying the
company of his family including his son
and grandson, both also named Erskine.

THE CHILDERS LETTERS

Letters written by President Erskine H. Childers are a rare find. The only president
of Ireland to die in office, his term came to a sudden and tragic end when he
collapsed and died in the arms of his youngest child Nessa in November 1974
after less than eighteen months in office.

But the following letter is even more of a rarity. It is of significant historical
importance, as the president writes with candour about running for the office
of Head of State against Tom O'Higgins, the nephew of the man who had signed
the death warrant on behalf of the State of his father, Erskine B. Childers, in
1922. He wrote that this 'incredible coincidence' was largely ignored by the Irish
press at the time.

Full of humour and warmth, this letter also shows a man who was politically
astute and gives us an insight into a president whom we didn't have long enough
to get to know.

It was written to his son Erskine and daughter-in-law Mallica in the days
after his election as the fourth president of Ireland in May 1973.

President Erskine H. Childers describes the fun and games, political and otherwise, on his successful presidential election campaign tour of Ireland in 1973. On winning the election by 48,000 votes, Childers said: 'Dev was weeping with joy on the phone. He told me I was elected on merit but that nevertheless the Irish people had expunged at least in part the crime of executing Grandfather.'

Letter 1

June 10

Phone 971902

68, HIGHFIELD ROAD
RATHGAR,
DUBLIN 6.

Dear Erskine & Mallacka,

We got your letter about your global job just as the Presidential Poll was about to take place and I told people you had a more important job than I might have. Rita and I should waved from the Bus painted in Presidential colours people and gold with my name the length of it for 25 days, sixteen hours a day. A car loudspoke our approaches and people came to the doors of their houses. The Bus played Irish music whole people could hear. A platform and loud speaker were attached. Press and camera crews travelled in it. We drove 4700 miles stopped 650 times and I made 250 speeches. The welcome became more and more enthusiastic. I was mobbed by young girls and women. The meetings were bigger than those at general Elections. I spoke on the new dimensions of the Presidential office. Planning for the younger generation preserving national identity. I said few Governments ever thought about what their countries should be like in 1998 etc etc.

Letter 2

One woman said to Rita "look after him he is precious I haven't been moved so much since ELVIS." This was an isolated remark..!! We won by 48000 votes. Rita was superb and spoke in College green very well indeed. In Donegal there were meetings of 400 to 500 at 12AM. 12.30. 1AM 1.30 AM 2AM 2.30AM (with a band playing most nights) 2.45 AM. We got to bed between 1AM & 2AM and got up at 8.30 AM. We were not tired at the end of the tour. I weeded the garden from 9AM till 2PM with a transistor and the Press caught me at it. All the papers carried the pictures. Nessa spoke over Radio so Rita and I feel still like a male and female Cinderella!! wondering when we are in the dark in bed whether it is true. Never had I dreamed of the possibility I refused publicly to stand till we were defeated because I wanted to continue as Minister for Health. An American Pressman travelled with us and attended the Election Committee briefings. He said we were like students compared with the heavy sophistication of USA politics

Phone 971902

68, HIGHFIELD ROAD,
RATHGAR,
DUBLIN 6.

I was going to leave Thinle Tawls at Arus
an Uachtarain. Tom O'Higgins rival was asked
question in Irish at University College Cork and could
not answer. I would not allow this to be published
when this was announced at my 1½ hours
successful seminar. The public thought he could
speak Irish because he read a script in Irish. I wanted
to win on mine own. As Minister for 22 years I
had a great advantage having built up many
personal contacts. The women gave me most
of my majority partly because of Health work
and partly because of my T.V. voice.
T.V and Radio. I think T.V confidence is like playing
the piano a gift

Nessa has gained three T.C.D honours in the
Matriculation Exam at 16 years and is going
to do the rest at Ringsend technical school.
More about the Election. The Coalition boosted
O'Higgins 7 children and spoke of him as
a family man. They deprecated the idea of
having a "Palo Vice Regal Lodge"
Jack Lynch answered the Coalition monstrously

by pointing out that Pearse was half Devonshire
and that about twenty other leaders had no
native Irish blood whatever! We produced 4 children
and five grandchildren the last day.
I think the Irish people are mature to elect
someone born in London ¼ American ¾ Irish
and the rest English or Scottish, educated
in England. I have as you, Presidential Blood
John Adams, and royal Edward Plantagenet—

Re making the Presidential Office well
will be very challenging
Dev was weeping while joy on the floor.
He told me I was elected in went
but nevertheless the Irish people had expunged
at least in part the crime of executing
Grandfather
The fact that the uncle of the Coalition candidate
ordered fathers executions was never mentioned
there was no civil war mention. Only the
British Press mentioned the astounding
coincidence. O'Higgins was decent his
supporters very mixed. Their campaign was
we must have a Coalition President—
Ours was we are putting up the best candidate
Come and stay with us soon.
I can't bear to think of you living in
New York but how wonderful + your
promotion is. Margaret is coming to
the inauguration

Lord the Rakes
June 2 & 4th 11 AM Ecumenical Service
St Patricks Cathedral 5 Faiths
12 PM St Patricks Hall Dublin Castle

5, Coolnah inch
Dundrum Rd
Dublin 14
11·1·75

Dear Mr President
          My son, who
is just ten years
old, would like to
be King of Irelands
Eye. So if you are
ever going to have
one, will you please
consider him for the
position

          His name is
Myles & he is an excellent

boy and would make
a very good Ruler.

          yours faithfully
          (Mrs) May Geiran

Dublin woman May Geiran asks
President Cearbhall Ó Dálaigh to
consider her son for the position of King
of Ireland's Eye in 1975. On the opposite
page, the president writes a considered
two-page reply.

PST/167 (6)

13ú Eanáir
975.

Dear Mrs Jennan,

I can well understand your son Myles' wish to be King of Ireland's Eye.

Does he know that Eye is a Norse word which means Island?

Ireland's Eye is a lovely Island and full of birds. The best time to go there is May.

Ireland's Eye looks across at Howth — Beann Éadair, a very famous place in Irish literature.

There is a great poem which begins: Aoibhinn bheith i mBinn Éadair

(7)

Whoever is going to be King of Ireland's Eye will have to send his messengers to do his shopping in Beann Éadair.

Any one who is as good as your son Myles could, one day, be invited to be King of Ireland's Eye, or even President of all Ireland

There is a story about a little boy — it is called The Little Prince — who lived on a planet much much smaller than Ireland's Eye. I shall see if I can get a copy: Myles would like it.

If any one would be like the little boy in the story he could become a Prince, or a King or a President.

Mise, le mórmeas
Cearbhall Ó Dálaigh

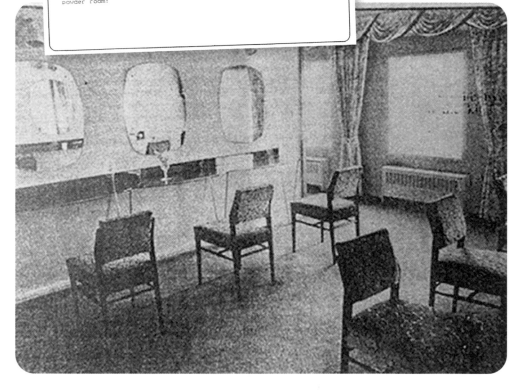

THE IRISH TIMES

The Irish Times Limited, P.O. Box 74, 11-15 D'Olier Street, Dublin 2
Telephone 792022. Telex 93639. Fax 793910

PERSONAL

9th November 1990

Mary Robinson
President-elect
43 Sandford Road
Dublin 6

Dear Mary,

Wonderful! Wonderful! Wonderful! For the past two weeks, I felt
that this election would tell us more about ourselves as a people than
anything else for a long time. And in the wake of the weekend smears
and the portrayal of Brian Lenihan as a true Irish martyr, I was fully
prepared for the worst.

But when I heard on the Pat Kenny's radio programme on Thursday
that the boxes from Kilronan, on Inishmore, gave you more votes than
Lenihan, I almost cried. Dublin you would expect, but the Aran
Islands? A pity Breandan O hEithir didn't live to see it and give us
the benefit of his islander's insight.

After all the defeats over all the years, it's really great for
once to be wholeheartedly on the winning side. And all I can say, as
I've been saying all day yesterday, is that this is a great little
country after all. More power to you - and the best of luck to
yourself, Nick and the children.

Sincerely,

Frank McDonald

PS Just in case you missed it, I'm enclosing a copy of an article I
wrote on the Aras last March. Whatever you do, keep that Fifties
powder room!

Environment editor of
The Irish Times, Frank
McDonald, congratulates
President-elect Mary
Robinson on her election
win in 1990, and implores
her not to do away
with the 1950s Ladies'
Powder Room at Áras an
Uachtaráin.

President Robinson —

Thank you very much for the loan of
Brave Hearts Must Travel.
Everyone enjoyed your painting,
and it gave a special dimension
to my venues in Ireland.

God bless you, and your people
your Excellency —
Yakoke / Slan

Gary White Deer
Choctaw

Gary White Deer, an elder of the Native
American Choctaw Nation, thanks President
Mary Robinson for lending him a painting for
an exhibition. In 1985 the president was made
an honorary member of the Choctaw Nation
during a visit to Oklahoma, where she thanked
the Choctaw people for the donation of money
sent to Ireland during the Great Famine of the
1840s. In 2020/21 thousands of Irish people
supported a fundraising campaign to help
the Choctaw Nation cope with the Covid-19
pandemic.

Dear Captain,

Could you please, on behalf of all the passengers (+ I am sure crew members), wish our President, Mary Robinson, a very pleasant + safe journey on to New Zealand.

Thank her for making this journey a very special + memorable one.

We are all even more enchanted by her, due to her surprise 'walk about' + wish her a safe journey onwards.

Thank you.

Note passed to the captain of a flight from Dublin to London asking him/her to wish President Mary Robinson well on her onward journey to New Zealand. The president was guest of honour at ceremonies marking the centenary of women's suffrage in New Zealand in September 1993.

13/20 English Market
Grand Parade
Cork.

Dear President Higgins,

I have just returned from a reception given by Queen Elizabeth and Prince Philip at Buckingham Palace

The welcome afforded us by the Queen and Prince Philip was superb, and everyone at the Palace, from the Police at the gate, the household staff and the Royal Family could not have been more accomodating. I must admit to feeling very proud to be Irish on that night.

I have no doubt you will have a highly successful State visit and will bring everyone involved another step along the road to more normal and friendlier relations with our neighbours. Enjoy your visit

Pat O'Connell
Fishmonger.

Pat O'Connell, a well-known fishmonger in the Old English Market in Cork, whose chat with Queen Elizabeth II was hailed as a highlight of her State Visit to Ireland in 2011, wishes President Michael D. Higgins well on his own State Visit to the United Kingdom. In doing so, he also lets the president know that he had made it to Buckingham Palace before him.

CONTRIBUTORS

SAMANTHA BARRY is the editor-in-chief of *Glamour*, one of the leading female-focused media titles in the US. She has transformed the Women of the Year Awards and reached record-breaking audiences across platforms. Recently, Barry interviewed the US First Lady, Dr Jill Biden, for *Glamour*'s College Women of the Year. Previously a reporter, producer and executive at CNN, BBC, ABC, RTÉ and Newstalk, Barry is a graduate of DCU with a master's in journalism. She was a fellow of Columbia University's Sulzberger programme and is a guest lecturer at Yale.

CATRIONA CROWE is former head of special projects at the National Archives of Ireland. She was manager of the census online project, which placed the Irish 1901 and 1911 censuses online and free to access. She is editor of *Dublin 1911*. She presented the RTÉ documentaries *Ireland Before the Rising*, broadcast in February 2016, and *Life After the Rising*, broadcast in January 1919. She is a member of the Royal Irish Academy.

Author and journalist **MARTINA DEVLIN** has written ten books, including *About Sisterland* and *The House Where It Happened*. Her latest is a short story collection, *Truth & Dare*, and one of those stories was adapted as a play, the political satire *What Would the Countess Say?* She is the recipient of the Royal Society of Literature's V.S. Pritchett Prize, a Hennessy Literary Award and three nominations for the Irish Book Awards. She writes a weekly current affairs column for the *Irish Independent* and has been named National Newspapers of Ireland commentator of the year.

LISE HAND is a journalist, broadcaster and a regular contributor to current affairs programmes and arts shows on national radio and television. She has worked at *The Sunday Times*, the *Irish Independent*, *The Sunday Tribune* and the *Sunday Independent*, covering the arts, current affairs and politics. For over a decade she held the position of parliamentary sketch writer for the *Irish Independent* and subsequently for *The Times* Ireland edition. She is currently battling disinformation with Kinzen media company.

TERRI KEARNEY has been the director of Skibbereen Heritage Centre since it opened in 2000. A West Cork native, she has published two books: *Lough Hyne: The Marine Researchers – in Pictures* and *Lough Hyne: From Prehistory to the Present* as well as co-authoring *Skibbereen: The Famine Story*. Terri initiated and manages the hugely successful folklore project Stories of the Revolution in which primary school pupils collect and record stories relating to the 1916–1923 revolutionary period in West Cork.

JUSTINE McCARTHY is an award-winning columnist and political correspondent with *The Sunday Times*. She is the author of *Mary McAleese: The Outsider* and *Deep Deception: Ireland's Swimming Scandals*.

DAVID McCULLAGH is a journalist and author. He is a presenter of *RTÉ News: Six One* and is a former political correspondent. He is the author of a biography of John A. Costello, *The Reluctant Taoiseach*, and a two-volume biography of Éamon de Valera, *Rise: 1882–1932* and *Rule: 1932–1975*.

HARRY McGEE is political correspondent with *The Irish Times*. He previously worked for RTÉ, *The Irish Examiner, The Sunday Tribune* and *Magill* magazine. He has also presented and written documentaries on politics. He is originally from Galway but now lives in Dublin. He comes from an Irish-speaking family.

Tá HARRY McGEE ina chomhfhreagraí polaitíochta leis *The Irish Times*. Chaith sé sealanna ag obair le RTÉ, *The Irish Examiner, The Sunday Tribune* agus *Magill*. Tá taithí fada aige chomh maith mar láithreoir agus scríbhneoir ar chláir theilifíse, go háirithe ar pholaitíocht. Is é Gaillimh a chathair dhúchais ach tá sé ina chonaí i mBaile Átha Cliath le fada an lá. Is le Gaeilge a tógadh a theaghlach.

RORY MONTGOMERY was an Irish diplomat from 1983 to 2019. He served as permanent representative to the European Union and Irish ambassador to France and as second secretary general at the Departments of the Taoiseach and of Foreign Affairs. He is now an honorary professor at the Mitchell Institute, Queen's University Belfast, and a writer and commentator. He was recently elected a member of the Royal Irish Academy.

JOSEPH O'CONNOR's 2019 novel, *Shadowplay*, won the An Post/Easons Irish Novel of the Year Award and was shortlisted for the Costa Book Award. He is the author of twenty-one books, including the international bestseller, *Star of the Sea*. He has been Harman Visiting Professor of Creative Writing at Baruch College, City University of New York, and a Cullman Fellow at New York Public Library. His work has been published in forty languages. He is the Frank McCourt professor and chair of creative writing at the University of Limerick.

PAUL ROUSE is a professor in the school of history at University College Dublin. He has written extensively on the history of Irish sport. His most recent books are *Sport and Ireland: A History* and *The Hurlers: The First All-Ireland and the Making of Modern Hurling*.

IMAGE CREDITS

Portraits of the Presidents

The official portrait of the President of Ireland is commissioned by the State, and portraits of the first eight presidents hang in the ceremonial Lafranchini Corridor at Áras an Uachtaráin along with busts of the presidents. However, protocol dictates that the official portrait of the sitting president does not join the others until after his/her term of office ends. Hence the official portrait of President Michael D. Higgins by Mick O'Dea PPRHA is currently on display at Leinster House in Dublin and is not yet permitted to be reproduced.

The official portraits (oil on canvas) of the first eight presidents, courtesy of Áras an Uachtaráin: President Douglas Hyde and President Seán T. O'Kelly by Leo Whelan RHA; President Éamon de Valera by Seán O'Sullivan RHA; President Erskine H. Childers by David Hone PPRHA; President Cearbhall Ó Dálaigh by Thomas Ryan PPRHA; President Patrick J. Hillery by John F. Kelly RHA; President Mary Robinson by Basil Blackshaw HRHA; President Mary McAleese by Joe Dunne RHA. The portrait of President Michael D. Higgins is by Stephen Bennett.

© *The Irish Times*

Pages 15, 19, 21, 55 (bottom), 93, 132 (bottom), 138, 154, 178 (main), 180 (centre), 180 (bottom), 184, 190, 191, 228 (bottom), 233 (bottom), 278 (bottom).

By kind permission, the archive of former President of Ireland, Mary McAleese

Pages 53, 181, 177 (and by kind permission the Scanlon Family), 54, 52, 173, 174, 231, 18, 40, 55 (top), 153, 128, 179 (top; and by kind permission the family of Shaun McLaughlin).

Courtesy of the National Archives of Ireland

Pages 4, 23, 24, 26, 26, 28, 29, 32, 36, 37, 42, 43, 45, 62, 63 (top), 67, 75, 94, 95, 96, 98, 99, 101, 114, 115, 116, 117, 118, 124 (top), 132 (top), 133 (right), 140–141, 143, 146, 159, 160, 162, 166, 168–169, 169 (bottom), 185, 186, 187, 189, 192, 197, 198, 198, 199, 200, 201 (Elina Sironen), 202 (bottom), 204 (top), 206, 207, 208, 209, 210, 211, 212, 217, 218, 219, 220, 223, 224, 225, 226, 238, 239, 243, 244, 245, 262, 265, 270, 271.

Courtesy of the National Archives of Ireland and © *The Irish Press*

Pages 124 (bottom), 131, 133 (left), 142, 188, 205, 221, 261, 272.
Courtesy of the National Archives of Ireland/*Yorkshire Evening News*: 3

Mary Robinson Archive: P143, James Hardiman Archives, NUI Galway

Pages 16 (bottom), 17, 39, 47, 48, 49, 60, 73, 74 (top), 76, 77, 78, 79, 80, 85, 88, 89, 90, 106, 107, 113, 125 (top), 126, 127, 151 (and by kind permission of the Le Brocquy Family), 152 (and by kind permission of Brendan Kennelly), 172, 229 (bottom), 230, 239, 246–247, 249, 250, 251, 278 (top), 279, 280.

the Embassy of Ireland, Belgium; 66 by kind permission the Royal Irish Academy © RIA; 70, 74 (bottom), 97, 130, 139, 156 (bottom), 175, 215, 255, 256 courtesy of Áras an Uachtaráin; 81 Leon Farrell / RollingNews.ie; 86–87, 150 by kind permission the Heaney Family / © Faber & Faber Ltd; 90 (inset) © Fennell Photography; 92 by kind permission the Douglas Hyde Centre, Frenchpark, Co. Roscommon; 102 © Lensman Collection, The Irish Photo Archive; 108 courtesy of Oideas Gael, Co. Donegal; 125 (bottom) by Flor MacCarthy; 129 (top) © PA Images; 129 (bottom) courtesy of *Warwick and Stanthorpe Today*; 134 by kind permission the Martin and Gaskin families; 135 (top) © Syracuse University Libraries, NY; 136 reproduced by kind permission and © Absolute Graphics; 145 (top) Allene Talmey, *Vogue* © Condé Nast; 145 (bottom) Irving Penn, *Vogue* © Condé Nast; 149 (top) by kind permission of the Grace Family; 154 (top) courtesy of Houses of the Oireachtas; 158 © British Pathé; 171 © Reuters; 180 (top) courtesy Special Olympics Ireland; 182 by kind permission the Smyth Family and St Seachnall's NS, Dunshaughlin, Co. Meath; 193 Royal Palace Archives, Monaco / by kind permission HRH Princess Caroline; 202 (top) © 1959 Disney; 203 (top) © Getty Images; 203 (bottom) © *New York Post Archive*; 204 (bottom) Alamy Stock Photo; 214 by kind permission of Shane Gillen; 222, 229 (top) by kind permission Sportsfile; 232 by kind permission Bagnelastown Cricket Club; 233 (top) courtesy of Hockey Ireland; 234 *Galway Advertiser*; 235 by kind permission of the Charlton family; 248 courtesy RTÉ Archives; 250 courtesy of Ms Costigan's sixth class (2019/2020), Duleek GNS, Co. Meath; 250 by kind permission Sacred Heart NS, Huntstown, Dublin; 257 courtesy of the Guilfoyle Family; 263 (bottom) courtesy of Westmeath Libraries (The Aidan Heavey Collection); 266 courtesy of the Sweeney Family; 269 by kind permission Dr Ida Milne; 273 by kind permission from Mallica Childers; 274–275 by kind permission from the Executor and the Estate of Erskine B. Childers.

ACKNOWLEDGEMENTS

About a decade ago I went in search of a book on letters to and from the presidents of Ireland. To my surprise, none existed. To my even greater surprise, I decided to write it myself. It wasn't until late 2018 that I ran the idea past Edwin Higel, publisher of New Island Books who, to my delight, responded immediately: 'Let's make this book!'

To Edwin, and to the dozens of people on whom I've called for help — not least to navigate through a pandemic — my sincerest gratitude. The team at New Island could not have been more brilliant, nor more patient, especially commissioning editor Aoife K. Walsh and editor Susan McKeever. Watching you both at work has been a masterclass in how to create a book (you'll be delighted to hear I'm ready for the next one!). Many thanks also to Mariel Deegan, Caoimhe Fox, Stephen Reid and to publicist extraordinaire, Peter O'Connell.

From the start I was fortunate enough to have the most generous support of former President Mary Robinson who granted me access to her archive, which is being catalogued in NUI Galway. Former President Mary McAleese provided invaluable advice and assistance too, and I'm enormously grateful to both of them for contributing to the book and for choosing correspondence from their respective terms in office.

At Áras an Uachtaráin, former Secretary General Art O'Leary gave me excellent overviews on the protocols of the presidency; and thanks also to Head of Communications Hans Zomer. And at the Department of Foreign Affairs, my thanks for their support: former Secretary General Niall Burgess, Deputy Secretary General Brendan Rogers, Aingeal O'Donoghue, EU Division and Cultural Director Eugene Downes. For their great assistance and advice, my thanks to Ambassador Daniel Mulhall in Washington DC and Orla Keane, Consul General in Los Angeles; Ambassador Patricia O'Brien and Liam O' Flaherty at the Irish Embassy in Paris; Fionnuala Callanan at the Irish Embassy in London; Ambassador Helena Nolan and James O'Brien at the Irish Embassy in Brussels; and a special 'thank you' to former Ambassador Eamonn MacAodha in Brussels who started the ball rolling.

The families of late presidents were wonderfully enthusiastic and supportive of this project. My thanks especially to Ruairí Ó Cuiv, Erskine Childers and to Mary Sealy and Una Sealy. Thanks also to Dr Phyllis Gaffney and Jim Ryan, Dr John Hillery, Maeve Tannam and Liam Ó hAlmhain.

When lockdowns were lifted the archives became a second home. I learned so much from archivist Niamh Ní Charra who is archiving the Mary Robinson papers, and whose expertise is matched only by her endless good humour and boundless patience. Thank you, Niamh!

For their invaluable assistance, my thanks to Orlaith McBride, director of the National Archives of Ireland and to senior archivist Hazel Menton, whose advice saved this project more than once. Many thanks are due also to Kate Manning, principal archivist at UCD Archives, as well as archivists Selina Collard and Orna Sommerville. I'd like to thank Dr Sandra Collins, director of the National Library of Ireland, along with archivists Colette O'Flaherty, Nora Thornton and James Harte, for helping to source some important letters when the library was closed to the public. My thanks to the Royal Irish Academy, the Royal Archives, Windsor, and the Royal Palace Archives, Monaco.

To the following for their advice and assistance I'm enormously grateful: Bride Rosney, Helen Carney, Clíodhna Ní Anluain, Emer Beesley, Caroline Nash, Susan Byrne and Frank Mangan. For their expertise in the field of historical research, my thanks to Brian Murphy, Liam MacMathúna, Grace O'Keeffe, Maurice Manning, Mark Duncan, Conor Bolger, and my brother Dan MacCarthy. My former colleagues in RTÉ Sinéad Crowley, Sean Whelan, Marty Morrissey and Tony O'Donoghue never hesitated to help. And my colleagues at Oireachtas TV Aisling Brady and Matt Stapleton were great for (often unsolicited) advice. To Nora Byrne and to Jacqueline Finnegan, thanks for listening!

I feel privileged to have such an amazing group of writers and historians contributing to this book. Thank you so much Samantha Barry, Catriona Crowe, Martina Devlin, Lise Hand, Terri Kearney, Justine McCarthy, David McCullagh, Harry McGee, Rory Montgomery, Joseph O'Connor and Paul Rouse.

To each and every letter-writer (or their families or estates) for allowing me to publish their letters, a most heartfelt thank you.

Finally, I would need another chapter to even begin to express my gratitude to Paul Cunningham and our children Isabelle and James for their love, patience and deliveries of treats to my desk throughout the making of this book. I'm back, I promise!

© Barry Moore

ABOUT THE EDITOR

FLOR MacCARTHY is a journalist and broadcaster who hosts political debates on Oireachtas TV (Irish parliamentary TV), interviewing politicians and academics in Ireland and at the European Parliament. A former news reporter and newscaster with RTÉ, she also presented a variety of cultural programmes on radio and television and has acted as a consultant for several international human rights organisations. Freelancing these days, and with a passion for history and the arts, she has contributed to numerous events in Ireland's Decade of Centenaries. Flor is from West Cork and lives in Dun Laoghaire with her family. *The Presidents' Letters* is her first book.

Randolph S. Churchill

~~Pierre de Monaco~~

Edward Hempel

Mrs. Edward M. Kennedy

Dubglas de hÍde

+ John C. McQuaid.

Éamon De Valera

Grace de Monaco

Jacqueline Kennedy

Kenneth David Kaunda

Seán T. Ó Ceallaigh

caroline de (nO) Mo

Seán Ó Lionaigh

Alan Parker